Passionate
Centrism

One Rabbi's Judaism

David J. Fine

United Synagogue of Conservative Judaism

ROWMAN & LITTLEFIELD
Lanham • Boulder • New York • London

The publication of Passionate Centrism was made possible in part through the generosity of Freddie and Beth Kotek in honor of Rabbi David J. Fine.

Published by Rowman & Littlefield
A wholly owned subsidiary of
The Rowman & Littlefield Publishing Group, Inc.
4501 Forbes Boulevard, Suite 200, Lanham, Maryland 20706
www.rowman.com

Unit A, Whitacre Mews, 26-34 Stannary Street, London SE11 4AB,
United Kingdom

British Library Cataloguing in Publication Information Available

Library of Congress Cataloging-in-Publication Data Available
    ISBN 978-0-8381-0086-8 (pbk. : alk. paper)
    ISBN 978-0-8381-0088-2 (electronic)

The paper used in this publication meets the minimum requirements of American National Standard for Information Sciences—Permanence of Paper for Printed Library Materials, ANSI/NISO Z39.48-1992.

Printed in the United States of America

For Our Sons

Laurence and Ariel

"And you shall teach these things to your children."

Preface

I thought of the term "passionate centrism" when I was in rabbinical school. My fellow students seemed divided between those who were steeped in the legalistic traditionalism of halakhah and those who set themselves in rebellion against it. What excited me about the Judaism that I pursued was that it could change from the inside, that it could approach the radical challenges of the day such as feminism and sexual orientation and yet retain its historical and theological authenticity. I believed, and still believe, that Judaism has always behaved this way because it is a vibrant culture, and vibrant cultures know how to evolve through historical change in order to survive. I trace this approach to the Positive Historical Judaism first articulated in the nineteenth century by Zacharias Frankel. A historical-evolutionary approach to religious meaning entails an embrace of relativism, that no one generation can ever attain a certainty of fundamentally knowing what is true, that is, of understanding God. While I embraced that relativity as liberating, many of my classmates and friends, both from the right and the left, found it dry and cold, detachedly academic rather than burning with the fire of spirituality. In these pages I attempt to respond to that charge, to define the passion of my centrism.

The pages that follow were influenced by my many teachers through the years. First and foremost are my parents, Rabbi Robert and Helene Fine, who provided me with a dynamic and modern Judaism at home and in school so that I could grow and learn. The two most influential teachers of my undergraduate and rabbinical school years were Rabbi Joel Roth and Rabbi Neil Gillman. Rabbi Gillman was the kohen at my pidyon haben. I became re-acquainted with Rabbi Gillman in high school when, after reading an article of his in a journal that I found in the Camp Ramah library, my father encouraged me to contact him directly, explaining our connection going "way back." I took Rabbi Gillman's undergraduate Jewish thought course in the summer of 1990 just when his book *Sacred Fragments* was first published. That was the first college course I took, and it remains the most important. I first met Rabbi Roth at Camp Ramah at around the same time. The camp had just adopted the principles of Rabbi Roth's responsum on the participation of women in a minyan, and I read his paper with great interest, not even realizing that he was there at the same camp. When my parents came to visit one Shabbat, my father introduced me to Rabbi Roth, and I then had the opportunity to directly engage with the author of the historical argument that was responsible for the admission of women into the Conservative rabbinate. The most influential book that I read in my college years—though not assigned—was Rabbi Roth's *The Halakhic Process*. So many of my generation who went through the Seminary and its affiliated institutions found themselves influenced by either Neil Gillman or Joel Roth, but not both. I was so convinced of the compatibility of the two perspectives, one of liberal theology and the other of legal positivism, that I wrote a short essay in college—also unassigned—on a synthesis between "Gillmanian Theology and Rothian Halakhah." I think that "passionate centrism" is a better term.

Were it not for the opportunity to teach and discuss these ideas and learn from my own students over the past several years I would not have been able to write this volume. I am indebted to my congregants and adult education students at Temple Israel and Jewish Community Center in Ridgewood, New Jersey, my Melton students from all over Northern New Jersey, and my European rabbinical students whom I have taught at the Abraham Geiger and Zacharias Frankel Colleges in Berlin. There is a certain kind of learning that one can only acheive when one teaches.

I am grateful for my congregation in Ridgewood, New Jersey, for providing a wonderful place to work, teach, and learn, and I thank my synagogue presidents over the past seven years, Joshua Holden, Allan Alterman, and Denis Vogel, for giving me the time to teach in Berlin and to work on this writing. Special gratitude is due Professor Walter Homolka, rector of the Abraham Geiger College and executive director of the Zacharias Frankel College, for inviting me to join our Berlin faculty on an adjunct basis and for always encouraging me in my writing. Very special gratitude is owed to my friend Jane Rosen from Ridgewood for so carefully editing the first draft of this manuscript and showing me how to do better.

Many thanks to Dorrie Berkowitz for steering this process through at the United Synagogue of Conservative Judaism with discerning care.

I am grateful to the Rabbinical Assembly, the American Jewish Congress, and the Jewish Law Association for permission to reprint previously published material in the appendices.

Finally, I am grateful to my wife Alla and our sons, Laurence and Ariel. They have been patient with my absences to teach in Berlin and to write at "solitary retreat" in the Berkshires, and they provide a home for me of warmth and love of Judaism. It is from their support that I write these pages.

Contents

Chapter One

PRINCIPLES OF POSITIVE HISTORICAL JUDAISM

At the start of my first year of rabbinical school at the Jewish Theological Seminary, our first-year seminar professor devoted a class session to discussing a recent essay by a prominent Conservative rabbi critiquing the idea of "Positive Historical Judaism" as an outdated and archaic vision for a livable Judaism. But for me, this idea was what set me on my path towards the rabbinate. I was so unsettled by the scathing critique that I dashed off a "defense" of the ideas that spoke, and speak, to me. While those words I wrote then appear now to be quite sophomoric, they were published in my denomination's journal, *Conservative Judaism*, its editors granting the young "novice" a priceless affirmation that I was not speaking nonsense. Twenty years later, these pages are intended as a more mature articulation of what excites me from this clumsy nineteenth century "ism."

The greatest strength of the Positive Historical approach is also its greatest liability, in that it believes the sources and foundations of Judaism to be embedded in history, culture, and law rather than in faith in God and divine revelation. This is a strength because it presents a Judaism that is impervious to challenges of faith and the discoveries of science and critical scholarship. That is, the foundations of Judaism are rooted in the memories and experiences of the people through history rather than through supernatural events or questionable legendary episodes. But this approach that I will elaborate on in this book is also a weakness because history, culture, and law do not excite passions as do matters of faith — at least not for most. No crusade was ever launched over a footnote. But it is for this reason that some perspective on the origins of historicism in the nineteenth century German Romantic movement, from which Positive Historical Judaism arose, can help us recover a passion for history, culture, and law and thus reinvigorate a centrist approach to Judaism. We need to rediscover the sense of mission for those in the center, lest Jewish religious identity be ceded to the right and to the left. Additionally, an approach to Judaism based in culture over faith may offer a drastically needed solution to the alarming attrition in the

American Jewish community where more and more Jews are dissociating from an identity of Judaism as a religious belief. At a time when more and more Jews are seeing their identity as a "culture" rather than a "religion," we need to find a way to speak about Judaism as a culture but in a passionate and religious voice. In this volume, I attempt to address this challenge, thus concluding my argument with how we might still find God.

Positive Historical Judaism is a term coined by the nineteenth-century German rabbi, Zacharias Frankel. Frankel sought to establish a middle ground in the denominational struggles of his time. He identified as a Liberal rabbi and attended the seminal Liberal rabbinical conference in 1845 in Frankfurt am Main. He knew he had no place in the Orthodox world, a world from which he felt rejected, not only because of his amenability to moderate reform but also because of his historical and seemingly secular approach to the history of rabbinic literature. And yet he left the 1845 rabbinical conference determined that the Reform wing had gone too far in its rejection of Hebrew and core religious observances. He was unsuccessful in forming a middle way in the 1840s, but later became influential in being chosen to head the first modern Liberal Jewish seminary, the Jewish Theological Seminary in Breslau (then Germany, now Poland), in 1854. Some see Frankel as the forerunner of Conservative Judaism, the American denomination that developed around the seminary with the same name founded later in New York. But there were no institutional connections between the two, and Conservative Judaism has developed as a large mainstream denomination comprising a "big tent," with many different perspectives, values, and theologies finding a home under its wings.

It is not my intention here to write a philosophy of Conservative Judaism. What follows are one rabbi's meditations on the struggles of approaching and understanding Judaism and its meaning today. My Judaism is not necessarily the same as Frankel's, nor can it be, for we live in different times, and one of the principles of Positive Historical Judaism is that Judaism evolves through history, always adapting to new times and circumstances. The issues and challenges that I address are not the same as those faced by Frankel, nor are my solutions the solutions that he would have reached. But I am passionate about the centrism that Positive Historical Judaism represents because in certain fundamental ways Frankel's approach appeals and has always appealed to me. Additionally, I fear that the approach to Judaism articulated in these pages is one that has ceded too much ground to a combined though uncoordinated assault by resurgent theological fundamentalism, a new spiritualized mysticism in liberal guise, and a triumph of an agenda of radical change. The following pages are offered, then, as a kind of "return to basics," a re-assessment of the core principles of who we are, or at least who I am.

Five fundamental principles that I identify with Positive Historical Judaism are:

1. that Judaism is a culture of law;

2. that Judaism has a history and continues to evolve;

3. that Jewish texts need to be read historically;

4. that Jewish history needs to be experienced through religious observance;

5. that God can be found through the structure of tradition.

That Judaism is a culture of law. Law is what the "Positive" refers to in Positive Historical Judaism. Law is the substance that defines, or is "posited" in a culture. "Positivists" in legal theory understand law to be more than a series of regulations; it is an organic body that preserves the essence of the culture that it serves. Positivism is based on the premise that law is a social and historical product, rather than rooted in the legislation of a sovereign authority such as a king or a god. Frankel, like so many modern Jews, was a true child of two worlds, inspired both by the contemporary German and European ideas of positivism and historical development, and by the centrality of halakhah in Jewish culture. For Frankel, it was not the individual laws but the law as a whole that was essential for Judaism. While the idea of law as a— or *the*—defining element of a culture may seem rather dry to contemporary sensibilities, in Frankel's time this was the cutting edge of Romanticism, a re-imagining of what culture and identity mean. The nineteenth-century Romantic movement was a broad trend encompassing music, art, history, and politics. Most remembered today by the music of great composers such as Brahms and Tchaikovsky, the Romantics sought to distill and celebrate the souls of their nations. Through such creative efforts they—along with other artists, writers, historians, linguists, and jurists—"wrote" nationalisms that were just developing out of the older model where polities and dominions were not necessarily correlated to specific cultures and languages. As the celebration of individuality and brilliance in specific cultures were the marks of the Romantics, Frankel sought to describe Jewish law as the brilliant essence of what characterized the Jewish people through the crucible of history.

Using the Romantic terms of German theorist of legal positivism Friedrich Carl von Savigny, but also influenced no doubt by Johann Gottfried Herder, the champion Romantic theorist of German folklore, Positive Historical Judaism understood Judaism as a unique culture, the key element of which was law. Halakhah as a cultural system, as a means of relating to the past and the present and forming the Judaism of the future, is the particular insight of Positive Historical Judaism. The highest form of Jewish cultural activity has always been the study of law, whereas the highest responses to new historical challenges have always been phrased through the language of law. Halakhah represents the fabric that has held Jewish tradition together.

Understanding Judaism as a culture of law, it must be emphasized, stands independent of any theological dogma. The fact that an individual law in question may be attributed to God or to the ancient rabbis or to contemporary judgment is immaterial to the role of law in the culture. What is essential is not the origin of the law but rather that it is accepted by the culture as a part of the organic legal system. Thus, when Frankel argued in his historical studies of rabbinic law that the phrase *halakhah le-Mosheh mi-Sinai,* a "law of Moses from Sinai," does not literally mean a law dating from Moses at Sinai but rather is code for an unattributable tradition from hoary antiquity, he was accused of heresy by his Orthodox colleagues. For Positive Historical Judaism, law is the primary aspect of the culture because it articulates the culture's values. All laws and legal systems do that, but all the more so in a culture such as Judaism where the law is the primary mode of cultural expression. To say that the law is "the Will of God" is, when understood through the prism of Positive Historicism, ultimately a theological re-articulation of the understanding that the law expresses the values of its culture.

That Judaism has a history and continues to evolve. This is the "Historical" in Positive Historical Judaism. Judaism is a culture of law, but it is not static. Since law is a product of—as it is the primary expression of—the culture, it evolves as the culture changes through history. This was the basis for Frankel's idea of "moderate reform," that individual laws could change but only through loyalty to the foundational principles of the culture and legal tradition. The "Historical" aspect of Positive Historical Judaism serves to mitigate the positivist emphasis on law, qualifying law as dependent on historical circumstances. At the same time, the "Positive" aspect of Positive Historical Judaism serves to mitigate the historical emphasis on change, qualifying change as through the prism of a legal culture. This is the careful balance that was later articulated by Rabbi Mordecai Waxman as "Tradition and Change."

The emphasis on history as the context for culture placed Positive Historical Judaism clearly within the Romantic rebellion against both the rationalism of radical Reform and the religious fundamentalism of Orthodoxy. There was no pristine perfect form of Judaism that could be resurrected through an excision of medieval rabbinic piety. Judaism is what developed through time, and we must celebrate and build off of the Judaism that came before us, not deny and reject it and imagine some perfect ancient past that may never have existed. Positive Historical Judaism is Romantic then in its celebration of the Jewish experience and, ultimately, in its traditionalism and loyalty to the past. At the same time, its historicism fundamentally divides it from the religious right, which is not so different from the radical left in believing in certain perfect fundamental truths that were given in the founding era. The radical right and the radical left argue over which truths and which ideas are primary. For the religious fundamentalist, a "law of Moses from Sinai" (whichever one the particular brand of fundamentalism sees as fundamental) is divine and perfect, while for the Positive Historicist, ancient laws are products of their time, venerable because they are old.

That Jewish texts need to be read historically. If Judaism is a historical culture, then its cultural product, its sacred literature, should be subject to historical analysis. While Frankel devoted his career to the historical analysis of rabbinic literature, the critical process applies no less to how we read the Bible. While it is both natural and a function of good literature to find ourselves and our deepest concerns in what we read, Positive Historical Judaism reads the Bible and all of Jewish literature ultimately as the—or a—voice of Judaism at the time of the composition of that work. Biblical criticism must be embraced as the highest form of religious study for it strives to understand Torah on its own terms, that is, *lishmah*, without any ulterior motive of what it might mean for us and our own timely contemporary concerns. The highest form of learning is, then, the reading of sacred literature with an understanding of its historical context. This is referred to in rabbinics as *pshat*. The second level, the level of practical application, is when we read into the works our own concerns. Judaism as a legal culture teaches us how to do so, how to use sources as precedent and apply them to new circumstances even when the original source may have imagined something entirely differently. This is referred to in rabbinics as *drash*.

That Jewish history needs to be experienced through religious observance. Judaism is more than an intellectual exercise; it is a culture of a people, and as such it must serve to keep that sense of national consciousness alive among its adherents. The ancient rhythms of enslavement, redemption, exile, and redemption again must be relived; but the sacred re-enactment of the national saga must also account for the recent trauma of the Holocaust as well as the miracle of the establishment of the State of Israel. Positive Historical Judaism must find the balance in remembering both ancient and contemporary history so that Judaism remains relevant and yet avoids becoming mere service to the contemporary. The determination of which observances are retained and which are not, which are added and which are rejected as failed experiments, is a sacred communal process involving rabbinic reading of the law and teaching and congregational learning and doing. The community is the ultimate authority and history the ultimate arbiter of what becomes sacred.

That God can be found through the structure of tradition. This is the synthesis that justifies the "Judaism" in Positive Historical Judaism. In order to remain a form of religious expression and not a mere philosophy or theoretical justification of behavior, Positive Historical Judaism must find a way of finding God through the process of legal and historical culture. Rather than a force outside of history, God's commanding voice must be heard through history. In a contemporary context where we hear so much of God as a personal matter independent of religion and teachings and liturgy and observance, Positive Historical Judaism makes the case that God can be heard and experienced collectively in community, where humans always achieve their highest potential, whether it be their best or their worst.

Zacharias Frankel drew the line with his more radical Liberal colleagues over the issue of liturgy. In response to Abraham Geiger's notorious pronouncement at the 1845 rabbinical conference that a prayer in German might be more powerful than the same prayer in Hebrew, Frankel conceded that Geiger was correct that the halakhah does allow for prayer in other languages. Ours is not the first time that not all the Jews understood Hebrew. But Frankel went on to argue that while all languages are effective to their speakers, Hebrew is the historical language of Judaism. In culturally specific terms reminiscent of the nineteenth-century movements of nationalism and Romanticism (yet a half century before the development of Zionism), Frankel argued for the centrality of Hebrew, and that prayer in the language of Scripture connects us with the ancient Covenant that we strive to invoke in our prayers. The essential break between Frankel and Reform Judaism in his day, then, was not over halakhah but over the language of Jewish religious expression. For this reason, I both begin and conclude this meditation on Positive Historical Judaism with a discussion of liturgy.

The following chapter discusses issues in Jewish liturgy today, including the structure of the worship and nature of its expression as well as the substantive questions of reference to the sacrificial cult and the question of the inclusion of the Matriarchs alongside the Patriarchs and the concomitant questions of gender in prayer.

Chapter Three will continue the discussion of the role of gender in Judaism while turning the focus to halakhah in general. Other questions such as homosexuality and Shabbat and kashrut observance will be considered, as well as the question of the role of ethics in a system of ritual observance.

Chapter Four turns the discussion from sacred living to sacred text. This chapter will focus on the spirituality of study and the nature of *Torah Lishmah*, of study for its own sake, and how that challenges the way we read the Bible. The chapter will also address how we read the Christian Bible and how Positive Historical Judaism might offer new insight on building Christian-Jewish understanding.

Chapter Five returns to the question of Jewish observance, focusing on the challenges of faith posed by new historical understanding and developments. The chapter will address the celebration of Passover even as we confront questions about the historical reality of the Exodus. Here I also consider the importance of Tishah B'Av in commemorating the destruction of the past, in light of Yom Ha-atzma'ut, Israel's Independence Day. Finally, Shavuot, the festival that marks the giving of the Torah at Mount Sinai, will be presented in the context of an approach to Judaism that denies the Mosaic authenticity of the Torah.

The final chapter addresses how we may find God through history, concluding with a discussion of the theology of the High Holy Days liturgy and how that might offer a theological approach to modern belief.

This volume includes four appendices written in academic style including bibliographic notations. The first two of these are rabbinic responsa, one I wrote and the second co-written with two rabbinic colleagues. The first addresses the question of counting women in a minyan, while the second represents an attempt to resolve the halakhic challenges posed by same-sex marriage. I append them here not only because they relate to questions raised in this work, but also because they best represent my quest to apply the idea of Positive Historical Judaism to the practice and observance of Jewish law. The third and fourth appendices are two studies I wrote on Solomon Schechter, the preeminent voice of Positive Historical Judaism in the United States.

The chapters that follow represent a very personal grappling with the issues facing Judaism today. I first used the term "passionate centrism" when I was a rabbinical student. Spending time in an environment of soul-seekers where the loudest and most articulate voices were those from either the radical left or the conservative right—terms that are always relative to the context—I decided to become an extreme moderate. How strange that devotion to the centrist mainstream is itself an oxymoron! And yet, I went to rabbinical school when Bill Clinton was president of the United States and Yitzhak Rabin was prime minister of Israel. Both inspired me as passionate centrists. While religion and politics can be a dangerous mixture, the approach to the one can be informed by a successful approach to the other. The center ground must be embraced with passion and must speak with authority rather than cede its place to the right or the left. Passionate centrism is important not because it is safe. Neither of my political heroes was successful at consoling opposition. One was charged with impeachment and the other was assassinated. They did not pursue the moderate course to play it safe. It is easier to enjoy the embrace of the "true believers" from whichever wing they may hail. The center is often a lonely place to be, as its adherents lack enthusiasm. The crisis in political partisanship today is the same as that facing the mainline churches (and mainstream Judaism) today—the lack of a passionate centrism. From an analogy of military strategy, a general can employ fancy wing maneuvers, but they are useless if the center line does not hold. Passionate centrism is essential not only for its own adherents, but also for the strength of the entire enterprise, as it is the bridge that unites the whole. Perhaps that is why centrist leaders are so vulnerable to attack: because they work so hard to keep two independently irreconcilable sides together. But a passionate centrist also truly believes in what he or she professes with no less zeal than the less moderate.

I hope to articulate effectively what excites me about a passionate centrist approach to Judaism, an approach I identify with Positive Historical Judaism. It is my fervent prayer that my own musings will help others translate Judaism into their own terms, just as I have done by learning from and being inspired by my teachers and mentors and the writings of scholars throughout the ages.

Chapter Two

LITURGY: ADDRESSING THE SACRED

The Mishnah, the second-century codification of Jewish law that is the core of the Talmud, states that a prayer said by rote and without proper intention lacks supplicatory power. This oft-cited statement is a plea for *kavannah*, that is, proper intention, over mere *keva*, the set determinedness, or rote, of worship. The ancients, who understood the importance of regular liturgical offerings, emphasized the concomitant value of proper intention. We are to feel what we are saying, to be present in the worship. Today, it is often the opposite emphasis that must be articulated; that being present in worship, that seeking a sense of mere spirituality, is not enough, but that one must also commit to a regular regimen of set prayers in their set times. The tension between regulated and spontaneous prayer goes back to the time of the Mishnah. The standard approach has been to emphasize the tension, that neither keva nor kavannah are sufficient without the other. Judaism requires heartfelt prayer, but it also regulates the times and content of prayer. Finding the kavannah within the fixed regimen was considered easier than finding it without.

For Positive Historical Judaism, the tension between keva and kavannah is particularly acute because of the value of preserving the traditional liturgy in Hebrew. How can the worshipper achieve kavannah if he or she cannot understand the language of prayer?

At one level, the expectations of kavannah are, in the opinion of this rabbi, exaggerated and ultimately harmful to the efficacy of Jewish worship. Our enchantment at various levels with spirituality, mysticism, and kabbalah has desensitized today's worshippers to the power of traditional worship. Expecting some kind of spiritual "nirvana" during prayer, worshippers have given up on the traditional forms, looking outside of the synagogue for spirituality, or expecting some kind of magical transformation of the synagogue service if only the clergy and lay leadership would agree to a particular set of changes in the rules. The unrealistic expectations of the worshipper might be alleviated if we were to read the halakhah carefully with the understanding that the kavannah required for prayer is not an intensive spiritual plateau but simply the intention to fulfill the mitzvah of prayer. One does not fulfill the mitzvah of saying the Shema, for example, if one happened to have been studying Deuteronomy 6 where the Shema occurs. One must read the selections with the purposeful intention of doing so to fulfill the mitzvah of prayer. Rather than expect a heightened spiritual state, the halakhah merely requires that one pray with a mind towards praying. If the expectations are thus lowered, the experience becomes accessible.

But on another level, the above becomes a circular argument where kavannah becomes subsumed under keva. Isn't prayer supposed to have a spontaneous and meaningful element to it independent of regulated observance?

There is no easy resolution of the tension between spontaneity and form in prayer, but the suggestion of traditional Jewish worship is that the structure of regular prayer provides the atmosphere and the access where the spiritual moment can be realized. Regulated prayer brings one into the synagogue and provides moments of prayer. If one stands up for the Amidah (the statutory prayer) every time, one might occasionally pray.

While it is argued, and was argued at the seminal debate in 1845 between Abraham Geiger and Zacharias Frankel, that prayer is more effective in the language that speaks most naturally to the worshipper's heart, the counterargument that Frankel first articulated as Positive Historical Judaism is that prayer in Hebrew resonates a magical tone that cannot be effected in any other language. Hebrew ties us to the history of Jewish worship and tradition because the prayer book and the Bible itself were written in Hebrew. God can understand all languages, of course. The Mishnah's permission of prayer in Greek for those who can't read Hebrew is a legal concession to what should be obvious theologically. The question is not which language God best comprehends, but rather, which language our hearts best comprehend.

When we limit prayer to the intellectual level we condemn the entire worship enterprise to failure, for a rabbi composing a prayer on a laptop within the past decade can no better describe the yearnings of my heart than the rabbis of late antiquity committing their poetry to parchment. In some cases, the more contemporary a prayer is, the less power it has to reach the worshipper, for its horizon is shorter. Jewish worship is an act of appropriating the history of Judaism in a Romantic fashion at the same time as reaching inward to the depths of one's soul. The Hebrew language, the traditional structure of the worship, the modalities and rhythms, naturally guide worshippers to a higher plane, from the profane to the sacred. Prayer is more than an expression of what is written on the page; it is a lifting up off the page to a place in the past and through time.

The more flexible and individual that prayer is, the less powerful it becomes in elevating the individual to a higher spiritual plane. This counterintuitive notion is premised on the understanding that prayer is ultimately about surrender of the self. Prayer is meant to remind us that our hopes and dreams are not ours alone, that others have joy and sorrow, and that we are never alone. Jewish prayer is at root a communal exercise, a kind of group therapy. There are times for individual moments, as when reciting the statutory prayer—the Amidah—and then one stands, book closed, eyes closed, and takes a few moments to reflect on the self, to open one's heart to God. On weekday mornings, the supplicatory prayers (Tahanun) are a time for real introspection, a silent confession of faults between the worshipper and God, the Supreme Listener. Those moments come to the regular worshipper as times of comfort and consolation because the worshipper has already surrendered to the structure of worship established by its formality. To approach worship with a sense of the urgency of immediate and personal prayer is too difficult to require on a daily basis. But once submitting to the regimen, the moments come on their own.

Hebrew and the traditional structures of prayer are therefore essential for Positive Historical Judaism. Before I think about my own troubles, for example, I remember the trauma of the destruction of the Jerusalem Temple. Before I dwell on the problems in today's world, I remember the messianic hopes of the generations. Worship and liturgy bring structure to the chaos and insecurity of our own worlds and help us form the words that come from the soul.

And yet, the familiarity with traditional Jewish worship is not readily accessible, requiring regular attendance at services before the rhythms become natural, and many hours of study so that the Hebrew can be sung and read, and needless to say, understood. The "moderate reform" that Frankel supported consists of non-fundamental changes in worship so as to bring the whole enterprise of Jewish prayer to a place where it would be more accessible to the contemporary Jew. While Hebrew remains the primary language of public prayer, usable translations and transliterations are essential, as are readings in the vernacular. Moments of study and edification by the rabbi are critical, as is the aesthetic quality of the music provided by the cantor, and perhaps the choir or singing congregation. The role of music in the synagogue service has become a hotly contested topic today, no less so than in the nineteenth century when organs were first introduced to Jewish worship.

Music in the Synagogue Service

There are important halakhic issues regarding the use of musical instruments in the synagogue service. The practice of a cappella worship on Shabbat and festivals goes back two millennia. Besides the weight of tradition, opponents cite the *gezeira* (decree) of the ancient sages to forbid music in the synagogue to differentiate it from the destroyed Temple where there were acoustical instruments, as well as the concern that a musician will want to carry his or her instrument to the synagogue and would automatically seek to repair it, acts that are clearly forbidden on Shabbat. Advocates stress the association of musical instruments in Jewish culture with joy. Mourners avoid music, whereas musicians are required for a wedding. The decree against music on Shabbat represents a state of national mourning following the destruction of the Temple, advocates claim, which may have been appropriate in its time but is no longer so today, especially given the re-establishment of Jewish sovereignty in the land of Israel. The concern that a musician may carry or tune or repair the instrument on Shabbat can be alleviated by individual logistical arrangements and instructions from the rabbi. A recent unpublished yet masterful responsum by Rabbis Elliot N. Dorff and Elie Kaplan Spitz examines the halakhic issues and approaches to music on Shabbat in detail, carefully mapping a comprehensive halakhic approach to the use of musical instruments in Shabbat worship.

While these various halakhic issues are not insignificant, in reality the debates about usage of musical instruments in the contemporary synagogue tend to be no different in substance than dialogues about which melodies the cantor may select. Not to trivialize the matter, but the debates are more about the aesthetic quality of the service than its legal underpinnings, and aesthetics are ultimately a matter of subjective judgment.

The halakhic arguments against and justifications for musical instruments on Shabbat span over two hundred years. The determining factor must be what is best for the individual congregation. Will the addition of musical instruments add to the level of devotion or will it distract worshippers? Will it make the liturgy more accessible or will it destroy the more familiar rhythms and make it more distant? There is no simple answer to these questions, reminding us that worship is a communal affair.

When I was twelve and thirteen years old I attended a range of different synagogues, through what we call "the bar/bat mitzvah circuit." The one experience I had of musical instruments on Shabbat was jarring to my sophomoric ears. Since then, I have gradually become more accustomed to the benefit that instrumentation can bring to worship. Having spent my twenties in New York City, I learned to appreciate the softness that the organ can bring to the welcoming of Shabbat. In Manhattan, not surprisingly, one lives the frenetic energy of the workweek in the extreme. I would always catch the Friday evening radio broadcast of the organ service from Temple Emanu-El, which reminded the city that it was okay now to slow down the pace. While some find energy and spirit missing in the organ and look to different types of instrumentation to establish the kavannah of Friday night, I find that the deceleration that the organ invites is exactly what Friday night is about. I have found, at times, that it is what I need to help rest and truly celebrate.

About fifteen years after living in Manhattan, I engaged my congregation in New Jersey in a conversation about musical instruments on Shabbat. We experimented with an organ service, a guitar service, and a whole band service. Each type appealed to different worshippers, as does still the a cappella service. That was to be expected. The challenge that faces congregations is how to find the right approach that reaches the various individual worshippers so that they can pray together as a community.

Music, whether it be the voice of the cantor, the role of the choir, or the addition of musical instruments, is a tool to bridge the gap between worshipper and liturgy. For some, the strumming of a guitar can break the proverbial ice in the room and help worshippers open their mouths and then their hearts. For some, the clear voice of the cantor singing the traditional melodies without the addition of harmonies or musical accompaniment can attain a perfection in purity, an echo of a sound from years past. For others, the soft deep chords of the organ are felt within, elevating the worshippers from mundane concerns into the realm of the sacred. If the music helps bridge that gap, bringing us to the point of surrender, then it is appropriate and holy. If the use of music can reconcile the congregation to the Hebrew liturgy and its structure, then it is praiseworthy.

Substantive Challenges to Liturgy: The Sacrifices

A more significant challenge to traditional Jewish worship is changes of the text, specifically regarding the references to ancient sacrifices. The original liturgical formulations of the founders of Reform Judaism in the early nineteenth century avoided mentioning the sacrifices and the Temple primarily because those early Reform teachers denied the traditional messianic hope for the restoration of the Temple in Jerusalem. They preferred instead to have the location of Jewish destiny in their nation of residence and newly found emancipation. Before anyone imagined a political Zionism working to re-establish Jewish sovereignty in Palestine—or anywhere else, for that matter—the early Reformers' interest in censoring the liturgy to better represent the political hopes of their constituents is understandable. But their motivations went beyond the political. For them, the form of Jewish worship had evolved from sacrifices and a latent hope for their restoration to the more pure form of "the service of the heart." In this they could rely on the writing of Maimonides centuries before, that sacrifices, even though we prayed for their restoration, were but an initial step in the development of pure worship. Whereas Maimonides made no changes to the liturgy and detailed the sacrificial cult to the letter in his legal code, the Reformers sought to eliminate reference to the sacrifices in the liturgy, called their synagogues "temples" replacing the Temple of old, and eliminated the entire Musaf service from the liturgy. The Musaf is the additional statutory prayer recited only on Sabbaths and festivals and correlates directly to the Musaf, or additional, sacrificial services mandated by the Torah. The Musaf prayer refers directly to the Musaf sacrifice, citing the Toraitic instructions word-for-word. The Musaf service that concludes all Shabbat and festival services in Conservative and Orthodox congregations is missing from the more liberal liturgies. The presence or absence of the Musaf constitutes, in my view, the essential difference between Reform and Conservative Judaism today, not because of the Musaf itself, but because of the ideas that its inclusion or omission represent.

Not that the retention of the Musaf lacked ambivalence in the history of Conservative Jewish liturgy. In the early liturgical publications of the Conservative movement in the United States, the tense was changed in the Musaf, so that rather than a prayer for the restoration of the sacrifices that *we will do again*, the text cites the devotion of our ancestors in days of old and *what they did then*. This was a subtle grammatical change that satisfied those uncomfortable with the eschatological hopes of the Musaf text. Changes in Conservative liturgical texts published in the latter half of the twentieth century went further, relegating the text of the sacrifices to a footnote or offering "alternative" texts that avoided all reference to the sacrificial cult. Some have argued for a return to the traditional text. We should not take the prayers for restoration of the ancient sacrificial cult literally, it is argued, but rather understand it as a metaphor, pleading for a return to greater intimacy with God as was known in the mythic past. Others argue that only the new "alternative" versions should be preserved, that the details of sacrificial offerings have no place in contemporary liturgy.

In my opinion, the elimination of all reference to the sacrificial cult in the Musaf denies the foundation for the Musaf's presence in the liturgical structure in the first place. I am not bothered by the change of tense one way or the other, because in my view it is not just the reference to the past but the entrance of the worshipper into the experience of the past that is essential. Tense becomes irrelevant once one passes the threshold into historical memory and consciousness. For Positive Historical Judaism, the Musaf is the most critical of all elements of the liturgy because it brings the worshipper into history. Clearly this is the case on the High Holy Days when the Musaf elaborates on historical themes in the martyrology and Avodah (Temple cult) services. The weekly Musaf does this in a condensed form, bringing the worshipper into the past, reminding the worshipper of destruction and exile, and before that of the glory of the cult in the ancient city. The Musaf brings the worshipper into the drama of Jewish sacred history, giving context to the celebration of Shabbat or the festival and to the individual yearnings of the worshipper's heart.

Reference to the Temple cult connects the worshipper with the Judaism of old. Without that reference, Judaism loses its tie to the past, its authenticity, and its power to reach the worshipper. That connection with the past is what reminds me that I am not alone when I pray. Reciting that part of the liturgy does not mean that I dream of the restoration of the sacrifices in my future. But it does mean that I dream of being a Jew of the ancient past dreaming of the restoration of sacrifices in his or her future, and that future becomes mine when I am transported back to that moment. No mere metaphor, the desire is real in that historical moment of the past, real in the desire to re-establish a sense of the nearness of the transcendent, a nearness that I experience through the liturgy.

The earnestness of this connection with the past in the present is noted beautifully in the culminating verse of the Ein Keloheinu prayer, one of the concluding hymns of the Sabbath and festival morning service. After four verses about God as our God, Lord, King, and Savior, the hymn concludes with the striking prose that breaks the poetic form by declaring that "You are the One to Whom our ancestors offered their sacred incense." That last verse is often omitted in liberal liturgies because, besides the discomfort of its association with the Temple cult, it does not seem to fit the poem that precedes it. But understood differently, that last line brings comfort and consolation to the worshipper, reminding us that this God, Lord, King, and Savior to whom we have addressed our long morning liturgy is the same One Who was worshipped by our ancestors thousands of years ago. That identification, through time, is redemptive.

The retention of the Musaf, then, represents the Romantic stand of Positive Historical Judaism against the ahistorical rationalism of Classical Reform. Whereas the Reform liturgy represents a statement of the political and religious hopes of the present and future, the traditional liturgy as understood by Positive Historical Judaism represents a leap into the mentality of the past.

Priestly Class Without Sacrificial Cult

While the Musaf service references the ancient sacrificial cult, there is no real hope for its restoration outside of certain fundamentalist circles. Why then, it is often asked, must we preserve the priestly and Levitical classes? If there is no practical reason for their preservation, what does the distinction establish besides the maintenance of an embarrassingly non-egalitarian hereditary and elitist caste system within Judaism? Like the referencing of the sacrifices in the liturgy, the preservation of the *kohen* and *levi* lines represents a key distinction of Positive Historical Judaism.

The role of *kohanim* and *leviyim* in Conservative Judaism, like the retention of reference to the sacrifices, has been a matter of contention for some time. Some Conservative congregations have eliminated the practice of calling up kohanim for the first aliyah (honor to the Torah) and leviyim for the second, and many have eliminated the Birkat Kohanim, the Priestly Benediction (or *Dukhenen*) recited by the kohanim on festivals in the Diaspora and more regularly in Israel. Many find the distinctions, which are passed on through the male line, as insulting to the egalitarian ethos. The halakhic opinions, unique to Conservative Judaism, that argue that daughters of male kohanim and leviyim are kohanim and leviyim in every right except in their ability to pass the legacy to their children, mitigate the criticism only to an extent. In all the congregations that I have served, I have had women *dukhen*, that is, go up to the bimah on holidays and pronounce the priestly blessing together with the male kohanim. I call women for the kohen aliyah and levi aliyah. Our understanding of the roles of men and women in public worship has evolved, I believe, but that evolution does not eliminate our need to preserve a tie with the past.

The Mishnah, in explaining why the kohen should receive the honor of being called to the Torah to recite the benedictions before others, says this is so that there be peace in the congregation. In order that the worshippers not quarrel over who should have the honor of going first, the tradition decides the matter ahead of time in calling up the kohen. That this insight of the Talmud is not misguided was made evident to me when I attended services at my rabbinical seminary, where, at the main egalitarian services, kohanim and leviyim were not recognized for the first and second aliyot. When the seminary chancellor was present, he was always called for the first aliyah. When he was not, then the vice chancellor was called. If none of the vice chancellors was present, then a dean would be called, and if no dean, then a faculty member. How different from the more traditional service, which continued from the pre-egalitarian days, where a first-year undergraduate would be called to the first aliyah because he was a kohen, whereas the *yisrael* full professor of Talmud sat and said "amen." Which was more egalitarian?, I would ask myself. The older service where the female student would never be called for any aliyah, or the newer service where the female student would also never be called for the first aliyah because she was just a student? Of course, in the new service the female student could be called for other aliyot, and it was because of my commitment to the "moderate" changes in Jewish worship in opening its doors to women that I attended the newer over the older service. But in my own congregations that I served as a rabbi, I fought and still fight for the retention of the rights of the kohanim and leviyim. When a woman is called up for the first aliyah in my synagogue, she is not called a *bat kohen*, a "daughter of a kohen," but a *kohenet*, a "priestess" in her own right. Egalitarianism is not so black and white.

The retention of the classes of kohanim and leviyim are important as they serve as living ties to the past. For me, the most powerful line of the daily morning liturgy is the introduction to the Psalm of the Day, usually said at the end of the service, which states that this day is the such-and-such day of the week when the Levites would recite the following psalm in the Temple. I am transported at that moment to the Temple courtyard in the first century, straining to hear the chorus of the Levites and having become, and become again each morning, a part of ancient Israel even as I prepare to live my own life in my own time and place. And yet the Psalm of the Day is an oft-forgotten component of the daily liturgy, relegated to the preliminary pages in most of the Conservative prayer books of the twentieth century and omitted completely from *Mahzor Lev Shalem*, the new Conservative High Holy Day prayer book published in 2010. I would argue that the traditional daily morning liturgy concludes with the Psalm of the Day as the culmination of worship, marking the successful spiritual transformation of the worshipper from his or her daily morning rituals to the courtyards of the Temple of ancient Jerusalem.

The Priestly Benediction, recited in the Diaspora only on festivals, is the high point of worship for me. I, a yisrael, descend the bimah and stand with my family, my wife's and my tallitot (prayer shawls) spread over the heads of our children, as we listen to each word of the blessing sung by the cantor, repeated by the kohanim, and mouthed silently by myself for my children. "May the Lord bless you and keep you…" The "threefold blessing," found etched in silver in ancient Hebrew script (on display in the Israel Museum in Jerusalem), is the oldest surviving fragment of the Bible. The text of this blessing is the most ancient of prayers, and for it to be recited by descendants of the same priestly class, millennia later in my own synagogue, connects me from the core of my being to the soul of ancient Israel. Much like the sounding of the shofar, the Priestly Benediction has an almost magical effect on me. I remember how powerful the blessing sounded and felt in the traditional Conservative synagogue in Queens (New York) where I grew up. The cantor would sing out each word in his high baritone, and then the kohanim would sing each word after him. One of them, Mr. Lasky, must have been close to seven feet tall and had the deepest bass voice. Those bottom-of-the-register notes sung by Mr. Lasky, in response to the plaintive tones of the cantor, became the foundation of my worship experience. The tradition of not looking at the kohanim, and the irresistible temptation of children to peek, added to the special nature of this holiest of liturgies. The question of whether all kohanim—or any—are really directly related to the family of Aaron, and the knowledge that in ancient times it was only men, although I insist that women kohanim join in the blessing today, does not mitigate in any way the power of the ritual.

The sanctity (*kedushah*) of kohanim today is symbolic, not real. Kohanim are not in themselves more worthy than anyone else to recite blessings for the congregation, whether it be the blessings over the Torah or the Priestly Benediction itself. The Talmud recognized that kohanim are not any more worthy, and that was precisely why the halakhah determined that kohanim should receive the first aliyah. Rather than go to someone worthy, which by definition establishes real distinctions between people, the halakhah required that kohanim receive the first aliyah, who are no more worthy but are chosen simply by accident of birth. Submission to that birth connection requires us to allow ourselves to be lifted up by the power of historical memory through the liturgical structure. While the cantor can certainly sing the Priestly Benediction, and does in traditional worship on a regular basis, the allocation of those lines to the descendants of the kohanim on festivals connects us to that past when all Israel would strive to travel up to Jerusalem as a pilgrimage. Our re-enactment of that process through the Priestly Benediction, which is itself the culmination of our recollection of that process through the Musaf liturgy, connects us deeply with our sacred past.

The halakhah itself recognizes the pure symbolism of the retention of the kohen and levi classes. A kohen, for example, is supposed to avoid entering cemeteries so as not to acquire the ritual impurity of the dead. But if a kohen does acquire that impurity, either by accident or by attending the burial of a close relative, he or she is not relieved of the tradition of continuing to avoid entering cemeteries. Even though that impurity can never be alleviated (the purification ritual is no longer performed), the kohen must — and does

— still behave as a kohen by avoiding cemeteries, receiving the first aliyah, participating in the rituals for the redemption of the first-born (*Pidyon HaBen*), and reciting the Priestly Benediction. The kohen's role in Judaism today is not actual but symbolic. He or she functions as if he or she were to celebrate in the Temple, even though he is two thousand years too late and he is a she.

Substantive Challenges to Liturgy: Egalitarianism

Jewish feminists have contended that traditional Jewish liturgy with its male-oriented "God language" promotes a male-centered patriarchal view of God and hence of Judaism, excluding women and relegating women's experiences to the sidelines. They are certainly correct that the traditional liturgy is male-heavy in its imagery. The question that is more difficult to resolve is whether the traditional liturgy is salvageable from a feminist perspective or whether Jewish prayer must be rewritten to be more inclusive.

As the first part of this chapter has made clear, my preference for liturgical conservatism is central to my understanding of Positive Historical Judaism. And yet, there are certain outright misogynist passages in the traditional liturgy that, I believe, must be excised. The morning blessing thanking God for not making one a woman, still appearing in Orthodox prayer books, ought not be recited. The alternative for women, who are taught to thank God "for making me according to Your will," is an insufficient rejoinder, and no apologetics can mitigate the damaging way that the traditional benediction has been read. The Conservative liturgical innovation possibly first suggested by Rabbi Max Gelb and published by Rabbi Morris Silverman, thanking God "for making me in Your image," offers a creative alternative that references the equality of men and women created, according to Genesis 1, in the image of God. Similarly, the tradition of reciting the second chapter of Mishnah Shabbat on Friday evenings with its assertion that women die in childbirth for being lax in lighting Shabbat candles in the home was rightfully omitted from Conservative prayer books. These changes, important as they are, do not change the structure and feel of the liturgy the way that more radical changes in approach to God-language would.

Creative as it is, in the new Conservative High Holy Day mahzor, *Lev Shalem's* alternative Avinu Malkeinu ("our Father, our King") becomes, debatably, no longer recognizable as an "Avinu Malkeinu." More radically, a blessing that avoids or emends the traditional formula *Barukh Atah Adonai Eloheinu Melekh HaOlam* (Blessed are You O Lord our God King of the Universe), becomes, at a point, no longer a traditional blessing. Perhaps that is the point, to change the liturgy so that it offers old prayers in new ways. Such an approach may be meaningful and powerful for some — but not for all.

Is there a more moderate alternative to such liturgical creations? Is there a way to salvage how we think of the Hebrew in prayer without losing the historical connection to the traditional liturgy? In the final chapter, I will return to the way that we imagine God through the liturgy and the meaning of such terms as "Father" and "King." At this point, I contend that if there is a way to read the liturgy as inclusive rather than exclusive, then that is preferable to re-writing it. On the level of translation, the move away from male pronouns in reference to God is important and should be supported by all. Our liturgists are creative enough poets to find ways to refer to God without the use of pronouns while maintaining felicity of language and correct grammatical usage. The more challenging problem is the Hebrew itself and the imagery it evokes. One intermediary solution that falls shy of rewriting the liturgy entirely but seeks to fulfill the need to be more inclusive of women is the addition of prayers that bring women into the text.

The least objectionable means of doing so is the addition of new prayers to the liturgy that add the voice of women. This can be done easily in the High Holy Day service where the tradition of adding new compositions goes back centuries. More difficult are three relatively recent innovations to the regular weekday and Shabbat liturgy: reference to Miriam in the benediction after the Shema that recounts the crossing of the sea; the addition of the word *ve-imoteinu* ("and our mothers") whenever *avoteinu* ("our fathers") appears; and the added reference to Sarah, Rebecca, Rachel, and Leah in the first paragraph of the Amidah, the statutory prayer.

The reference to Miriam is both the most and least radical of the three innovations. It is most radical because it adds an entire new phrase whereas the other two innovations add names to a list or simply a qualifying noun. But it is also the least radical because the mention of Miriam singing at the sea is a direct contextual expansion of the liturgy's reference to Moses and the Israelites singing at the redemptive moment of the crossing of the sea when the exodus from Egypt is sealed with the destruction of Pharaoh's army. Leading up to the crescendo of the Mi Khamokha ("Who is like You...") at the end of the benediction, the additional reference to Miriam gives more than it takes away from the force of the liturgy. My hesitation in this particular case has more to do with the glorification of a person, here Miriam, who sings and dances at the destruction of the enemy. While praise of God would have been appropriate after a dramatic victory, I have always read Miriam's outburst of dance as a bit "over the top." Miriam's dancing upon the death of the Egyptians, as well as her later notorious criticism of Moses for his marriage to the non-Israelite Tziporrah, has always made me wonder why she has been chosen as a heroine for a Jewish feminist reading of the Bible. Of course, the Bible does not offer us many good women exemplars (as Biblical women have the same flaws as Biblical men!), but does that mean that we are left to work only with what we have?

On a related note, I have always been uncomfortable with the tradition of a Miriam's Cup at the Passover Seder. While I appreciate the instinct to see the Seder ritual as an open table for new rituals to help us tell our story, and that women need to be a part of that story, my discomfort flows from the traditional Haggadah's careful omission of Moses from the narrative. Pharaoh is mentioned, but there are no Israelite heroes; only God. Following the traditional teaching of "not by an angel nor other agent but by God alone were the Israelites taken out of Egypt," the Haggadah is poignantly careful to avoid a glorification of Moses. Neither Moses nor Aaron is celebrated and neither should Miriam be. To have Miriam as a counterpart to Elijah is confusing, as Elijah's Cup is used at the closing of the Seder to welcome him in as the harbinger of the Messiah. Miriam is associated with the Exodus, looking back rather than forward, and to do so, to focus on her personal role, seems to me to go against the careful approach of the tradition in how to tell the story.

The other Biblical women who have been added to the liturgy are Sarah, Rebecca, Rachel, and Leah, whether directly after reference to the three Patriarchs, or simply by the addition of "and our mothers" following "our fathers." The word avoteinu can also be translated as "our ancestors," avoiding the male gendering. Part of the challenge is that Hebrew has no gender neutral usage, so the masculine can either be male-specific or can be more general as the default grammatical form. For example, whereas the word banot means "daughters," the word banim can mean either "sons" or

"children," depending on the context. The ambiguity of the ˈ
cause significant debate, as in the Talmudic discussion over wheth..
Torah commands us to teach our "sons" or our "children," where a point of
grammar makes a difference in whether girls are to be educated equally with
boys. Here, the intent of adding *ve-imoteinu* is to emphasize that the liturgy
is reflecting on the Matriarchs as well as the Patriarchs. While I understand
the motivation, I am troubled by the result of the addition, forcing the
word *avoteinu* to take on the male-specific meaning rather than the more
gender neutral and inclusive meaning. That is, the addition of the gender-
specific *ve-imoteinu* seems to hinder the general attempt to read the liturgy
in more gender-inclusive terms. I prefer to read *avoteinu* as referring to
"our ancestors" who are both male and female and neither male nor female.
"Our ancestors" is a nonspecific reference to the nation of old, referring to
the past, back to that place I seek to be transported to through the act of
worship. To limit the term to men serves to, in a sense, emasculate its power.

On the Inclusion or Exclusion of the Matriarchs

There is no ambiguity, though, that Abraham, Isaac, and Jacob were men.
The statutory prayer, the Amidah, always begins with the words: "Blessed
are You, our God and God of our ancestors/fathers, God of Abraham, God
of Isaac, God of Jacob." In his responsum that was accepted by Conservative
Judaism's Committee on Jewish Law and Standards on the question of "the
inclusion of the Imahot [Matriarchs] in the Amidah," Rabbi Joel Rembaum
argued that there was ample halakhic precedent for the adjustment of the
wording of the individual benedictions of the Amidah, so long as the number
of benedictions with their specific themes were maintained. Therefore he,
and the Law Committee in lending its support, saw no objection to the
addition of the phrase, "God of Sarah, God of Rebecca, God of Rachel, and
God of Leah." Opponents of Rabbi Rembaum's position, and of the inclusion
of the Imahot in the Amidah, argued that there was a difference between
"unconscious" evolution of liturgical text and conscious agenda-driven
changes. While evolution may creep into the standardized liturgical texts
because of errors of transmission, I find it difficult to believe that there was
never a role for scribal subjectivity in deciding how to set a prayer for a
particular community. I prefer to look at the question of the inclusion of
the Matriarchs from the perspective of historical tradition rather than law.

,oing back to the great debate on the language of prayer in 1845, Frankel could not dispute Geiger's claim that the halakhah permitted prayer in any language. Here, too, I cannot discount the halakhic arguments in favor of at least this particular liturgical change. For that reason—among other more properly political considerations—I have never seriously considered resisting the decisions of the congregations I have served as rabbi in adding the Matriarchs to the Amidah. When I lead the congregation in the public recitation of the Amidah, I always add the Matriarchs out of respect for the congregation's tradition. And I have no doubt that for those growing up with this liturgy it will seem as perfectly natural as it seems unnatural to me. For like Frankel, I do not see this as a halakhic issue but rather a Romantic (i.e., emotional) issue about the feel of prayer. The rhythms of the first paragraph of the Amidah are so ingrained in me that any change, no matter how long I try and no matter how principled it may be, will never have the resonance of the magic of the way I first learned the prayer, like the magic for Frankel of the Hebrew language as the mother-tongue of prayer itself.

And there are other reasons beyond mere habit for why I resist the inclusion of the Imahot, reasons that are also rooted in the historical approach to Judaism. The motivation behind the inclusion of the Imahot is that the initial covenant was with the Matriarchs as well as the Patriarchs; rather than only focus on the men, we must reclaim the women as co-principals of the story. I recognize in this contemporary feminist enterprise the very traditional hermeneutic of rabbinic midrash, an attempt to reread the text so that it says what we now hear it to say. But this is a traditional approach to reading texts that I can no longer accept. I can admire it and learn how it works in classical rabbinics, but I cannot apply it to texts myself. As a Positive Historical Jew, I am committed to reading texts *in context,* as opposed to reading them midrashically, which means acontextually and ahistorically. As I read it, the Matriarchs were not co-principals of the story. Genesis portrays a very patriarchal system; perhaps the very cultural model for patriarchy. Attempts to read in equality of the women are apologetics directed at a text that is ultimately unredeemable from this perspective. While I am committed to an egalitarian religious expression where men and women are equal, I cannot pretend that such was always the case, or even was meant to always be the case. Rather than argue that egalitarianism was embedded in the original pristine idea of Judaism and was somehow lost along the way, only to be recovered now, I prefer to accept that egalitarianism is a new value, a product of our time, introduced and grafted onto an older non-egalitarian tradition. To do otherwise would seem to deny and cover up the unjustness of what came before. I am not troubled that my vision of Judaism is not reflected in its pristine origins because, as a Positive Historical Jew, I deny that there ever was an original perfect pristine Judaism. The perfection is a moving target, flowing and evolving in every age. I omit the Imahot in my private devotions because I recognize that the God I pray to was not the god of the mothers of old, even if She is the God of my sisters today.

Chapter Three

HALAKHAH: LIVING THE SACRED

If Judaism is a legal culture, then the system of law can promote change as much as it can champion rigidity. Comprehending the history of the tradition can orient us toward accepting changes just as it can prejudice us against it. In the previous chapter, I argued how a Positive Historical orientation can promote liturgical conservatism. In this chapter, I argue how halakhic thinking can promote what might be interpreted as radical change. I will examine questions in the areas of the role of women in Jewish law, driving to synagogue on Shabbat, observance of kashrut (the dietary laws), the role of ethics in halakhah, and the halakhah of same-sex relationships. In each of these areas, I will demonstrate how the perspective of Positive Historical Judaism influences an approach that I believe reaches the standard of what Frankel called "moderate reform," even if he would not have recognized the specific results.

On the Role of Women

In Zacharias Frankel's synagogue, the men and women sat separately and only the men participated publicly in worship. What had changed in the nineteenth century, though, was that women were beginning to receive the same education as men. Religious education was particularly important for women in the modern era as women were seen to be the protectors of tradition in the home. It was they who kept the kitchens kosher and ensured that the children received the basics of Jewish education while the men often strayed too far into the non-Jewish world. As women sought and achieved more of the public status once reserved only for men, an increasing public role for women, specifically in worship, became both an ethical and a practical desideratum. In the 1970s and 1980s, when the more liberal denominations opened the doors of the synagogue and the rabbinate to women, and the Orthodox circled the wagons to defend the traditional division of roles, Conservative Judaism found itself embroiled in a heated and divisive struggle over these questions. The fault lines of the conflict were drawn on careful readings of obscure passages from halakhic literature. What were the precise qualifications necessary to serve in the rabbinate? On what basis did one count towards the minyan (quorum) for prayer? What was the level of a woman's obligation towards mitzvot (religious observances) traditionally performed by men? What was the status of a lone opinion that permits a woman to count toward a minyan for saying Birkat Hamazon (Grace after Meals)? What were the distinctions between established custom and legislation, and what was the authority of the contemporary rabbinate to overturn precedent? A debate about the role of women morphed into a philosophical discussion about the role of halakhah in contemporary Judaism and whether one could maintain loyalty to the halakhic system—if not to halakhic precedent—while promoting change. In the end, the majority of the Conservative rabbinate reconciled itself with change argued through halakhic terms, although they could never agree on which terms made the best argument.

In Appendix 1, the reader will find the text of a responsum covering these questions in historical and legal detail, which I wrote for the Law Committee and was accepted in 2002. My paper has a retrospective sense to it, reflecting on a generation of debate about egalitarianism. I came of age in the midst of the struggle in the 1980s and was blessed to have had the opportunity to study personally from many of the principal voices on the issue. At the time when the Conservative movement seemed poised to split over the question of women rabbis, I was a Solomon Schechter student and Ramah camper. My school and camp had — overnight — set up a choice of two services, one egalitarian and one not. Synagogues were choosing in which direction to go, and the Movement-wide institutions were trying to stay neutral. I remember answering for myself in both places why I, an apparently *frum* (observant) young man, would attend the egalitarian services. At the time it was the natural thing for me to do because my father was a Conservative rabbi who, with the majority of his colleagues, had voted for the admission of women to the Rabbinical Assembly and was working to bring more egalitarian worship into his congregation. But after being challenged in school and camp, I studied the rabbinic responsa with great interest and engaged my teachers in helping me figure out how the practice I supported was correct.

About twenty years later, I wrote my paper as an attempt to bring order to the plethora of legal approaches to the question, which I limited to the inclusion of women in the minyan and service as prayer leaders. While

I offered my own view that I had developed over those twenty years and hoped would have resolved many of the still-open questions, I found that, in order to win consensus, I had to phrase the paper as permitting women to count in the minyan through various legal means, by which my approach was but one of many. The debate revolved around the same issue covered in the previous chapter on the inclusion or exclusion of the Imahot in the Amidah. Is Judaism a tradition that changes and evolves through time, or is there a fundamental(ist) truth, in this case egalitarianism, that goes back to an authentic pristine core of Judaism's mythic origins?

In my responsum, I described the two concepts as representing two different schools of approach to the halakhic process. The appeal to a new reading of the "original" halakhah I attribute to the contributions of Rabbis Judith Hauptman and David Golinkin, both of whom argue, separately, that the halakhah always intended women to have the same obligations, thus the same privileges, as men in prayer and public worship. The culture developed where women were treated differently from men, but now we can revert to the original intent of the law and restore the full rights of women. The second approach, which I attribute to Rabbi Joel Roth and then to my own thinking, argues that there is no way to read the traditional precedents as having intended that women have equal obligations, rights, and privileges in public worship with men. We would not read the legal tradition in what was, we argued separately, an ahistorical and acontextual, or forced, meaning. We suggested that we must accept the tradition for what it is, but allow the process to evolve so that today, women may achieve the equal status to men that they could not achieve in the past. Now, of course, Rabbis Hauptman and Golinkin would argue that their readings of the halakhic tradition are not forced, just as feminist readers of the Bible argue that the Matriarchs were co-principals of the Genesis narrative. The discriminating student must decide, then, if a reading that goes against the way the text or tradition was always read and yet conforms beautifully with the contemporary agenda of the ones proposing the reading is as defensible as the alternative.

Not that the alternative approach is without its drawbacks! The Positive Historical approach to halakhic change lacks the aura of appeal to "original intent" and stands on its own, trusting that the religious leadership of the time has chosen the correct path for halakhic development. Conscious change lacks the authentic certainty of "correction" and requires greater faith in the evolutionary methodology of the halakhic process. And yet, it is this break with fundamentalism that is the hallmark of Positive Historical Judaism. It is this break that distinguishes Positive Historical Judaism on the one hand from the rigidities of Orthodoxy and on the other hand distinguishes it from the faith in a return to the pristine Prophetic religion of ancient Israel championed by the proponents of Classical Reform.

The interested reader can explore the details of the halakhic debate in Appendix 1. In brief, the argument proposed may be explained in three steps: 1) that a woman was traditionally excluded from counting in the minyan because her level of obligation in terms of regular daily prayer did not equal a man's (as argued in 1973 by Rabbi David Feldman); 2) that a woman could elect to assume an equal level of obligation in terms of regular daily prayer and thereby acquire the privilege of counting in the minyan and serving as prayer leader (as argued in 1979 by Rabbi Joel Roth); and 3) that after a generation of egalitarian worship in Conservative congregations, it can be assumed that women today understand that their obligations in terms of regular prayer are equal to those of a man's.

At the root of my argument on women and minyan was a belief that men and women both understand halakhah to be an obligation. Today, in non-Orthodox congregations, it is commonplace to find women rabbis and cantors and women reading Torah more often than men. We are starting to see more women wear tallit and tefillin, although there is still much work to be done there. But the question remains whether there is any sense of obligation towards halakhah in non-Orthodox communities. How can an argument permitting women to count in the minyan be based on the premise that they accept halakhic obligations when non-Orthodox Judaism as a whole rejects such obligations, argues the critique. In the responsum I argued that the fact that non-Orthodox Jews do not as a whole observe halakhah does not necessarily imply that they do not consider it to be obligatory. Offering what was perhaps an overly technical approach, I wrote that it is not the observance of the law but the acknowledgment of the sovereignty of the law that is requisite. People who drive above the speed limit, for example, know that the law forbids them from doing so, even if they have no expectation of punishment because they are driving, let us say, less than ten miles per hour above the limit. Enforcement power, I argued, is not a prerequisite for sovereignty, because then there would be no justification for Jewish law at all unless we were to really believe that God punishes us for transgressions. The paucity of halakhic observance on the part of non-Orthodox Jews is a challenge of behavior, not attitude.

The contemporary Jew, in my opinion, understands traditional Jewish practice as something that he or she *ought* to perform, whether or not one actually does so. I believe this not only because I recognize the prominence of "guilt" in Jewish culture, but more so because of the prominence of law. Halakhah remains the language and forum for discussion of the role of women in Judaism as it remains so for all other contemporary issues, and the predominance of the halakhic context is found across the denominations. Judaism is a culture of law, a Positive Historical tradition.

Driving to Synagogue on Shabbat

When Conservative Judaism, through its Committee on Jewish Law and Standards, decided in 1950 to permit driving to synagogue on Shabbat, it was seen as making a fundamental break with Orthodoxy. While mixed seating was already prevalent in Conservative synagogues, and many Conservative Jews drove to synagogue, often parking discreetly around the corner, it was this pronouncement of the clergy rather than the practice or custom of the people that drew a line in the sand between the Conservatives and the Orthodox. While subsequent decisions such as the admission into the rabbinate of women and, later, gay and lesbian Jews, counting women in the minyan, and performing same-sex marriages would seem to signify far greater changes in practice than the permission to use an automobile on the Sabbath, the celebrated 1950 decision is still looked upon by many as an "error" and miscalculation. Understood broadly as a concession to the realities of suburban life where Jews lived too far from their synagogues to reach them by foot, the decision to permit driving was offered in the context of revitalizing Shabbat observance. Yet it is remembered chiefly for permitting something that changed the nature of Shabbat and thereby delegitimized the claims to authenticity of non-Orthodox Judaism.

While there remain many non-Orthodox Jews who do not drive on the Sabbath, the overwhelming majority, including those who are committed in other respects to traditional Jewish living, do drive to synagogue. I have found it absolutely necessary as a rabbi to defend the legitimacy and integrity of the decision of 1950 and by extension those committed Jews who live by it. While I myself have preferred not to drive on Shabbat, I completely accept the halakhic legitimacy to do so. First, I am respectful of the very careful halakhic argumentation offered in the original decision by Rabbis Morris Adler, Jacob Agus, and Theodore Friedman. The ignition of the spark that starts the combustion engine does appear to be like lighting a fire, but one does not do so in the way that one lights a fire and for the purpose of lighting a fire. While resulting in an inevitable violation of Shabbat, when the violation is so technical and unintended, and when the intended result helps in the performance of a mitzvah, then there are grounds for allowing the violation. Second, I approach the question with a sense of humility. A true submission to the authority of halakhah is to accept the process independent of the argumentation of individual decisions. In any legal system one must submit to the results of the process even if one does not agree with the resolution. The United States has persisted under a single Constitution for more than two hundred years because the legal culture insists that the citizenry as well as the different parties accept the results of elections, legislation, and judicial rulings, whether they personally agree with them or not. Faith in the constitutional system supersedes individual disputes. All the more so in Judaism, where the legal culture is embedded in millennia of history; one must be able to accept a decision independent of how one feels about the issues involved. Third, as a matter of morale, it would be very difficult if I could not find the actions of my fellow congregants redeemable in how they attend regular Sabbath worship. Ultimately, law will always come to reflect the values of the community it represents, and in this case, the majority of the people invested in regular Sabbath worship attendance see driving to synagogue as necessary and therefore acceptable.

Finally, in historical perspective, driving to synagogue on Shabbat and the attendant issues of the use of electricity on the Sabbath do not mark a break with historical patterns because the decision was penned only a few decades after the advent of the automobile. Driving an automobile is as new a development in history as is suburban sprawl. Neither could have been imagined by rabbis living at the time of Frankel, a hundred years earlier. A car does not have to be cared for and fed and worked in the same way that one works an animal of burden. Unlike a horse, a car can be refueled and serviced during the week. Unlike fire, electricity is never truly ignited nor extinguished. Those authorities in the Conservative movement who have permitted the use of electricity on Shabbat liken its nature more to water (opening up a flow) than to fire (igniting and extinguishing a flame). The nature of the automobile and the use of electricity are new developments in technology not unrelated to the demographic spread of Jewish populations. I do not see the use of electricity or the automobile in driving to synagogue as a break with historical tradition, but rather as a new development offering different paths for halakhic development and evolution.

Keeping Kosher and "Eating Hot Dairy Out"

Together with the Sabbath, the discipline of keeping kosher is the principal mark of the halakhically observant Jew. Halakhic living is meant to encompass every moment of life, so that one does not put food into the mouth to satisfy the most basic appetite of hunger before thinking of what is permitted and what is forbidden. Keeping kosher establishes the hegemony of law over appetite, of culture over instinct. The ongoing debate over the meaning of the dietary restrictions becomes irrelevant when one considers them in these terms. Keeping kosher is a mark of being a fully cultured human being, like learning to eat with a knife and fork. The mechanics of eating are culturally determined. The Chinese consider it barbaric to pierce food as one does with knives and forks, and so they use chopsticks. Whatever the Torah intended by forbidding the boiling of a kid in its mother's milk, the law's prohibition of eating meat and milk together is not an ethical but a cultural observance. While the Jewish legal system seeks to codify ethics as law, laws can also reflect cultural preferences that are devoid of ethical value. Kashrut is an essential element of the legal culture that defines Judaism.

So much of the kosher-eating culture today has been consumed by discussions of what may not be eaten over what may be eaten. Higher and higher standards of rabbinic supervision, of slaughtering requirements, and of the washing of vegetables has stratified the kosher-eating world to the point where what is kosher for one Jew is not kosher for another, and what is kosher for that second Jew is still not kosher for a third. At the opposite end of the spectrum is the long-standing practice of committed non-Orthodox Jews—and some Orthodox Jews as well—of keeping kosher homes and what has come to be called "eating hot dairy out." Such Jews will eat in non-kosher restaurants but will avoid ordering any meat or shellfish. Shellfish can never be kosher, and no meat is kosher unless it has undergone ritual slaughter called *shehitah*. However, vegetables, dairy products, and most fish are, in theory, kosher. (There is a question about the rennet, or curdling agent, used to produce cheeses, but Rabbi Isaac Klein argued for the Law Committee that rennet should not be considered non-kosher because it goes through a chemically transformative process and becomes a new substance, a *davar hadash*, losing its prior identity as the product of an animal's stomach. Rabbi Klein similarly argued for the kashrut of gelatins, and also wrote an important responsum on the kashrut of swordfish.) The primary halakhic objection to "eating hot dairy out" is that when the food is cooked with the utensils that were used to cook non-kosher meats and shellfish or to mix meat and milk, the kashrut of the potentially kosher items becomes compromised. Is there any halakhic legitimacy, though, to the practice of eating hot dairy out?

While this reflection is not intended as a halakhic argument—in a word, yes. While eating in a kosher restaurant is certainly easier to justify, much like walking to synagogue on Shabbat, the practice of eating hot dairy out is observed by such a large number of committed Jews that it, like driving to synagogue on Shabbat, merits serious consideration.

In a responsum written for the Law Committee in 1940, Rabbi Max Arzt argued that it is reasonable to assume that no restaurant would ever prepare fish with the same utensils or on the same part of the grill as it prepares other foods because the smell of the fish would compromise the other food items. I once grilled hamburgers that smelled like salmon—a mistake that I will make only once. Rabbi Arzt argued that because in the majority of cases the fish would be prepared with its own dedicated utensils, one may, in halakhic judgment, "go with the majority," even if such is not always the case, and assume that the kashrut of the fish was not compromised by being cooked with utensils that are also used to cook meat. This responsum was limited to the question of fish, although it was depended on in practice to justify eating any hot "dairy" items out (with "dairy" used in the general sense of non-meat since fish is not dairy but "parve").

How might one justify the wider practice? Following the line of argument suggested by Rabbi Arzt, one might contend that there is a difference between an active and a passive role in the preparation of food. When one is preparing food in one's own kitchen, one cannot depend on assumptions but must act in accordance with the requirements of the law. All utensils must be kept separate and only kosher products may be brought into the kitchen. Meat and milk items can never be cooked or served together. But when one eats in another person's dining room, one may rely on the honesty of the server to not be deceptive by serving something that is not kosher. Sometimes, in the interest of peace, one learns not to ask too many questions. If I am invited to a home for Passover, for example, and the hosts claim that they are kosher for Passover, I do not question whether they kashered their kitchens properly or bought only specially hekshered (certified) Passover items. I rely on them to serve me what is proper and not what is improper. For me, the value of being able to eat in someone else's home as their guest takes precedence over the minutiae of kashrut. I do not need to discover something I don't need to know. Similarly, if invited to someone's home on a Saturday night, I do not need to interrogate my host to discern that no food items were cooked on Shabbat. I will simply assume that that was not the case, even if it actually was. The halakhah itself permits us to presume that all Jews observe halakhah, even if we know that that is not true, so I will avoid any specific information and presume, halakhically, that everything was prepared as I would have prepared it in my own home. This is a critical point because there are too many "newly minted" pious Jews in our day who will refuse to eat in the homes of their parents because they have chosen to observe a higher level of kashrut. Keeping kosher is not so inflexible a discipline as to exempt one from the obligation of honoring one's father and mother.

Eating in a non-kosher restaurant is more complicated than eating in someone else's home, but the principles are the same. True, in a restaurant there is no concern for insulting the host because the host is generally a business that we choose to patronize rather than a parent or neighbor or friend. And it is also true that one can often manage to eat in only kosher restaurants (depending on where one lives) and still survive socially and professionally in the modern world, as modern Orthodoxy has demonstrated. It is also true that one can live close to a synagogue so that one does not need to drive. For me, though, halakhah needs the flexibility to reach Jews where they are. No one can convince me that a Jew who never orders meat or shellfish in a restaurant is nevertheless an *okhlei treifos befarhesia*, an eater of forbidden foods in public. On the contrary, the Jew who only eats dairy in public is sanctifying God's name by demonstrating that he or she is committed to Jewish living at all times and in all places, not just on Shabbat and in the synagogue.

The principle of passive as opposed to active food preparation should still apply. If I am sitting in a restaurant and order hot dairy, I have no specific information that my food has been compromised by being cooked in a utensil that was used to cook meat within the past twenty-four hours (being the specific data that would compromise the kashrut). It is true that such an approach does require selective attention to one's surroundings. At the counter in a pizzeria, for example, the Jew who eats hot dairy out needs to not notice the pepperoni pizza coming out of the same oven that was used to bake the plain pizza. But here it must be emphasized that traditional kashrut requires no less an appreciation of reality. The laws of kashrut governing when flavors transfer from the food to the pot and back to the food, and what procedures are necessary to purify, or kasher, the utensil so that it can be used again, are almost impossible to justify when applied to the standards of food science. The halakhah, like any legal system, makes certain assumptions that may be informed by but are never determined by scientific knowledge. When one is truly at home in a legal culture, one can learn to live with some disparity between a scientific reality on the one hand and a legal reality—or presumption—on the other. To take an example from the field of criminal or civil jurisprudence, we understand that there may be a fact that is known to be true even when it cannot be proven legally, just as there are legal presumptions of facts even if they cannot be proven in reality. The decision, therefore, to make certain assumptions of law in regard to food preparation is not necessarily unreasonable from a legal perspective even if it may not be likely from a realistic perspective.

When one understands that halakhic observance is symbolic of adherence to a legal system of culture, one can be secure in one's adherence to that culture without needing to rely on the strictest avenue of practice and interpretation. Clearly one who orders only hot dairy in a restaurant is living a life according to a disciplined code of cultural conduct. If that code can be interpreted flexibly to permit one to live more comfortably in the world in a context where we mix with different people and travel to different places in ways unimaginable only a century ago, then such an interpretation would seem to preserve the general adherence to and survivability of that culture. That is the approach and the goal of Positive Historical Judaism.

On the Ethical and the Halakhic

While I have been discussing kashrut as an example of ritual adherence to a legal culture, kashrut has also been at the forefront of the discussion on the intersection of halakhah and ethics. Recent investigations have revealed large-scale abuses in the kosher meat industry in the United States in the areas of both labor relations and animal care. New efforts such as the Magen Tzedek program have developed that seek to examine the ethical standards of kosher food providers as an additional certification meant to complement the ritual certification of the kashrut authorities. The kashrut requirements themselves are not immune from ethical concerns. The smooth stroke of the carefully sharpened knife into the neck, so that blood and airflow to the brain are stopped thus causing the animal to faint, is analogous to the mercy killing of a bullet to the head. The requirement to bury the blood that flows from the chicken as well as the removal of the bulk of the remaining blood before the food can be eaten represents a respect for what the Torah calls "the life force" of the animal (Gen. 9:4). When laws are followed by the letter without concern for the spirit behind them, the culture of law that supports the structure begins to calcify. While a calf kept in a tiny pen its entire life might produce glatt kosher veal, the truly pious Jew should think twice before eating it. A complex negotiation must take place between the practicalities of the industrial world and the values of the consumers who support and fund it. The ethics of halakhah require that we learn more about how food is produced and how labor and animals are treated. The truly halakhic Jew will not use a kashrut certification as an excuse to disregard the ethical concerns that underlie the spirit of the law.

There is a particular pressure on a legal culture such as Judaism to read the ethical into the letter and spirit of the law even when it is not readily apparent. If the law represents the distilled values of the culture, then how can values or ethics be assessed when they fall outside of the law, or even of its spirit? The question begs another question: If the value or ethic is foreign to the spirit of the law, then from where did it originate? It can be either a "new idea," or more likely "borrowed" from another culture. Today the situation is even more complex because we live in multiple cultures that overlap into each other's jurisdictions, like a Venn diagram. If we live in the United States, for example, then it is natural that we take on certain American values as our own. They become part of how we see the world or how we believe the world ought to be, even if those values are not "authentically" Jewish. But if we believe in the halakhic system, then it must be able to encompass all of our values lest it become too parochial and ultimately irrelevant. That is what has unfortunately occurred already for too many modern Jews, a compartmentalizing of Judaism where it concerns only the "religious" parts of life rather than the claims to wholeness that every culture desires.

Why, one might ask, can we not believe in certain ethical values independent of Judaism? Why must there be a correlation between what is right and what is halakhic? Of course there are always cultural values that are ethically neutral. In Jewish thought we would call such values *ritual commandments*. But we recognize that there are also the *ethical commandments* which we consider paramount because they are not mere symbols; they effect relationships with the world around us, whether they are people, animals, or the environment. The problem is that when we accept an ethical value that seems to have no expression in our corpus of cultural values, the very cultural system starts to lose its force, as the culture has been judged to fall short of a higher ethical standard. We start to ask, Is there something wrong or inadequate in a culture that fails to recognize something that is so obvious to us? To translate this discussion into theological terms, if by "a legal system represents the articulation or codification of a culture's values" we mean "Halakhah is the Will of God," then why would God not have commanded something that is the right thing to do? How can there be any kind of ethical mandate outside of the Will of God?

While it may be too radical to claim that the Will of God changes through time, a more conservative approach to the theological problem would be to claim that while God's Will is perfect, the human—or the culture's—understanding of God's Will changes through time. This is precisely the approach of Positive Historical Judaism. A healthy legal culture with a functioning flexible legal system will always be able to adapt new ideas and values into its corpus. The law changes through time but at any one time the law is the Will of God for that particular point in time. The legal process as the method of understanding God's Will to figure out what is right is a process of historical evolution. As long as that process remains true to the broader legal culture, it can adapt and survive. Judaism has been accepting and offering values between itself and other cultures throughout its history. A value is only "foreign" until it is made "Jewish." Once it has become a part of Judaism it is authentically Jewish just as the respective Jewish and pagan elements in Christianity are now authentically Christian.

Homosexuality and Halakhah

The question of the status of homosexuality in halakhah, with the connected issues of whether gay and lesbian Jews could be ordained as rabbis and if rabbis could officiate at same-sex ceremonies, pushed the question of the intersection of halakhah and ethics to the forefront. While this question did not cause the same kind of divisiveness on the congregational level as did the debate over women's participation in public worship and women in the rabbinate, it raised more complex theoretical challenges. The public divisiveness was not as significant as the struggles over egalitarianism because, unlike a woman rabbi, a gay rabbi looks the same as any other. Unlike a public worship service with women's participation and officiated by women, a same-sex ceremony was a private affair. But on the theoretical level the stakes were higher. Whereas some made the claim that the ethical standard of the innate equality between men and women required the halakhah to adapt, one was hard-pressed to find clear statements in the halakhah to the contrary. Women were, as argued above, treated differently than men by the halakhah, but that could be understood, at least through a historicist reading of Jewish law, as a function of the role of women in society at the time. There were no overarching principles in the law demanding that women be unequal to men. The account in Genesis 2 of the woman's creation from the man's rib appears to be superseded in the Torah itself by the alternative account of Genesis 1 stating that men and women were created simultaneously in the image of God. Not so the case with homosexuality, which the Torah appeared to clearly understand as an abomination (Lev. 18:22). Nowhere does the Torah state that a woman may not be a rabbi or that women may not count in a minyan and lead the congregation in prayer. The fact that the Torah does not know about rabbis, minyans, and public prayer only emphasizes the theoretical difference between the two questions. The problem of homosexuality and halakhah as raised in the 1990s brought into direct conflict the ethical value of the dignity of all human beings with the status of the Torah and the halakhic system as an articulation—cultural and religious—of the right and the good.

On one side of the spectrum were those who condemned the Torah and halakhah as an anachronistic guide to ethical values, while on the other side of the spectrum were those who insisted that, as with egalitarianism, contemporary values foreign to Judaism were being promoted, values that violated the God-willed order of the world. Like the ancient idolatry that needed to be stamped out by the Prophets of old, so the "true believers" rallied against those who argued that the Jewish world find room for gays and lesbians.

Most responses fell between these two extremes. The Orthodox leader Rabbi Norman Lamm argued as early as 1974 (and for a wide audience in the annual supplement to the *Encyclopaedia Judaica*) that gay and lesbian Jews needed to be accepted with compassion, recognizing that sexual orientation may not be a conscious choice. Within Conservative Judaism, Rabbi Joel Roth argued in 1992 in his responsum for the Law Committee that the halakhah makes no prohibition or judgment as to sexual orientation and is solely concerned with sexual acts. Recognizing —while avoiding any assertion — that homosexuality may be innate or irrepressible, Rabbi Roth allows that a gay or lesbian Jew could be a rabbi as long as he or she represses acting on what he legally terms a "temptation" (*hirhur* in halakhic terms). In his paper, Rabbi Roth also makes a critical claim that could only come from a Positive Historical perspective, that when the Torah understands homosexual behavior to be abominable, the term it uses, *toʿevah*, refers to *attributed* rather than *inherent* abhorrence. Seeing how the same term is used to refer to the abhorrence of the Egyptians to sharing a table with Semitic nomads (Gen. 43:32), Rabbi Roth argues that the Torah's judgment against homosexual acts is an assertion of culture rather than a law of nature. Clearly distinguishing himself from those on the far right of the spectrum who understood homosexuality as a crime against nature, Rabbi Roth now had to explain why the halakhic system ought to retain such a culturally determined value. His explanation, rooted in Talmudic and medieval rabbinic commentaries, was that the halakhah was concerned with the values of marriage, family, and children. Homosexual behavior needed to be checked culturally in order to prevent men and women from deciding to avoid marrying, building families, and raising children.

My own response to Rabbi Roth, written for the 2006 deliberation of the Law Committee, together with Rabbi Myron S. Geller and my father, Rabbi Robert E. Fine, appears at the end of this volume as Appendix 2. That paper was a culmination of fourteen years of wrestling with the challenge of the intersection of halakhah and ethics in the case of homosexuality. I was an undergraduate in 1992 when the Law Committee deliberated on Rabbi Roth's and a series of other papers. I sat with dozens of other observers at the final meeting, held in the auditorium at the Seminary, experiencing the tension among students, professors, and rabbis as we watched the Law Committee vote. Fourteen years later, after much private and public debate, I was honored to have my own paper voted on by that Committee, although the outcome was not exactly what I wanted.

From 1992 to 2006, I was fascinated and challenged by the question of Judaism and homosexuality. I read the 1992 papers that were proposed by the Law Committee and attended the final session with great interest as a Conservative Jew, recognizing in this question a test of the mettle of how Conservative Judaism and its approach to halakhah can respond to a question like this with such a seemingly clear conflict between the halakhic and the ethical. For me this was an intellectual problem about Conservative Judaism. I was not interested in the question because of anyone I knew who was gay or because of any political concerns. I found the papers lively and exciting and the deliberations in New York dramatic. I then returned to Wesleyan, my small New England college, where I was enjoying my sophomore year, eager to share the ideas that were expressed and my first-hand account of what had transpired. My student community at Wesleyan, consisting of some graduate students and mostly undergraduates of various Jewish backgrounds, was well informed and keenly interested in what I had to share. That year, I had already become one of the core leaders of the Jewish student community. After sharing with my new community my excitement over the ideas, I was unprepared for the emotional response of those directly invested in the outcome of the Law Committee's proceedings.

What was for me an intellectual challenge, was for my friends an existential question. While I was invested existentially in the viability of Conservative Judaism as the central component (as it was) of my Jewish identity, for my friends the issue was so much more personal. I should have known better and prepared myself for the pain of deeply committed Jewish gays and lesbians upon reading Joel Roth's paper—which I admired—and hearing of the Committee's decision to maintain what was then the status quo. My own journey from the theoretical to the real was and is mirrored in the continuing movement to recognize the lives of same-sex couples. For myself, I was fortunate to have experienced the very varied undergraduate environment that Wesleyan offered where I was pushed, both socially and intellectually, emotionally and existentially, to grow. In my senior year, for example, I registered for an anthropology course on sexuality and the law. It actually took me several class sessions until I realized that, sitting among twenty students and a professor, I was the only straight person in the room. True education happens when the perfect balance is reached between being challenged and feeling safe. Wesleyan was that perfect place for me.

Writing my term paper for that seminar was my first attempt to see how Jewish law might respond to gay and lesbian Jews in a different manner than the 1992 decision of the Law Committee. A few years later, while in Israel for my third year of rabbinical school, I wrote a Hebrew responsum on this question for a seminar on responsa literature. My professor, Rabbi David Golinkin, told me he disagreed with every word I wrote but gave me an A. I continued the project at the Seminary as another term paper, this time for a course on jurisprudence with Rabbi Gordon Tucker. My part of the paper mentioned earlier, submitted to the Law Committee for deliberation in 2006 with my father and Rabbi Geller, was the culmination of those fourteen years of research, writing, arguing, teaching, learning, and growing.

The paper we wrote for the Law Committee agrees in principle with Rabbi Roth's understanding of the value underlying the law, with the concern for marriage and children. But, in our view, the nature of society has changed so that today, where same-sex couples are able to marry and raise children as they were never able to do in the past, the reasons for the law's stringency and negative valuation no longer apply. On the contrary, the overriding concern of the culture as articulated in the law — that Jews seek marriage and children — would support an overturning of the precedent today. In our responsum we proposed that the change in law be understood systemically, as a limitation of the original law (*mi'ut* in halakhic terms), so that the prohibition could not apply to our society where same-sex couples are able to marry and have children.

Both Rabbi Roth's and my approach sit squarely within the perspective of Positive Historical Judaism. We both understand the law to be culturally determined and subject to historical development. Our difference lies only in our subjective assessment of the case at hand: whether society has changed enough to warrant an adjustment of the law and whether such a change would and can uphold the overriding principles of the law. A sad and frustrating moment for me, then, was when that same Law Committee, before whom we argued this approach, determined through special procedural means that Rabbis Geller, Fine, and I failed to meet the standard of judicial halakhic discretion. Arguing that our methodology was more legislative fiat than judicial interpretation, that we depended too much on unproven sociological developments such as the acceptance of same-sex marriages and unions in civil jurisdictions, and that our approach was, in essence, too radical, the Committee voted to raise the threshold of the vote that would be taken on the validity of our paper, a higher threshold that we would surely fail to reach.

I made a speech that day to the Law Committee that I still believe was the most important speech of my life. It was not easy to do. I already had been working as a congregational rabbi for five years, and a man had just died after a long illness, leaving behind a widow and young children. The funeral was the morning of that final day of the Law Committee's deliberations. I officiated at the service, attended by hundreds of people, and then rushed to the Park Avenue Synagogue in Manhattan where the Law Committee was meeting, sending my cantor to preside over the burial. That decision was not without some political cost to me in my congregation. More immediate for me at the time was the personal sadness in not being able to complete the burial for the family and be there at that moment of profound closure. But I had learned what I did not understand fourteen years before, that the results of this sacred deliberation of the Law Committee would affect the lives of many people, could replace sadness with joy, and might even save lives. I also believed I was defending Torah, maintaining its relevance for a new generation. While not usually stated in such dramatic terms, rabbis must make choices where a decision to be present in one place means we are absent in another.

And so I delivered my speech to the Law Committee, articulating an approach to Jewish law that argued for broad judicial discretion, an acknowledgment of the evolutionary process and how the text is understood, and the critical importance of recognizing societal changes as the fundamental canvas of history upon which all our traditions rest. I argued for Positive Historical Judaism as it applied to change in Jewish law, as I saw it. It was the most important and most difficult speech I ever gave, not only because so much was riding on it, but also because the odds were against me. In the end, I lost. My teacher, Rabbi Roth, did not vote with the majority that found our approach extraordinarily radical requiring the higher threshold. Joel Roth's approval at that moment, for my methodology if not for my conclusions, was very meaningful, even as we lost the vote 12 to 9. The fact that the following decade saw more and more dramatic changes in laws, culminating in the 2015 U.S. Supreme Court ruling in *Obergefell v. Hodges* guaranteeing a constitutional right to same-sex marriage and supporting our conclusion that society had changed, the fact that a survey of Conservative rabbis and other leaders indicated that a majority agreed with our approach, the fact that the Rabbinical Assembly itself subsequently decided to eliminate the special procedure that the Law Committee had invoked to defeat our responsum, and the fact that another opinion was approved that did allow for gay and lesbian rabbis in the Conservative movement, did not mitigate the realization that in 2006 the Conservative movement was not yet ready to hear what we were saying. However, we are as much a product of our disappointments as we are of our successes.

By taking the time to reflect on that decision, my motivation is not to rehash old struggles but to elucidate the theoretical perspective of Positive Historical Judaism as opposed to another approach that was, in my estimation, more fundamentalist. Conservative Judaism's Committee on Jewish Law and Standards did, in 2006, approve the responsum that authorized the ordination of gay and lesbian rabbis and the celebration of same-sex ceremonies, even as it also confirmed a restatement by Rabbi Roth as well as a responsum by Rabbi Leonard Levy that suggested that gay and lesbian Jews seek therapeutic efforts to "overcome" their homosexual tendencies. Rabbi Roth's responsum, like his 1992 contribution, made no such claims on the merits of therapy and accepted the stipulation that homosexuality was not a "choice" of the gay or lesbian Jew, the "choice" being homosexual behavior. Rabbi Roth's emphasis on the choice of behavioral action is important as it not only distinguished him from the approach of Rabbi Lamm, which he criticized, but also from the responsum that the Committee accepted authorizing the ordination of gay and lesbian rabbis and the celebration of same-sex ceremonies that was penned by Rabbis Elliot N. Dorff, Daniel S. Nevins, and Avram I. Reisner. Rabbis Dorff, Nevins, and Reisner, following the approach of Rabbi Lamm, argued that the halakhah must recognize, as it perhaps did not recognize in the past, that one who is gay or lesbian has no real choice in the matter and therefore falls under the category of one who is compelled to do something, where the state of compulsion (*ones* in halakhic terms) overcomes the transgression. Rabbi Roth, in his 1992 paper, rejected this entire approach to the question of homosexuality by relying on Talmudic precedent that there can be no compulsion in sexual action. That is, one may be raped (including a man) but one may not claim compulsion when one has actively initiated a sexual act. Rabbi Roth's argument was that sexual orientation could not be used as an argument for compulsion, that one has no choice, any more so than a heterosexual man could not claim compulsion due to his heterosexual orientation when he committed a forbidden heterosexual act such as adultery. This insight points to another significant weakness in the approach of Rabbis Dorff, Nevins, and Reisner that their responsum, even its permissive conclusion, reads as if it is a concession.

Let me state here unambiguously that I fully support the decision that Conservative Judaism reached in 2006 through the action of the Law Committee on the responsum by Rabbis Dorff, Nevins, and Reisner, and the subsequent acceptance of gay and lesbian Jews by the Ziegler School of Rabbinic Studies of American Jewish University and by the Jewish Theological Seminary into their rabbinical and cantorial programs on the basis of that decision. And, as it should be assumed without saying, I hold Rabbis Dorff, Nevins, and Reisner in the greatest respect as scholars, and I value their friendship. My disagreement with them falls under the category *mahloket leshem Shamayim,* a "controversy for the sake of Heaven." As I wrote earlier in regard to the 1950 decision on driving to synagogue on the Sabbath, one can, and must, accept the decisions of the systemic authority even if one does not agree. In this case I do wholeheartedly agree with the overall results of the decisions. My disagreement remains chiefly theoretical although with some practical aspects, and for those reasons Rabbis Geller and Fine and I (as did Rabbi Gordon Tucker with his similarly rejected paper) submitted our responsum as a dissenting opinion in 2006. The reader may refer to Appendix 2 for the details of the halakhic disagreement. I will focus here on the theoretical substance and how it relates to the principles of Positive Historical Judaism. My impetus is not to re-argue the case but rather to address the important issues of theory — of how law can evolve — which was the problem that drove me to write the responsum in the first place.

Rabbis Dorff, Nevins, and Reisner read the prohibition of the Torah in Leviticus very carefully as applying, first, only to male-male intercourse, as made clear in the text itself, and, second, as applying only to anal intercourse, as made clear in the Talmud's legal commentary. On these points all agreed. The next step in their argument, that all other forms of sexual intimacy between men and all forms of sexual intimacy between women were not forbidden by the Torah but (only) by subsequent rabbinic legislation, was contested, at least in part, by Rabbi Roth. The distinction between Toraitic law (*de'oraita* in halakhic terms) and rabbinic law (*derabbanan* in halakhic terms) is a complex theoretical determination since so much of rabbinic law is derived through midrashic (acontextual) inference from the Torah. The theoretical pitfalls of the discussion were articulated best by Rabbi Tucker who said, in the context of this discussion, that "the definition of what is *de'oraita* is itself *derabbanan*." The distinction, though, does play an important systemic role when conflicts between laws occur. In general, the halakhic system is stricter with its treatment of Toraitic (or primary) legislation and more lenient with its treatment of rabbinic (or secondary) legislation. I will return to the theoretical difference between Toraitic and rabbinic law in the following chapter. The distinction was important here because Rabbis Dorff, Nevins, and Reisner introduced the competing claim of human dignity (*kevod habriyot* in halakhic terms). Understanding that gay and lesbian Jews have no choice regarding their sexual orientation, they argued, human dignity demands that we acknowledge and respect them for who they are, and embrace them and their lives within the fold of the Jewish community. The argument of human dignity was essential because, in the halakhic system, it can override rabbinic prohibitions. The problem is that human dignity as a halakhic concept does not override Toraitic prohibitions. So the third and resolving tier of their argument was that all of the rabbinic prohibitions relating to homosexuality, that is, all of them save for male-male anal intercourse, are overturned. Gay and lesbian Jews may live together as couples and may become rabbis and cantors. Only gay men must avoid anal sex.

The strength of the argument put forward by Rabbis Dorff, Nevins, and Reisner, and the reason it was able to win consensus support, was that it found a way to reach the desired halakhic change without significant change to the way the Torah itself was read. Adjustment to the meaning of a clear voice in the Torah was seen by too many as a line that could not be crossed if Conservative Judaism was to retain its authenticity as a form of halakhic Judaism. And yet it is precisely that strength that also marks the weakness in the argument.

The approach of Rabbis Dorff, Nevins, and Reisner represented, on one level, an appeal to the fundamentalists in Conservative Judaism who could not comprehend a system where the Torah's meaning could be adjustable. While the responsum succeeded in adjusting policy in accord with contemporary values, there were a number of unresolved issues. I will limit the discussion here to three concerns: sexual relations between men; bisexuals; and the question of how to read the Torah.

Sexual relations between men. This is perhaps the most obvious liability of the responsum of Rabbis Dorff, Nevins, and Reisner. They find no way to halakhically justify anal sex between men. In our dissenting opinion, Rabbis Geller and Fine and I argued that we found this approach inconsistent with Jewish sexual ethics where all forms of sexual intimacy are permitted within the sanctified context of marriage. Neither can one argue that the restrictions of the responsum are only technical and best left to the private domain. Some years after the decision was published, I was contacted by a prospective cantorial student who confided his struggle with applying to the Jewish Theological Seminary if he were forced to keep the nature of his sexual life "in the closet." While no one at the Seminary was going to ask him specifically about his intimate life, this prospective student could not see himself committing to an institution still pursuing a policy of "don't ask, don't tell." In a sense, nothing had changed, at least in the mind of this prospective student, who decided not to apply and perhaps not even pursue his dream of becoming a cantor. Overall, the restrictive aspects of the responsum seemed to many as too tentative and prurient as to offer a compelling vision of Jewish sexual ethics for our day.

Bisexuals. What about the Jew who is capable of feeling attraction towards men and women but has chosen to be with a partner of the same sex? The responsum of Rabbis Dorff, Nevins, and Reisner seems to offer little help in such a circumstance because so much of their argument is based on the use of the concept of human dignity as a concession to the sexual orientation of the individual rather than to the conscious choice of the individual to be with another human being of the same sex. Their argument is based on the assumption that sexual orientation is inherent and cannot be changed. But what if it *is* a choice? For the bisexual the choice is recognized by definition. Alternatively, the approach offered by Rabbis Geller and Fine and myself stands independent of the nature of the sexual attraction. There is no concession in our paper as to whether or not one has a choice in being gay. Our focus was on the cultural value of marriage, family, and children. The entire body of prohibitions does not apply when the same-sex couple is able to form a family. Our halakhic ruling applies independent of the sexual orientation of the Jew, but rather is dependent on the social possibility that the Jew can marry and form a family.

The question of how to read the Torah. The difficulty—or inability—of applying the responsum by Rabbis Dorff, Nevins, and Reisner to bisexuals draws attention to the most significant problem with their paper: They seem to support the preference of heterosexual relationships over same-sex relationships. This preference becomes clear when one asks how, according to their paper, does one read Leviticus 18:22? By opting to uphold the traditional, if restrictive, understanding of the prohibition in the Torah, Rabbis Dorff, Nevins, and Reisner seem to say that there is still something "abhorrent" in male-male relations. One may ask, then, what is it? Is it only anal sex per se that is abhorrent, while all other forms of same-sex intimacy are not? And if so, what is it, then, about anal sex between men that is so abhorrent when it is specifically permitted by halakhah (along with all other forms of consensual intimacy) between husbands and wives? Or, alternatively, are they suggesting that all same-sex relations are abhorrent, but we still permit other forms as a concession to human dignity? Or perhaps only male-male intimacy is still regarded as abhorrent while female-female intimacy is not? These questions remain unresolved by their approach because theirs is essentially a systemic elimination of a whole area of law without offering a new reading of the Torah verse that drives that same area of law in the first place. That is, they have eliminated an entire body of law that they have determined to be rabbinic law, without—by design—touching the status of the Toraitic law that inspired all of the supportive rabbinic prohibitions. Because the initial reading of the Torah law is preserved, the cultural value inherent in the law seems to remain as well.

Judaism is a legal culture in which laws describe the values of the culture. If the original verse from the Torah represents a value that is still held by the culture, then so be it. But if not, then it must be reread in a way that expresses a cultural value. The Torah must be read in a way that maintains its use as a cultural code. There will be parts of the Torah that do not speak to us today. Some laws fall into misuse such as those governing slavery, but others will maintain their force, even if revised and reinterpreted. I am not suggesting that we in any way "pretend" that the Torah always meant that two men and two women could marry and raise children. As with the earlier discussion on the role of women in public worship, we cannot rewrite the history of the law. But we must allow history to continue its progress. What are our values today? How do we understand God's Will today? How do we read the Torah today?

Homosexuality is just one area where our contemporary ethical values seem to come into conflict with the precedents of the halakhah. My reflections on the halakhic issues are presented at length because this is the perfect case to exemplify the conflict and possible resolutions between halakhah and ethics. Another classic example of such conflict is the relative disability of women as opposed to men in marriage law. That is, according to Jewish law the man "acquires" the woman as a wife and only he can initiate a divorce. Many have suggested that the marriage ceremony be changed so that the man and the woman enter the marriage as equal legal partners and each have authority to initiate dissolution. While such an idea is certainly more equitable, and is the best approach in developing the new structures of same-sex marriage in the Jewish context, I do not support the change for heterosexual marriage. Consistent with my reasons for liturgical conservatism outlined in the previous chapter, I believe that more is lost than gained when we forgo traditional formulae. When I officiate at the marriage between a man and a woman I always say, in introducing the *ketubah* document, that the Aramaic is the same as that used by Jewish men and women over two millennia, "except that this one has your names on it." The issues of equity can be, and are, resolved through agreed handling of property disputes (either through the civil courts, arbitration, or mediation), and by rabbinic annulment of marriages (practiced by the Rabbinical Assembly as *hafka'at kiddushin*) when the husband refuses to authorize dissolution.

Sometimes form is just form. Other times the form of law communicates a value that stands at odds with our understanding of what is right, that is, of God's Will. It is ultimately a subjective judgment when and how the halakhah requires movement. My answers do not stand alone. They are genuine, but also invite disagreement. Only an engaged community and a responsive rabbinate can maintain the vibrancy of the culture of law that we call halakhah.

Taking a Step Back

While this discussion has focused on matters of legal interpretation and theory, we must remember that Jewish observance is ultimately an emotional rather than a philosophical action. Traditional observance is at once the affirmation of a culture's values through living and also a poetic clinging to one's need for order, structure, and meaning. The very limited discussion of halakhah in this chapter has focused on Shabbat, kashrut, and marriage because these are three key areas where the halakhah demonstrates its cultural power. In each case, the legal culture engages with the individual in establishing a discipline that embeds the cultural process into the realities of life. There is no more basic element of society than commerce, the interaction of human beings with each other for trade and the pursuit of gain. Shabbat disciplines that enterprise by demanding that we cease from commerce, to the extent defined by the law, for one out of every seven days. There is no more basic need than to eat and no more basic instinct than sex, and yet in both cases the halakhah channels and controls our actions so that we learn to establish culture over more base desires. By channeling commerce, food, and sex, the culture of halakhah teaches the Jew how to make life holy, living the sacred.

Chapter Four

SACRED TEXT

If Judaism is a legal culture, it is also a textual culture. The entire structure of the law can be understood as a commentary on the text, a map or path—literally "halakhah"—on how to live in light of the text. In the traditional understanding, God gives the text, from which flows the halakhah, to which the people respond in every generation. From the perspective of Positive Historical Judaism, however, the elements are the same but the order is flipped. The people write their own culture through history, informed by what came before but also by the continuing process of distillation of values and customs. Each generation produces texts that take their place in the literary corpus of the culture, describing and articulating the lives and hopes of the people, and those texts are themselves distilled and accepted by future generations as representing, at least in part, the Will of God.

While recognizing that this "flipping of the order" in process may be revolutionary, one must still ask whether it fundamentally changes the nature of the process. One way to approach this question is to understand the three distinct acts of doing, writing, and reading. The previous two chapters discussed "doing" and "writing" Judaism. That is, how does the perspective of Positive Historical Judaism change the way one behaves as a Jew in terms of the observance of Jewish law? And how does the perspective change the way one engages in the halakhic process in terms of crafting rabbinic legal opinions? However, the observance of halakhah should stand independently of how one understands the source of its authority. The history of Jewish thought is filled with different motivations for the observance of mitzvot. Any motivation was considered acceptable and authentic if it succeeded in supporting compliance and fidelity. The feelings of one observing a law that is understood to be sanctified through the process of history, rather than by direct command of the Divine Will, of course will be different from those of one who believes otherwise. Also, the feelings of one who observes a law because one finds its specific reasons to be compelling will be different from those of one who observes out of general loyalty to the system. One who observes because one wants to secure a place in the afterlife is different from one who observes the law in order to hasten the advent of the Messiah in this world, just as one who observes for the joy of communal celebration is different from one who observes to achieve a private mystical state. The inner spirituality of the observing Jew varies from person to person. What unites each type, including the Positive Historical Jew, is living the culture.

"Writing" Judaism is not that different. The individual theology of the rabbi answering a halakhic question is not significant as long as the rabbi answers within the systemic language (or cultural code) that attains authenticity for the writer and the (sub)community for which he or she writes. No one can ever, or has ever, achieved recognition of authenticity from the whole Jewish people in his or her own day. Jewish culture is too dialectical for anything of substance to be contributed without a corresponding rebuttal. The greater the substance, the greater the controversy. This was the case, for example, with the work of Maimonides, arguably the greatest rabbi of all time. This extraordinary legalist and philosopher was the source of polarizing conflict in the worlds of halakhah and Jewish theology.

While no rabbi has managed to avoid controversy, a rabbi who can write authentically for his or her community falls squarely within the history of halakhic literature. Some claim, though, that there is a difference when one understands the process as historical rather than revelational. Is there a difference, the question is asked, when one is consciously contributing to a historical process rather than trying to understand what God willed in the original texts? The claim is made that those who are (more) conscious of the historical process are more comfortable in applying flexibility to halakhic precedent. Is it an accident that a Positive Historical perspective might support women rabbis, driving to synagogue on Shabbat, eating hot dairy out, and same-sex marriage; none of which are championed in the Orthodox world? Perhaps not. The argument of much of this volume's second chapter was that a historicist perspective can just as easily support a conservative over a liberal (or radical) perspective, and that Frankel himself articulated the idea of Positive Historical Judaism to argue for the retention of Hebrew as the traditional language of prayer. The American heirs of Frankel's Positive Historical Judaism called themselves "Conservative" because of this very relationship between history and tradition. Nevertheless, Conservative rabbis influenced by historicist thinking tend to be more liberal in their reading of halakhah than are Orthodox rabbis. But to add another level of complexity, much of the detailed argument in the previous chapter, combined with the first two appendices, supports the position that there are liberal opinions on halakhic questions that are rooted in a more fundamentalist or ahistorical reading of texts, just as there are more conservative opinions that are rooted in historicist reading. While it is possible that the historicist perspective fosters greater halakhic flexibility, it is by no means certain. Another possible explanation for the generally more lenient view of Conservative rabbis toward halakhic questions, compared to the views of Orthodox rabbis, may be rooted in the nature of the communities that Conservative rabbis serve, as opposed to those served by Orthodox rabbis. Conservative rabbis, if they are to become authentic rabbis for their communities, have to read halakhah more flexibly, just as Orthodox rabbis must read the tradition more strictly. What is key to this broader question is that the way that one "writes" Judaism is based on the way that one "reads" Judaism.

Are sacred texts, then, read differently by readers who recognize that their sacredness is rooted in their canonization by the people through history rather than through their direct revelation from God? Perhaps, although this is by no means merely a modern question. The Catholic writer James Carroll suggested in *Constantine's Sword,* his monumental and popular volume on Church-Jewish relations, that it should be easier for Catholics than for Protestants to "rewrite" the "mistakes" of the first generation of Christians who wrongly wrote anti-Judaism into their foundational texts:

> What has been distinctive about the Catholic tradition ever since Martin Luther raised the banner of *sola scriptura,* or "Scripture alone," as the measure of truth has been its emphasis on the claim that the normative literature of our community was produced by that community, and not the other way around. The New Testament, that is, was made by the Church; the Church was not made by the New Testament. That is why, speaking generally, Catholics differ from Protestants in the importance given to the authority of the Bible on the one hand, and the authority of the Church on the other. Therefore, Catholics more than Protestants would tend to say that the community has authority over its normative literature (Carroll, *Constantine's Sword,* p. 103).

We may be too dependent on Protestant influences when we view the Bible as the end of God's word rather than the beginning. The idea that the Jewish community or the rabbis or historical development determines how we read and understand Torah is not a revolutionary idea, as it has deep roots in the Catholicism that James Carroll describes. If Catholics can say that the text does not determine God's Will but only serves as guidance to the decisions of the Church, why can't we? If Catholics can recognize that the understanding of God's Will is an ongoing revelation between God and the faith community of the Church—whether embodied in a pope, a synod, a Vatican conference, or the Church as a whole—why can't we understand the same role for "Catholic Israel" (to borrow Solomon Schechter's phrase)?

At the same time, modern Judaism is indebted to nineteenth-century German liberal Protestantism for its evolution of Martin Luther's emphasis on "Scripture alone" to what we call today modern biblical research. German Protestant scholars applied the tools of historical and literary analysis to the Bible, reconstructing not only our understanding of the New Testament, but of the Hebrew Bible as well. The so-called "Documentary Hypothesis" of the origins of the Torah was famously summarized in 1878 by the German Protestant scholar Julius Wellhausen, who identified the J, E, P, and D sources, later redacted together into the Pentateuch. According to Wellhausen's description, the Yahwist source (J, pronounced in German as a Y) is marked by the use of YHWH for God's name in Genesis, whereas the Elohist source (E) is marked by the use of *Elohim* for God's name in Genesis. Each represents two complete versions of the texts that were later combined into a JE narrative. The Priestly source (P) is generally marked by priestly concerns related to the Temple cult, ritual purity, and genealogies. The Deuteronomist source (D) is generally marked by a concern for the centralization of worship and a theology of covenant and exile that is the overriding thesis of the broader "Deuteronimistic History" that dominates the subsequent Biblical narrative telling the history of ancient Israel through the fall of Jerusalem in 586 BCE. While the specifics of the Documentary Hypothesis have been debated and adjusted ever since its first publication, the basic premise — that the Torah is a composite human document — has been the accepted consensus of biblical scholarship in the academic world. And yet, its "discovery" by individuals who grew up with more traditional conceptions of God and Torah is often made with resistance. The fundamental premise of traditional Judaism is that God gave the Torah to the

People at Mount Sinai through Moses. How to respond to the Documentary Hypothesis has been one of the central questions of Jewish thought since the late nineteenth century. While much of Orthodoxy has drawn a line in the sand in remaining steadfast to "Torah True Judaism," we have seen in the last chapter how devotion to text plays a strong role in non-Orthodox Judaism as well. The devotion of traditional Jewish thinking to the literary unity of the Pentateuch is strikingly different from the Christian acceptance of four different evangelical testimonies: Matthew, Mark, Luke, and John. The voices of J, E, P, and D are more univocal than those of the Evangelists because they were so masterfully redacted into the composite document that is the Pentateuch.

The encounter with the academic views on the origins of the Pentateuch is often an acute spiritual crisis. Whether early in life, in university classrooms, or at seminary, the realization that the Torah is not what we thought it was and not what we had been taught is a difficult transition. I have long thought that we need to do a better job in religious education in teaching what we really believe if we want our "Torah" to last in the minds of thinking Jews. It is in that spirit that I have written this book.

My own crisis came when I was thirteen years old, just a few months after my bar mitzvah, enjoying a summer at Camp Ramah. Part of the camp program was a Bible course, and my teacher was Rabbi Gerald Skolnik, who was later to serve as president of the Rabbinical Assembly. The crisis came one day in Rabbi Skolnik's class. We were studying the first book of Samuel and had just read the eighth chapter where the people ask Samuel for a king, anticipating Saul, the first king of Israel. Although the people prevail in the end, Samuel tries to convince them that they do not need a king because God is their king. In class, Rabbi Skolnik then taught us the law of the king from Deuteronomy 17, instructing what to do when the people ask for a king and what the limitations of the king should be. Samuel seemed unaware of those instructions and of the limitations, such as building a cavalry of Egyptian horses, having many wives, and amassing gold and silver to excess. (These limitations, I would later learn, are clearly based on the negative assessment of King Solomon in First Kings 10 and 11, an assessment that, like First Samuel 8, seems unaware of Deuteronomy 17.) As I wrote in a letter home to my parents on August 7, 1986:

We studied today in Rabbi Skolnik's class ch[apter] 8 [of 1 Samuel], which is when the people ask for a king. We discussed Shmuel's [Samuel's] despondent response of rejection. Then Rabbi Skolnik read several words from Sefer Devarim [Deuteronomy] saying that if the people ask for a king they shall get one—and then several rules. Wouldn't Shmuel have known that and not reacted the way he did? When he prayed to God, He [God] would have said: "As I told Moses so shall you do." The people would have said: "Give us our right from the Torah!" The answer is because Sefer Devarim was written after the story of Shmuel. Rabbi Skolnik even called it a "response." I asked why the author of Devarim wrote that. Rabbi Skolnik said that it was to allow the King to reign and to solve problems with the King. But then Sefer Devarim is a political lie undeserving of its kedushah [holiness]. What did Moses say? Did he give such speeches before he died or was Kriat Shma [the reading of the Shma: the passages from Deuteronomy 6, Deuteronomy 11 and Numbers 15 read each morning and evening] written by one of David's scribes in the name of Moses? What is true and what's not of the Torah? What gave the author the right to call his book "law"? But the first part of Devarim is written like any other prophetary volume; it begins in [the] third person (these are the words of Moses at so and so a place which he said to etc. etc.). Then Moses speaks. Could some of the speeches have survived the Exodus? Obviously, the part about the King didn't. But if it [the law about the king] was for political purposes, what makes it holy? How could a man sanctify something and make it holy if it was not? What if the whole idea of Shabbat was made up by a king of Judah? Why should Shabbat be holy then? I don't know. Who installed the priesthood? Was there an Aharon [Aaron], Eliezer, and Pinchas [Phineas]? Was there a Moses? How could all of the locations listed in Bamidbar [Numbers] and Devarim [have] been remembered over the generations? What about the first chapters of Bereishit [Genesis]? Where did they come from? What about the Ten Commandments? If none of these came from Sinai then what did? What is Sinai? Was there a revelation? If not, where did the Mishkan [Tabernacle] develop? How could a king write the Ten Commandments in the name of God? If it was a navi [prophet], it would have been mentioned in the book of the navi. I think you get my point. What is Torah?

My father wrote back, promising to answer all my questions upon my return from camp. At home he explained to me about the different concepts of "revelation" and gave me a volume of Heschel to read, a book that I dissected. In his response to me on August 13, 1986, my father wrote: "[Your questions] ultimately culminate in a big one: What is Torah? That is the question that divides the Jewish world today into different camps. How we define Torah is the central ideological issue of the Jewish world today. But we'll discuss it all when you get home."

In another letter to my parents dated August 11, 1986, I wrote:

> For eight years I've been going to Solomon Schechter Conservative day schools. I know that the Torah is the basis of Jewish law. I learned (in school) that it was given to Bnei Yisrael [the Israelites] at Har Sinai [Mount Sinai]. I imagined the Ark with two stone tablets and five leather-bound books in it. Then when I learned that books were written on scrolls I imagined five Sifrei Torah [Torah scrolls]. I thought that later in history it was written on one scroll. Such was my belief….After all those years in school, the teachers, the five leather-bound books in the ark…I assumed, after all, that the Torah came from Sinai.

Reading these letters so many years later, I believe that my early idea that the original Torah was written in five leather-bound books was inspired by a deluxe set of the Torah as five separate little books that my father used to keep on his desk in his synagogue office. So much of the world we construct is based on the images around us that we absorb as young children. I had already realized, before my bar mitzvah year in 1986, that the original Torah could not have looked as I imagined it, because books were not bound in leather in the time of scrolls. I already knew of the conflict between the creation story and the findings of science. I had already started to read different perspectives on the origins of ancient Israel, perspectives that were critical of the Pentateuchal narrative. But it was in early August of 1986 that it all came together for me—or rather, all fell apart—and I realized that the Torah was not at all the same book that I thought it was.

While I believe we must reconsider how we teach the Bible to children, so as to mitigate the crisis of skepticism that comes at some point, the Positive Historical school of Zacharias Frankel in Germany and later of

Solomon Schechter in the United States was not so quick to embrace biblical criticism. See Appendix 3 for a study of how difficult it was for Schechter and his followers to accept fully the implications of the critical study of Judaism (in German, *Wissenschaft des Judentums*). Those who championed biblical scholarship and the historicist approach to Judaism eventually came to follow the suggestion that Schechter first articulated in 1896 (ninety years before my class with Gerald Skolnik at Camp Ramah), that the source of religious authority was no longer the Bible but rather what he termed "Catholic Israel." By "Catholic Israel" Schechter meant the expression of the totality of Jewish history and culture. (See Appendix 4, where I argue that Schechter's phrase was a translation of the rabbinic term *Kenesset Israel.*) Schechter's notorious choice of term "Catholic Israel" has always been understood in the context of his late nineteenth-century felicitous English usage when everyone knew that "catholic" meant universal and total. But one wonders whether Schechter might have had a second meaning in mind given James Carroll's reflection on Catholicism and Church authority.

An irony of Positive Historical Judaism is that it offers a Catholic solution to a Protestant problem. If the entire enterprise of modern biblical scholarship was founded by German Protestant scholars in pursuit of Luther's charge to pursue the text itself without the dogmatic readings of the Church, then Schechter suggested that we return to the Church—or the Synagogue in our case—to discern God's Will. Schechter both embraced and rejected the world of German Protestant scholarship. His appeal to "Catholic Israel" was his turn to the Romanticism that the Catholic Church represented to so many of his contemporaries. The late nineteenth century saw a significant turn to Catholicism by individuals seeking the traditionalism, pageantry, and high ritual of the Catholic Church that was missing in much of liberal Protestantism. The turn to history with its embrace of emotion over rationalism was the essence of the Romantic reaction to the Age of Reason. Following Schechter's model, Positive Historical Judaism adapts the best of both the Protestant and Catholic ethos: Historical scholarship is embraced as a value in its own right, but the authority of tradition and the community is maintained over that of the text. In rabbinic terms, the pursuit of critical scholarship is reflected in the value of *Torah Lishmah*, whereas the authority of the community over the text is reflected in the dogma of *Torah Shebe'al Peh*.

Torah Lishmah (Torah for Its Own Sake)

One of the extraordinary values of traditional Jewish culture is its respect for theoretical over practical learning. That this long-standing value has become embedded in Jewish behavior may be expressed in the disproportionate representation of American Jews enrolled in liberal arts colleges. In Jewish culture, learning for its own sake has always been prioritized, and this is especially true when the subject is Torah. By its very name, Rabbinic Judaism styles itself after the rabbis, the teachers of Torah. Rabbinic ordination marked achievement at the highest level of Torah scholarship, the mastery of the Talmud and other rabbinic texts. While rabbis did fulfill various functions in the Jewish community, rabbinic education was never directly linked with a specific profession until the nineteenth century, just as rabbis were not generally paid a living wage for their services until modern times. To this day, rabbinical seminaries debate how much of their curricula need be devoted to "practical" and "professional" education and how much should be preserved for the study of texts "for their own sake." In Talmud courses, the debate is over whether texts should be selected that have "practical applications," whereas in Bible courses the debate is over whether biblical criticism must be taught over homiletical insights. Traditionally, the less practical application the texts had, the higher the religious value of the study. The sections of Leviticus detailing the sacrificial order and mishnaic texts on ancient agricultural laws were deemed superior to the sections on current ritual concerns such as Sabbath and festival observance, much less codes of ethical behavior. Talmud courses on ancient torts would be considered superior to courses on Jewish laws observed today, which were relegated to the term "practical halakhah." Today, of course, rabbis require practical preparation, yet theoretical learning is still prioritized in the same way that law schools debate the extent to which their curricula need focus on practical matters rather than legal theory. But in Judaism, the preference for theory has more than just disciplinary pride of place. And neither is it rooted in an ascetic removal from the concerns of living communities. Jewish learning prioritizes theoretical learning and non-applicable matters because it understands learning, specifically Torah learning, as a form of worship.

When the Second Temple in Jerusalem was destroyed in 70 CE, Judaism lost its cult of divine worship. Christianity, which began as a Jewish sect, transferred the locus of divine worship from the Temple to the personhood of Jesus. For Rabbinic Judaism, the locus was transferred to Torah. Yes, the Divine could be experienced through prayer and ritual observance, but Torah study was the most direct approach to "communion" with God. When study is understood as worship, then the less practically applicable the study, the more pure the worship. This is the meaning of Torah Lishmah, of study for its own sake. Torah Lishmah is pure study with no practical motive other than the act of study itself.

It was this very predisposition for Torah for its own sake that facilitated the application of the methodologies of the German university to Jewish scholarship. The rabbinical seminaries and eventually the great universities of the world became centers for the study of Judaism for its own sake. The challenge of the modern study of religion is that the material is dismantled for the student who is then left alone to reconstruct for him or herself a usable religious tradition. Rather than retreat to medieval scholasticism, seminaries need to embrace critical scholarship but then complete the spiritual process by reconstructing the inheritance of the past into something usable. A devotee of the tradition should not fear the study of its texts and history according to the best methodologies available any more than the stargazer should fear astronomy. If one truly loves the text, one should want to learn as much about it as possible according to the most cutting-edge scholarship in the field. But the seminarian does not study the Bible alone. Ready to aid and guide the student in the discovery of Holy Writ are the teachings of the Church. The fact that the Bible has a history of cultural reception does not mitigate its holiness; it defines its holiness. In Jewish terms, the fact that the Torah is a human document does not mitigate its holiness because its holiness does not derive from the Torah itself but from the way it was—and is—read by the community. That is what is termed Torah Shebe'al Peh.

Torah Shebe'al Peh (The Oral Torah)

The halakhic system categorizes laws into the categories of *de'oraita*, or Toraitic law, and *derabbanan*, or Rabbinic law. While *de'oraita* legislation is given the primacy of primary law and *derabbanan* legislation as secondary, in practice this prioritization is flipped. As in Rabbi Gordon Tucker's articulation, mentioned in the previous chapter, "the definition of what is *de'oraita* is itself *derabbanan*." In other words, the normative status of the text is determined not by the text itself but by what the community accepts as normative. This idea, which is fundamental to Positive Historical Judaism, is asserted by the ancient Rabbis themselves through the theological doctrine of the Oral Torah, the Torah Shebe'al Peh.

In traditional terms, God gave the Torah to Israel at Mount Sinai through Moses. The Torah consisted of a written component, which is the Pentateuch, and an oral component, which is the understanding, interpretation, and meaning of the text that Moses proceeded to teach the People. Moses is called *Mosheh Rabbenu,* "our Rabbi Moses," not because he received the Written Torah, which, theoretically, any literate person can read, but because he received the Oral Torah, which only the Rabbis possessed. The doctrine of Oral Torah is a product of Rabbinic Judaism, not the other way around. Never mentioned or even hinted at in the Bible, the Oral Torah is an idea by which the Rabbis were able to assert their authority as rightful heirs of Torah, not only over rival Jewish sects but even over the text itself. The doctrine of Oral Torah establishes the primacy, in practice, of *derabbanan* over *de'oraita,* or, in other terms, of the Church over the Bible. In the terminology of Positive Historical Judaism, this is what is meant by the identification of history and culture as the source of law and tradition.

That Oral Torah was a metaphor for the authority of community and not believed literally should be clear to anyone who studies rabbinic literature. The Mishnah and Talmud, the supposed collections of the Oral Law, are obsessed with attributions of teachings, often citing three generations of "chains of transmission." While one might argue that the reported chains of transmission are to prove authenticity going back to Moses, the chains never go back more than a few generations. The more likely explanation for this aspect of rabbinic literature was the concern to give credit where credit was due, to cite sources properly, as one must take care to do when transmitting oral teachings. The laws and teachings recorded in the Mishnah and Talmud were oral before their written codifications, but they were oral creations, not receptions from a more ancient period. The Rabbis did not believe that they and their teachers were merely passing down the teachings of Moses. Rather, they knew they were contributing to the Tradition, and they also believed that their contributions became part of Oral Torah. As long as certain rules were followed — a specific rabbinic hermeneutic code — their own teachings fell under the rubric of the Oral Torah. Through midrash the Rabbis read the Torah, narratively and halakhically, reading their own teachings into Moses' "mouth" from "Sinai."

I call the doctrine of Oral Torah a "doctrine" because, for example, it is not unlike the Catholic doctrine of papal infallibility. The Pope as the personification of the Church has the authority to interpret God's Will, and that Will, as interpreted by the Pope, would exceed, in theory, even the plain meaning of Scripture itself. Similarly, constitutional courts claim the right to interpret constitutions, and their interpretations become the meaning of the constitutions even if they appear to violate the plain meaning of those texts. The ambiguity of Oral Torah lies in the nature of Rabbinic Judaism, that rather than in a single person (the Pope) or a clearly defined judicial institution (the courts), rabbis become rabbis by virtue of their education and acceptance by their communities. A rabbi to one Jewish community can be condemned as a heretic by another. This ambiguity provides a flexibility that defers to history the ultimate authority to determine which teachings become Torah for future generations.

The concepts of Torah Lishmah and Torah Shebe'al Peh function as two poles allowing a religious culture based on sacred text to survive. Torah Lishmah encourages us to understand the text on its own terms, contextually, whereas Torah Shebe'al Peh teaches us to read the text the way it has been understood and codified by the culture, reading often acontextually, a reading tied more to the context of the interpreter. I might say that Torah Lishmah keeps me honest while Torah Shebe'al Peh keeps me Jewish. However, I recognize that it is my Jewishness that drives me to read the text critically just as it is my honesty that reminds me that the Torah Shebe'al Peh is the product of later history and culture and not to be confused with the text itself, a product of its own history and culture. The Positive Historical Jew can read a text critically, unraveling it down to its component parts, but also knows how to put it back together to what it meant for those who wrote it, edited it, read it, lived by it, and died by it in subsequent periods of history. The Positive Historical Jew dismantles the text as an act of worship and recognizes the readings of culture and history as authoritative. The Positive Historical Jew's understanding of the Tradition as an acontextual reading should not make adherence to that Tradition any less commanding than the Positive Historical Jew's critical reading of the text's context makes it any less worshipful.

And yet there is a difference. The difference is the role of God. It must be more than a coincidence that rabbis who understand halakhah to be the product of Jewish culture tend to rule more leniently on most questions than do rabbis who understand it to be the product of God's Will. The former must worry about being true and authentic to the weight of Tradition whereas the latter must worry about disappointing the Master of the Universe. Both believe that the halakhah they determine, or the way they read the text, is the Will of God. However, the latter know that God knows if he or she was correct whereas the former know that only future generations can make that determination. Both speak with the authority of Tradition, but the latter seek to approximate the Will of God whereas the former seek to determine it. That theological posture can make all the difference between emboldening and intimidating the rabbi. It also makes a difference in terms of how we understand sacred text and talk about it with others.

Confronting Christian Scripture

In May of 2010, I saw the Passion Play at Oberammergau in Bavaria. I was present with a group of young American Jews brought by the American Jewish Committee to dialogue with the Passion Play producers and German seminarians about the anti-Jewish elements of the play. The Oberammergau Passion Play is the most well known of the widespread medieval custom of producing plays of the Passion Narrative, dramatizing the suffering and crucifixion of Jesus in small towns as acts of repentance to avoid the plague. Oberammergau has been producing a Passion Play every ten years since the seventeenth century, and its latest productions have attracted visitors from across the globe. In the past these Passion Plays were significant sources of the spreading of antisemitic stereotypes, as the Jews were presented as evil, vicious Christ killers. In the years following the Second Vatican Council and in response to Church directives not to blame the Jews for the death of Jesus, the Oberammergau production made significant changes to the way the story was presented. The most significant development in the 2010 production is the embrace of the Jewishness of Jesus. Jesus is now presented in the Oberammergau play as a rabbi, wearing a tallit (prayer shawl) and reading from a Torah scroll in Hebrew as he enters the Temple. The Last Supper is introduced by Jesus leading the Kiddush benediction over the wine in Hebrew, and his disciples and the whole ensemble sing a key Torah passage (the Shema) in Hebrew in a new, powerful musical setting. The current director, Christian Stueckl, explained to me that this was particularly important to do in Oberammergau, where the elderly citizens (still participating in the play) remember Adolf Hitler attending productions when they were children and praising the anti-Jewish elements. Stueckl has taught these elderly villagers today to stand on the stage and sing in Hebrew, celebrating the religion and people that Hitler sought to destroy. He explained to me that in preparation for the 2000 and 2010 performances, he brought the principal actors to Israel—not just to visit the sites in Jerusalem associated with the Passion narrative, but also to visit Yad Vashem, Israel's Holocaust memorial and museum.

I was overwhelmed by these efforts and the resulting production, with the idea of presenting Jesus as a first-century rabbi, of the celebration and respect for Judaism, and the determination to tell the Passion story in such a powerful and dramatic fashion. Yet a number of Jewish and Christian leaders still pointed to flaws in the production. Many focused on the way the Jews in the story are presented, specifically of the High Priest Caiaphas calling for Jesus' execution, rejecting Jesus, and causing his suffering. Well-meaning scholarly research and doctrinal pronouncements from the Vatican and other major Christian denominations have focused on the Romans as the crucifiers rather than the Jews. They explain the attention of the Gospel accounts on the Jews as due to later divisions between Christians and the rest of the Jewish people, with the turn of Christianity toward Gentile converts and the evolution of Jews as "the Other," and to the need to down-play the conflict with Rome when Christianity was looking for a broader non-Jewish base within the Roman Empire. The producers of the Oberammergau Passion Play went to great lengths to present Jesus and his followers as a sect among the larger Jewish people, with Judaism itself respected as the "mother church" from which Christianity emerged. But the role of "the Jews" from the Gospels was still preserved; the High Priest Caiaphas still called for Jesus' execution, and the people, the hundreds of members of the ensemble on the stage representing the Jews of Jerusalem, all still yell, "Crucify him! Crucify him!"

Perhaps it is true that the Jews played no role in the crucifixion. It makes little sense, historically, why any Jew would have. There was certainly much contention among differing Jewish groups in the first century, but there is no evidence—outside of the Christian scriptures—of Jews turning against each other or turning other Jews over to the Romans for execution. Not until the outbreak of the Great Revolt in 66 CE did the Zealots—perhaps—turn to violence against other Jews. It is true, of course, that the Jewish authorities would not have had the power to execute, so the Gospel accounts make sense in allocating that role to the Romans. But it is difficult to imagine that a High Priest, and the Jews of Jerusalem in aggregate, would have called for an execution of one of their own, especially given the long-standing Jewish discomfort with capital punishment and the concern with proper care for the dead, both running at odds—not by mere coincidence—with Roman practice. So while it is true that one can argue that the Gospel accounts, which point fingers at the Jews, are inaccurate, and one can argue that what actually happened may have been quite different from what was remembered, and one can look to new efforts in interfaith dialogue to rewrite the relationship between Judaism and Christianity, one cannot rewrite the New Testament. Historically accurate or not, Christian scripture is codified and says what it says. And the story is more powerful the way it is told. The point of the story is that Jesus suffers while his own people, the ones for whom he suffered, look away. The point is that the prophet is rejected and hated in his own city.

If the narrative is told the way it was written, then "the Jews" should be seen not as the hated Other but as the erring Self. Jew-hatred needs to be eliminated, but the Jews cannot be taken out of the story. The "audience" is supposed to identify with the Jews. This was particularly poignant for me at Oberammergau, where the audience was being asked to identify not only with the Jews of the ensemble but, more painfully, with the audience who sat in that space three generations before, an audience who turned against their own, turning their neighbors over to the authorities for execution. The point is that "the Jews" are not demonized; they are ordinary people, they are the audience. And ordinary people do terrible things, even turning on their own. The role of Judas Iscariot in the play is pivotal, the tragic figure who betrays his master and then kills himself in agony over his act. In earlier times, when the Oberammergau play truly was antisemitic, no one in the village wanted to play Judas, and the one who did was often ostracized as if he himself were associated with the treachery he performed on stage. But today, as Stueckl explained to me, the role of Judas is the most coveted, even above Jesus. Because it is the most challenging to perform. Because it is the most human.

And yet, the Oberammergau production did try to present the Romans as the real executioners, as the ancient "Nazis." Pontius Pilate is the villain, the Roman authority intent on controlling the people and his own position at any cost. I saw Pilate as manipulating Caiaphas into persecuting Jesus while pretending to be forced into the role of executioner, when in fact he was pulling all the strings. At the end of the important scene when Judas makes the deal with Caiaphas and the other priestly leaders, Caiaphas closes the scene with: "Everything is set up perfectly according to our wishes. Soon the false prophet will be in our hands. Pilate, you shall have him!" In a bizarre development of pure coincidence, the final line, "Pilate, you shall have him!" which I thought revealed that Caiaphas was responding directly to Pilate's urging to deliver Jesus to him — a radical retelling of the story — was omitted from the published libretto. It was never read by the teams of international scholars and clerics studying and critiquing the script and was heard only by those who came to see the production. Without that final line, the question becomes more ambiguous as to who the true villain is, Caiaphas or Pilate. That ambiguity is inherent in the implication in the New Testament as to how the Jews are seen and portrayed and will be thought of for centuries to come.

I offer this analysis of the Oberammergau Passion Play because of what I learned there about how Jews need to think about Christian scripture. The Positive Historical Jew who understands that his or her own scripture is a product of history and culture and is to be revered and studied and struggled with because of that history needs to allow for the same devotion of other cultures to their scriptures. One cannot simply say, "I don't believe in your scriptures, they are incorrect," because they are no more correct than anyone else's or mine. If sacred texts are the products of cultures, then each culture has its own sacred text, which is as sacred to itself as one's own is to one's self. What is essential is not the veracity of the texts, but that they have been accepted by the cultures to which they belong as sacred through history.

Just as an honest appraisal of the fittingness of the Matriarchs in the opening paragraph of the Amidah, or of the history of women in Jewish law, would bring one to acknowledge that women were excluded, or that gays and lesbians were discriminated against by halakhic culture, so too does an honest reading of the Passion narratives prevent us from pretending that "the Jews" of the story were all virtuous. The Positive Historical perspective requires one to read the past honestly and dispassionately and to find a way to use that past in the present, to transmit and translate the inheritance of tradition. We must read the text *lishmah*, understanding it on its own terms, and at the same time find a way to retell it *be'al Peh*, with the authority of tradition and community.

Judaism needs to accept the Christian story irrespective of "what really happened," just as Christianity needs to find a way to tell that story in a way that does not cultivate continued hatred of Jews. Perhaps the Passion Play at Oberammergau today is a way to begin doing that.

Understanding Chosenness

If our sacred texts are mere products of our history, and other cultures' sacred texts are products of their histories, then does the concept of the Chosen People have any meaning? Mordecai Kaplan found the concept so offensive that he struck it from the Reconstructionist prayer book. Is it possible for Positive Historical Judaism to retain the concept of the Chosen People, to continue saying the same liturgies, while responding to the ethical objections of Kaplan and to the historical relativity of the concept given our understanding of history?

Looking at the ethical challenge first, we should understand that there are dangerous and tragic consequences to believing that one's people are greater in merit than another's. A certain amount of self-pride is of course important for morale, but that fine line between nationalism and jingoism must be guarded. Having been on the victim's side of the worst explosion of jingoist chauvinism in world history, the Jewish People should be particularly sensitive to the notion that any one people or race is more superior to another. And yet it was a healthy dose of faith in Chosenness that might have contributed to so much of Jewish survival through the Holocaust. Belief in Chosenness drove the Zionist movement to rebuild the Land of Israel for the Jewish People and defend it against those who sought its destruction. But excessive Chosenness has also driven an enmity between Jew and Arab in the Land and has become one of several stumbling blocks towards a peaceful resolution of the conflict. When Chosenness encourages one to raise oneself above others, then the ethical faults of the concept erupt.

Historically, it is natural for a culture to imagine itself as the center of the world. While the Western tradition views Jerusalem as the center, or "navel," of the world, for the Chinese the very name "China" means "Middle

Kingdom." The French had their "civilizing mission," whereas the Americans had "Manifest Destiny." To the student of history, then, it is as natural for Islam to "correct" the Hebrew scriptures and "remember" Ishmael as the favored son of Abraham as it is for the Church to see itself as the "true Israel." Once one can accept one's own sacred text as a cultural rather than divine product and yet continue to revere it as sacred, then one can also learn to better respect the sacred texts of others as resting on similar cultural and historical foundations.

If Jews can acknowledge that from the Muslim perspective it was Ishmael — not Isaac — whom Abraham brought to Mount Moriah, and that this sacred memory is just as true for Muslims as the binding of Isaac is for Jews, and vice-versa for Muslims, then each should better be able to appreciate the other's claims to Covenant and Land and Chosenness. But before one can change a geopolitical fault-line, one must first change one's own internal perspective. What can it mean to be chosen by God?

It is natural and healthy for every culture to have pride and faith in itself, what might be called "Chosenness," just as it is for any individual to have self-confidence and self-love. While dangerous in extreme doses, both for individuals and nations, some sense of self-importance is essential for survival. Rather than deny Chosenness, as Mordecai Kaplan and his Reconstructionist movement suggested, Chosenness should be embraced, but understood in new Positive Historical terms. When the root of Chosenness is recognized as coming from *within* the historical culture rather than coming from *without*, then the sense of national pride can be retained but absent the concomitant assertion of exclusivity. That is, since the act of God's choosing a people originates with each nation individually, then the relationship between that people and its God is only exclusive in the terms of that people's understanding of God.

The ancient pagans understood this. Athenians knew that their having been chosen by Athena did not mean that Zeus did not choose the Olympians. When an ancient people conquered another god's city, many understood one god as having defeated another. Surely the Babylonians of Nebuchadnezzar's army in 586 BCE believed, as they watched the Temple of Solomon burn, that Marduk had defeated the god of Jerusalem. But the prophets of ancient Israel preached otherwise, believing that God was the god of all the world and that the election of Israel was eternal, even when the people were in exile. While I am not advocating a return to pagan ideas of multiple gods and their eternal conflicts, I am suggesting that Chosenness does not have to be exclusive.

Monotheism does not have to lead to chauvinism. A parent can have more than one child, and each child can feel individually loved and cherished by the parent even though the same parent can have a special relationship with each child. Each child develops his or her own relationship with the parent based upon the child's experiences. Similarly, each people can be "chosen" by God and have a special relationship with God, without requiring God to not have special relationships with any other people.

This approach to Chosenness has some roots in the Bible itself, with, for example, God caring for the Ninevites in the Book of Jonah, the seat of Assyria, Israel's nemesis. But once one adds the perspective of Positive Historical Judaism it becomes easier to embrace, because the historical perspective allows us to recognize that the very image of the parent is conceived separately by each child. Positive Historical Judaism allows us to embrace the concept of being chosen without denying that innate concept to any and all others.

A more relative and non-exclusivist understanding of Chosenness is necessary in order for the relationship between different faiths to evolve from tolerance and acceptance to mutual partnership and friendship. For an example of this necessary change of paradigm, let us consider Gotthold Eprhaim Lessing's parable of the ring. Lessing, the late eighteenth-century German playwright and close associate of the Jewish thinker Moses Mendelssohn, wrote *Nathan the Wise,* the play that includes the famous parable about a king who had three sons. When the king was about to die, he wanted to give his precious ring to his favorite son. However, not wanting to disappoint his other two sons, the king ordered two replicas of the ring to be made so that the true ring was indistinguishable from the copies. When the king died, each son received his ring and believed that his was genuine. But none could prove such to the others. Lessing's lesson is that Christianity must accept Judaism's and Islam's claims to truth as no more or less rational than its own. While Lesssing's parable is a beautiful articulation of the Enlightenment principle of tolerance, it also identifies the limitations of tolerance. Even though Enlightened Christianity must give up the quest to convince everyone else that it is the true religion, the Enlightened Christian can still believe that he alone is in possession of the unique truth. There is still only one genuine ring and, of course, Lessing believed that it was Christianity.

Only a post-Einstein appreciation of the relativity of truth can allow us a different way to approach the problem of different religions claiming to be true to the exclusion of others. There is not one simple truth just as there is not one simple reality. What we perceive in the world is a function of when and where we are in relation to the object of our observation. So if we were to rewrite Lessing's parable, we would not have the king order two copies of his one true ring, because we know that there is not one true ring. We would have the king melt down the metal and use it to produce three identical and indistinguishable rings, each with an element of the original. All three rings, then, would be true. This contemporary corrective of Lessing's parable should help clarify the way Positive Historical Judaism needs to understand Chosenness. All religions have a claim to Chosenness as each is the genuine product of a culture and community in history. If history is the source of authority, then any—and every—historical tradition has a claim to authenticity.

The traditional liturgy, in both the Friday night Kiddush and the blessing before reading from the Torah, praises God for "choosing us from among the nations." Similarly, the Havdalah, the special liturgy at the conclusion of the Sabbath, praises God for "distinguishing Israel from the nations." Israel was "chosen" for these things, for the Sabbath, and for the Torah. These are the specific cultural treasures of the Jewish People, the essence of its distinctiveness and sanctity. These are the products of its history and culture. To accept this Chosenness is to keep the text sacred.

Chapter Five

SACRED HISTORY

The Positive Historical Jew must distinguish between real history and sacred history. The concept of sacred history, called *Heilsgeschichte* in German, has special meaning for the Positive Historical Jew, for whom history is the source of the sacred. The challenge that the Positive Historical Jew must address is that the seminal events of the spiritual history of the People often fail to meet the burden of historical proof. We can understand easily enough the cosmic and prehistoric legends of Genesis as representing mythic conceptions of the origins of life and God's role in the world. The creation stories are parables meant to teach lessons about God's relationship to the world, not accounts of natural, geological, or astronomical history. But what of the accounts of the Patriarchs and Matriarchs? Why be so concerned about who is mentioned in the Amidah when we cannot verify any of them as historical personages? And what of the Exodus from Egypt and the events at Mount Sinai?

The Book of Genesis reports that the Hebrews began as a nomadic clan. There is no reason to deny the plausibility of that claim. Some scholars have suggested that claiming Mesopotamian roots added a higher cultural status to the Hebrews over the indigenous Canaanite tribes, and some scholars have proposed that the Israelites were simply the most successful of the Canaanite peoples in establishing their culture across the land. Clearly, though, according to Genesis, there is an overriding theme of distrust of cities, from the story of the Tower of Babel to the destruction of Sodom and Gomorrah to the rift with Shechem to the tension with neighboring "kings" and with Egypt. The people had to have begun as nomads. If they were an urban people their stories of cities would have been quite different.

The original Hebrews, then, must have lived much as Abraham, Isaac, and Jacob did. It should not really matter who the first Patriarchs were as much as the fact that the later developing culture understood its ancestors to have been Abraham, Isaac, and Jacob; Sarah, Rebecca, Rachel, and Leah; and Bilhah and Zilpah. They are remembered as imperfect human beings who yet had faith that they were chosen by God to found a new People. The fact that their descendants were around to tell the tale was evidence enough that the blessing of Chosenness was real.

Remembering the Exodus from Egypt

Every Friday night the observant Jew makes Kiddush over wine, sanctifying the Sabbath "for the memory of the Exodus from Egypt." The Exodus is also recalled in the daily morning and evening liturgies and at the Passover Seder, the most widely observed of all Jewish rites. Each participant, after eating of the matzah and the bitter herbs, is asked to feel as if he or she was redeemed personally from Egypt. Can we assume there was an Exodus as we can assume the existence of some kind of patriarchal and matriarchal ancestry? And if not, how do we say these prayers and celebrate Passover?

Rabbis have found it difficult to suggest in public that there may not have been an Exodus. Much like a Christian pastor questioning the existence of the historical Jesus, the Exodus is one of those events where the discipline of history challenges the faith of religious communities. Unlike the Bible's account of creation, which is "correctible" by ample scientific evidence, the Exodus, like the historical Jesus, is questioned because there is no evidence to support it. The only first-century reference to Jesus outside the New Testament is a passage from Josephus that many assume to be a later Christian gloss. There are no extrabiblical sources attesting to the Exodus. Even the Bible itself, outside of the Pentateuch, has few references to the Exodus, causing some scholars to suggest that the Exodus tradition may have originated with only one segment of the People. While it is true that we would not expect the ancient Egyptians to have memorialized the loss of so many slaves or their pharaoh's defeat by a shepherd prince — even one of courtly origins — we might have expected to uncover in the Sinai desert some trace of a nation passing through over a forty-year period. There is an Egyptian source about Israel from this period, the oldest recorded reference to the People of Israel, in the famous Stele of Merneptah. This thirteenth-century BCE granite monument, currently housed at the Egyptian Museum in Cairo, celebrates the victories of the pharaoh Merneptah, including a note at the end that, among other Canaanite nations, "Israel's seed is laid waste."

Thus, the only actual source we have of ancient Israel, from the time that most assume the Exodus was to have occurred, reports that the Israelites were living in Canaan and lost a war with Egypt, with no reference to them being slaves or former slaves, escaped or free. While there is no way to prove that the Exodus did not happen—unlike the creation story which cannot sustain itself against scientific evidence—there is also no way to assume that it did happen, especially according to the discipline of history, which requires source evidence to establish facts.

While one approach might be to argue vociferously for the historicity (that is, the historical truth) of the Exodus, the Positive Historical Jew does not need to, nor should, do so. Just as Positive Historical Judaism understands the commandedness of Jewish law as originating in its acceptance by the People through history rather than having been pronounced by a deity at the top of a mountain in the Sinai desert, so too does the sacred memory of the Exodus, along with its understanding of God as redeemer, originate not from the details of ancient Egyptian and Near Eastern history but rather from its acceptance through history by the culture that wrote it into its Biblical narrative and into its daily, weekly, and annual rites. We should be free to study history *lishmah*, for its own sake, without any preconceived conclusions of what must have happened and how. We should be able to accept the sacred history of the Bible as Torah Shebe'al Peh, as what the culture recalled from the past, even if that is not identical in every detail to what may have actually taken place.

When the Exodus is remembered as the archetypical event of sacred history that it is rather than as a matter of shaky historical veracity, it becomes easier to fulfill the tradition's mandate of feeling as if one has been redeemed personally from Egypt. Even in the Passover Haggadah itself, the traditional text used at the Seder, the Exodus is remembered without any mention of Moses. As noted in the second chapter, traditionally this is explained as an effort to remove any focus on the agency of Moses and reserve all praise for God; it can also be understood as a hint that the Exodus is not to be remembered in the same way as other historical events. The "truth" of the Exodus lies not in the details of the history but in the realization of what it means to be redeemed. The evidence for sacred history lies not in the retelling of events but with the culture that recalls them.

Observing Tishah B'Av, Yom HaShoah, and Yom Ha-atzma'ut

I have, in my experience as a rabbi in Conservative congregations, often found the observance of Tishah B'Av, the fast of the Ninth of Av, to be a challenging "sell." Even among those who come to hear the recitation of the Book of Lamentations on a summer evening in July or August, few will observe the fast. And I know that has nothing to do with the hardships of fasting, because plenty of people manage to fast on Yom Kippur. Why is it then that the fast of Tishah B'Av is so under-observed?

There was discussion at the Law Committee of the Rabbinical Assembly of Israel on the question of whether one might only fast through the early afternoon on Tishah B'Av rather than the entire day. Those who argued for this mitigated observance claimed that given the reality of the miraculous existence of the State of Israel, one should not mourn for the destruction of the Temple and Jerusalem of old in the same way. I understand that it is the existence of the State of Israel that brings the observance of Tishah B'Av into question. Now that the Jewish people have a sovereign state, why should we continue to mourn the loss of the first and second commonwealths in 586 BCE and 70 CE?

While I recognize the challenge of making Tishah B'Av meaningful, I believe that challenge is essential for Positive Historical Judaism. Tishah B'Av stands in polarity with Yom Kippur as the second and "other" major 24-hour (actually 25-hour) fast of the liturgical year. Yom Kippur is called the White Fast, the festival of atonement, whereas Tishah B'Av is the Black Fast, the national day of mourning and sadness. Yom Kippur, while a fast day, is not a sad day. Tradition specifically says that Yom Kippur is a happy though solemn day because on that day our sins are forgiven. On Yom Kippur we fast not out of sadness for the sins we committed, but in optimistic demonstration to God of our genuineness in having made repentance and in starting the new year as better people than we were before. On Tishah B'Av we fast and mourn. While fasting is not a sign of mourning in Judaism—anyone who has been to a shiva house knows that mourners are supposed to eat—on Tishah B'Av we fast to mimic the response of the ancient Israelites who always fasted to beg God for forgiveness, believing that it could only have been because of the weight of our sins that God would have allowed the Temple to burn. Some say that they are offended by the notion that catastrophe should have occurred "because of our sins." This was, of course, the brilliant response of the ancient Israelites to the notion that Marduk, and later, Jupiter, had triumphed over God. It was not that God was defeated, only that God's favor was withdrawn from Israel. This classical Jewish response to catastrophe, while repeated throughout history, was called into question and rejected by many Jews after the trauma of the Holocaust. While there are still some ultra-Orthodox theologians who continue to rely on this ancient theodicy, most modern Jews find it blasphemous to presume that God was responsible for the Holocaust, allowing it to occur as a punishment for Jewish sins.

I agree with that post-Holocaust critique, and it is for that reason that I agree with the notion that while previously seen as the day to commemorate all catastrophes faced by the Jewish people through history, Tishah B'Av should not commemorate the Holocaust. The Holocaust is unique in the long catalogue of catastrophes of Jewish history and therefore requires its own day of commemoration: Yom HaShoah, Holocaust Memorial Day. Renewed efforts need to be made to keep the observance of Yom HaShoah meaningful when there are fewer and fewer survivors to light candles and speak. The tone of Yom HaShoah must remain that of mourning. It must have none of the trappings of the theodicy of blame that is inherent in the observance of Tishah B'Av. Therefore, one must neither fast on Yom HaShoah nor wear white (a Yom Kippur practice), implying that we are now innocent of sin. Yom HaShoah must have its own remembrance, but that should not take away from the overall importance and role of Tishah B'Av.

To fast on Tishah B'Av is not to say that I believe that God punished Israel for its sins and allowed the Babylonians, and later, the Romans, to destroy the Temple. To fast on Tishah B'Av means that I can feel as if I myself had been there watching the Temple burn, and that had I been, I would have believed that God was punishing Israel for its sins, and I would have fasted. On Tishah B'Av one must transport oneself into that theological history—even if one does not believe its premise—just as on Passover one must transport oneself into the foundational event of the Exodus—even if one does not believe that it actually happened. Observance of Tishah B'Av in the traditional way is essential for the Positive Historical Jew because the Positive Historical Jew's sense of the sacred is bound up with the experience of the totality of Jewish history.

How are we to truly appreciate the miraculous existence of the State of Israel if we do not experience the loss of the Temple and the defeat of

Jewish arms against the Babylonians and the Romans in antiquity? Only by experiencing the loss, by feeling as if we were there watching Jerusalem burn, can we truly rejoice over the establishment and independence of the State of Israel.

We must feel as if we were personally redeemed from Egypt when we eat the matzah at the Seder. We must feel the loss of the Temple when we fast on Tishah B'Av. We must imagine ourselves at Auschwitz when we light a memorial candle on Yom HaShoah. And we must imagine hearing David Ben-Gurion reading the Declaration of Independence of the State of Israel when we make a barbeque on Yom Ha-atzma'ut, Israel's Independence Day. The separate observance of Yom HaShoah allows us to observe Tishah B'Av without offending our understanding of the Holocaust. The observance of Tishah B'Av, more than Yom HaShoah, allows us to truly understand Yom Ha-atzma'ut, because the State of Israel did not just rise out of the ashes of the Holocaust, it arose from a hope of two thousand years (*hatikvah bat shnot alpayim*).

On Shavuot and Conversion

For the Positive Historical Jew, identification with the key moments of Jewish history is critical, making history sacred. This must be done for the real events of the recent past, such as the Holocaust and the establishment of the State of Israel, as well as for events of the ancient past, such as the fall of Jerusalem, and even, and especially, of the legendary past, such as the Exodus from Egypt. What meaning, though, can be associated with remembering the revelation at Sinai, as commemorated on the festival of Shavuot, when the very idea of Positive Historical Judaism proposes a concept of Torah that is completely contrary to the narrative about Sinai?

I believe that the Torah, including of course the Oral Torah, is the product of Israelite and Jewish culture and history. I do not believe that God gave anything to Moses on Mount Sinai. I do not know whether the People ever gathered at that mountain, or where that mountain would have been, when it would have been, and whether or not there was ever a real person named Moses. But I do believe that the Torah is an attempt to articulate the Will of God. Abraham Joshua Heschel famously said, in his masterpiece *God in Search of Man*, that "as a report about revelation, the Bible itself is a midrash."

The account of the meeting of God and Israel in the Bible is a metaphor, a poem, a painting of an ineffable process, the meeting of the human and the divine. If we believe that process to have been protracted—as the ancient Rabbis must have believed in their understanding of the development of the Oral Torah—then that does not in any way diminish the power of the poem about Sinai. On the contrary, the poem, as a poem, is even more powerful and poignant. The more historically the process of revelation is drawn out, the more concise, emotive, and dreamlike the story about Sinai becomes. And so it is that each year on the festival of Shavuot we are to imagine as if we were there at Sinai, as God opened the heavens and presented us with the Torah.

When I was seven years old, I traveled with my father and my uncle to Mount Sinai. It was the summer of 1981, when Israel was in the midst of a scaled pull-back from Sinai per the Camp David peace accords with Egypt. The border that summer went right down the center of the desert peninsula, with the mountain that the Arabs call "Jabal Musa" (the mount of Moses) just on the Egyptian side. When I reflect on this time, the experience of the temporary border as the history of the Egyptian-Israeli peace was being written was far more real than my sense of the place's supposed pedigree. Christian tradition has recognized Jabal Musa as Mount Sinai since the fourth century. The monastery of Saint Catherine's, at the foot of the mountain, is one of the oldest still-functioning monasteries in the world. It is built around a bush that was identified by Helena, mother of the emperor Constantine, as the bush that burned but was not consumed when Moses was first commissioned by God. There is now a modern town of Saint Catherine next to the monastery with hotels and up-to-date amenities for tourists. But when I was there in 1981 none of that existed. We slept in the monastery, in a stone-walled room with bunk beds and several dozen people. We did not need to sleep long, however, as we woke early to ascend the mountain in time for sunrise. After a steep trek on a winding trail up the mountain, we enjoyed the sunrise over the desert peaks. We then descended an ancient trail of stone steps going straight down the slopes. Later, sitting on the patio that night, I enjoyed the brilliant sky as my father pointed out the Big Dipper and the North Star. I remember being far more inspired by that than by the large bush growing out of the wall of the ancient chapel built by Helena, just around the corner from where we were sitting. That the bush was the Burning Bush was too much for my already skeptical mind to accept.

Had I visited Mount Sinai but a few months before, it would still have been under Israeli control. It did not matter, of course, because the peace treaty allowed for tourism and the border was open. But it could not have felt more different from the sites that I had visited that summer in Israel, my first trip to the Holy Land (excluding an earlier visit I was too young to remember) and, therefore, my first experiences of the places of sacred history. Jerusalem felt sacred and authentic. Sinai did not. I remember the Sinai trip well, because it was an exciting adventure as it would have been for anyone then, but especially for a seven-year-old with his father and uncle, having left his mother, aunt, young brothers, and cousins behind at the hotel in the comfortable Israeli Red Sea resort of Eilat. Maybe Mount Sinai did not feel authentic because Jewish tradition did not celebrate it as a holy place in the way that it celebrated Mount Zion (that is, Jerusalem). But what I can better understand now is that Jewish tradition had always made a subtle distinction between real history and the history of myth and legend.

Mount Sinai belongs to the history of myth and legend. It is a poem, not a place. The metaphor-over-history nature of the Sinai experience is all the more meaningful when we consider the convert to Judaism. The Rabbis, very consciously, selected the Book of Ruth to be read liturgically on Shavuot. They saw in Ruth the first convert to Judaism because she accepted the Covenant of Sinai and the destiny of Israel as her own. A convert, at the moment of immersion in the mikveh (the ritual bath), becomes, somewhat magically, a descendant of Abraham and Sarah. The convert becomes a part of the Jewish People, covered under the Covenant *as if* his or her ancestor accepted it along with the ancestors of genetically descended Jews. The *as if* is critical, for it must also apply to most genetically descended Jews as well. I can vouch for my Jewishness through several generations back to the nineteenth century in Eastern Europe. But for three thousand years? However, I believe *as if* I am a descendant of Abraham and Sarah, and that *as if* is sufficient. Similarly, a kohen today, a Jew whose father is a kohen, is considered *as if* he (or she) is a direct descendant of Aaron the Priest, despite the multiple assumptions of pedigree that such a claim entails. Similarly, a convert is considered Jewish *as if* descended from someone at Sinai. All Jews are *as if* descended from the generation that stood before the mountain. *As if* a generation of Israelites stood before a mountain.

Chapter Six

FINDING GOD IN HISTORY

If the sacred texts and sacred tales of Judaism are all rooted in history, if our very understanding of God and God's Will is a product of this historical culture, if it is within the national experience that we should look rather than without, then where can we find God? What do we mean when we speak about God, if we understand the stories we tell about God as originating in history? Is there a God outside of history?

Before these questions can be answered, we must first clarify what it can mean, from the perspective of Positive Historical Judaism, to call God a "God of History." In the traditional sense, in the sense of the revolutionary sermons of the prophets of ancient Israel, the God of Israel was a God of History, in contrast to the pantheon of ancient Near Eastern gods who controlled the various forces of nature. The God of Israel, too, controlled nature, but the field of God's actions moves from nature, given "short shrift" in the first few chapters of Genesis, to history. The "proof" of God's benevolence, the terms of God's Covenant with Israel, are not—or not only—the cooperation of nature, but also and primarily the continuing historical fortunes of the People in their land. This revolutionary approach was what allowed the religion of Israel to survive destruction and exile. Loss of land and ultimate restoration are the terms of God's involvement in the world, the plane of God's activity. While the second paragraph of the Shema, recited twice daily in the liturgy, still presents God as a rain god (that is, as a god who grants rain), it is through the experience of exile, more than through drought, that God's wrath is most evident.

Traces of God as a rain god are interesting to uncover, for they help us trace the development of the God idea in Judaism. In the first chapter of Genesis, God is described as separating the "upper waters" from the "lower waters" with the "expanse" or "firmament" (*rakia* in Hebrew) between them. Then, God parts the lower waters to establish land. Part of God's role— temporarily retracted during the Flood—is to keep the waters in the seas so they do not flood the land. But God's other role is to provide rain in its season: not too much rain lest there be floods, but not too little either lest lack of water prevent the growth of crops and other life. The "upper waters" is the sea that is suspended above the earth. Representing an ancient theory of where the rains originate, and why the sky is blue, humanity depends on God to open up the "valves"—for lack of a better term—in the sky to let just the right amount of water through, when necessary. To open those valves too much, or to keep them closed too long, would each be disastrous. Survival depended upon God's doing God's part in the sky. The Israelites were no different than other ancient peoples in seeking to appease this God of Nature through sacrifices.

In the Torah, while sacrifices are still omnipresent, a new element is introduced: the concept of Covenant. God promises to do God's part if the People agree to do theirs. The People's responsibility is not phrased as sacrifices, which remain the primary domain of the priests, but fidelity to the Torah and its mitzvot, a special code of conduct. The rain god of the second paragraph of the Shema is a god who is interested in the culture of people, not just sweet-scented sacrifices. This paragraph, omitted in most liberal liturgies because of its implication that God is a God of Reward and Punishment, represents an important transition from the concept of a God of Nature to a God of History. Because the ultimate punishment, elaborated on in the Torah, is not natural disaster but historical disaster.

Continued recitation of the second paragraph of the Shema is important, not only because it is a codified tradition, but because it puts us inside the minds of the ancient Israelites who were terrified by the prospect of no rain and lacked an understanding of the vicissitudes of the seasons outside of the power of God. We must place ourselves *in their minds* just as we place ourselves at the moment of the Exodus, at Sinai, at the destruction of the First and Second Temples, in the Holocaust, at the proclamation of the State of Israel in Tel Aviv in 1948, and where we stand today. And thus the seasonal passage in the Amidah, praising God as "causing the wind to return and the rain to fall," connects us not only to the need for rain in Israel today, but to that need, and that sense of hope reaching from helplessness, from millennia ago.

The transition from a God of Nature to a God of History was essential for a religion to survive not only the upheavals of destruction and exile but also new geographic and historical realities. Life in Europe was not as dependent on rain seasons as was the Near East. The new anxieties of security lay more in historical conditions — in relations with one's neighbors and authorities — than with the weather. Faith in a God of History, a God who preserved the Jews as God's faithful remnant, gave the People a way to preserve their sense of Chosenness during the long period of Exile.

But when Europe turned to secularism in the Age of Enlightenment, the insight of the ancient prophets, that God controlled the fortunes of nations, began to be reconsidered. One did not have to wait until the horror of the Holocaust to doubt whether God truly controlled history. Positive Historical Judaism grew out of the new secular approach to history, that history was the product of human culture, not divine fiat. If human history was the domain of human action alone, where was its God?

Rather than the Master of History, God then became the product of history. My teacher Rabbi Neil Gillman taught me that any words, stories, or ideas that we use to describe God must be understood as mythic because they represent our human attempts to understand what stands, by definition, beyond description in human terms. Rabbi Gillman emphasized that he was not saying that there was no God, just that any attempt to explain God is limited and incomplete, a metaphor, a myth. But after living with these ideas now for decades, as both a student and a teacher, as a practicing Jew and a rabbi, I find this explanation inadequate. It is not enough to say, as Heschel did, that as a report on revelation the Bible itself is a midrash. We must go in the direction pointed to by Mordecai Kaplan, that the idea of God is not a report on something outside, but a description of an idea from within. It is a product of Jewish history and culture. I wonder, as well, whether that might have been what Rabbi Gillman was hinting at all along.

A myth is a poetic explanation of a complex phenomenon. It is an explanation of a reality in specific cultural codes. But what is the reality that the God idea is meant to describe? Rather than understand God as a god who controls history, let us consider what God would look like as a product of history.

The most important distinction is that such a God cannot be blamed for the problems that occur in our lives or the tragedies that unfold in this world. The old God of History controls everything, from the international to the personal. Prayers for world peace are intermingled with prayers for success at work; petitions for strength are intermingled with prayers to be cured from cancer. But consider: if God can heal a hurt finger, then God should be able to cure cancer, whereas if God cannot (or will not) cure cancer, then how can God (or why would God) heal a finger? If God can bring peace to warring nations, then God should be able to ensure that a young woman accepts a ring, and if not, then why not? I have often wondered what is truly in the heart of the worshipper who prays for God to bring healing or in the mind of the physician who says "It's in God's hands now." What kind of a capricious God would grant some such requests, but deny others? What kind of a loving God would allow good people to suffer? What kind of a moral God would permit the unspeakable horror of the Holocaust?

The answer that works for me is that God does not allow these things because God does not have that power. Rabbi Harold Kushner emboldened me to say this when I first read *When Bad Things Happen to Good People*. That bestseller and critical contribution to Jewish thought was assigned to me by Rabbi Gillman in the first college course I took after graduating from high school. And yet, a generation had to pass until I could find the strength, or chutzpah, to write that idea in my own words. I first typed this chapter with a bandage covering a severed fingertip. While I did not pray for God to heal my finger, I did marvel at the ability of the body to heal itself. And I was grateful for the good skill of the surgeon who worked on me. When I put on my tefillin, I thanked God for taking me out of Egypt.

The God Who Controls History still keeps a strong hold on the Jewish soul. And yet, I have seen too many circumstances where this theology drives people away from religion instead of towards it, where it establishes distance between us and God rather than immediacy.

Rabbi Kushner suggests that rather than controlling things in the world, God gives us the strength to cope with adversity. That is a beautiful pastoral articulation, and I have continued to use it in my work as a rabbi. But as I think about what it means, I understand it to say that God is a source of comfort and support that we can draw upon, a reminder of the values that we hold dear and the people we strive to become. That is to say, God is an articulation of the sacred incarnate, a sense, an understanding, of what I know from my history and culture.

The God who is the product of our collective Jewish history and culture is sanctified, then, by our acknowledgment of God, much like the body of Tradition, the commandedness of halakhah, and the sacredness of certain times are sanctified by our observance. God is God because we make God God. The unique contribution of Positive Historical Judaism here is that this determination is not an individual matter subject to whim and circumstance. The very existence of God has been codified by tradition over time, just like the truth of the Exodus and the body of Jewish law. And just as we can place ourselves in the Exodus irrespective of its veracity in real history, so can we feel ourselves to be in the presence of God, even if we know that that very idea is the product of our historical evolution. If we can observe the dictates of the Oral Torah—and the Written as well—as if they were commanded to Moses at Sinai, can we pray to God as if God is listening? Is it possible to pray to God as if God can cure cancer, even if we know that God cannot?

We must find God in order for the religious cultural system to work and have meaning. The way to find God, in the context of traditional Judaism, is through that system. The tradition gives us the support of knowing that we are not alone. The tradition reminds us that we are a part of a community through both space and time, connected to others throughout the world and throughout history. The rites and rhythms of halakhic living and traditional prayer align our hopes with the community to which we affix our destinies. If we are to pray to a god, then why not to the God of Israel who has the depth and breadth of historical millennia?

Rabbi Gillman used to tell us that the question is not ritual or no ritual but which ritual. He would talk about the atheist tennis player who insisted that no one take up the racket in the club without white shorts. We studied classics of cultural anthropology, learning how the most primitive and most complex cultures all invent rituals to bring order to the chaos of life. If one is to mark life through the structure of ritual, as all human beings do, then why not use the rituals that have accumulated meaning and power through centuries of Jewish practice? The same should apply to God.

The advantage of Positive Historical Judaism is that it provides us with a legal, cultural, and religious structure that has withstood the tests of time. But that very pedigree raises the challenge of destiny: If God did not choose us for this Tradition, but rather is its product, why then must I comply? Of course, I choose to comply, as anyone can "opt out" of the cultural system.

Apostasy, while an extreme action, is an ancient alternative. The challenge is to accept the Tradition, to feel as if we are at Sinai.

The way this is done, especially in terms of finding God, is not through any intellectual process, but rather through the emotional sense of surrender that the liturgy helps us attain. The nineteenth-century Romantic movement helped Zacharias Frankel understand that Judaism was more than a series of rational principles. Positive Historical Judaism is not a mere intellectual survey of the past. It is an emotional "Romantic" assertion of that past, forging a meaningful present and future.

I began this reflection with a discussion of liturgy, and to that I now return. Jewish prayer is not an intellectual process. The phenomenon, as is most evident when expressed in its most dramatic form on the High Holy Days of Rosh HaShanah and Yom Kippur, is one of surrender. Surrender is not an easy thing for us, living in a broader culture that champions individualism. But this is precisely why the process of prayer can be so transformative. We must allow the synagogue to become a sanctuary, a place where we may find peace and security. We must allow the Tradition to return us to our sacred history. We must allow the words of the Torah to become our sacred text. And we must allow God to be God.

How we think about God and describe God is almost a more difficult question than whether or not there is a God. There have been many attempts from within the non-Orthodox world to find new ways to address God, avoiding the masculine hierarchical language of old. One must consider the challenge raised by feminist theologian Judith Plaskow, that when we speak of God solely in male terms we ignore the Women's Torah and help preserve a male-centered patriarchal system. I was privileged to hear Plaskow speak when I was an undergraduate at Wesleyan University, and I have been wrestling with her words ever since. I have learned to eliminate the use of male pronouns when speaking of God in English. But I know that, as difficult as that is in English, it is impossible in Hebrew. And I know as well that Judith Plaskow challenges us to think about more than grammar. The very metaphors we use about God paint the picture of a male ruler, as much as we might reference the feminine aspect of the Shekhinah, the Divine Presence. That, I have come to understand, is an exception that proves the rule. The traditional Jewish God is a male Near Eastern king. God is called "the King of Kings" in the fashion of the Great King of the Persian Empire, a king whom other kings worshiped, the most powerful entity in the world. That is the original authentic metaphor. It is male centered, it is patriarchal, and it is hierarchical. Yet I prefer to maintain it because I believe that I would be giving up too much to let it go.

As a Positive Historical Jew, I am not looking for a new God to cling to in the image of twenty-first-century sensibilities. I look to an ancient God. It is that ancientness, that finding of God in history, that establishes God's realness for me. When I say that as a Positive Historical Jew I pray to God *as if* there is a God who hears, I am not professing agnosticism. Rather, mine is a faith, a leap of faith into history, a clinging to a wisdom from the past to show me who God is. I cannot let go of the authentic historical imagery of God any more than I can make up my own religion. I can understand God in new ways so that I do not blame God for things that are not God's fault and beyond God's control. I can reinterpret God's law so that I stay true to both it and to my sense of the right and ethical. I can make sense of the traditional God in a way that speaks to my own yearnings and hopes and fears. But I cannot think of God differently any more than I can let go of my own yearnings and hopes and fears. At some point I must surrender to the King of Kings, as the King of Kings.

While acknowledging, then, the liabilities of tying ourselves to ancient imagery and language—just as we tie ourselves to ancient practices and texts—we can still continue the process of understanding what those terms mean *on their own terms*, that is, systemically. What does it mean for God to be King? On Rosh HaShanah and Yom Kippur and in the days between, the regular liturgy adjusts so that the Kingship of God is emphasized. Many find this element of the liturgy uncomfortable, as a cause for distance between the worshiper and the worshiped. Many High Holy Day prayer books from the non-Orthodox world have proposed alternatives to the famous Avinu Malkeinu prayer, ranging from an avoidance of a direct translation of "Our Father our King" to an introduction of new imagery and phrasing. But while it is true that God as King does use an ancient and patriarchal model, it is not true that the image is meant to establish distance. Rather, it should establish intimacy.

Martin Buber was the great teacher who pointed out that when, in the German (and old English) Bible translations God speaks to us as "thou," it is to teach us that our relationship with God is to be one of immediacy and

PASSIONATE CENTRISM   •   88

intimacy, not distance and formality. The "thou," while it seems so formal because it has become archaic, is the informal second person. In German and other European languages, one must take special care to know when to use the informal second person and when to use the formal. Buber teaches us that the God-human relationship is to be one of *Ich und Du,* of "I and Thou." God is immanent, not transcendent. This immanence of God is to be keenly felt at the High Holy Days when we approach God as king, even though this sense is so often missed.

The reason God's kingship is stressed in the High Holy Day liturgy is that we are describing the metaphor of petitioners before a king. We have been sentenced for our sins, and we are appealing to the king for mercy. The king, unlike the sheriff or the judge, has the opportunity to show mercy and compassion because of the king's direct relationship with the subject. The king, that is, has the power to pardon. The king is approached by the petitioner, not because the king is distant, but because the king is near, loving, and compassionate. This role of the king as compassionate pardoner is retained in our American system where the chief executive — a governor or president — has the power to set aside a sentence. It is in this same sense that God is King on Rosh HaShanah and Yom Kippur. We appear in synagogue to surrender ourselves to God's mercy as the King of Kings and thereby to feel the immanence of God's love.

The physical motions of standing and bowing in Jewish prayer, and the ideas described in the poems of the liturgy, are meant to bring us to the point where we surrender our individual pride and discover humility. This process cannot be more critical to striving for perfection as human beings. For that reason, we are taught to apply ourselves to the process on a daily basis. Jewish prayer is not only meant to be recited on Rosh HaShanah and Yom Kippur, for we are challenged to be human each and every day. When I wrap my tefillin every weekday morning, I take that moment to remember that I am binding myself to God and Torah and to all of the values and responsibilities that come with the Covenant, accepted and codified through history. I am affirming, and I am also praying.

And so, we do pray to God to help us, to heal us, to protect us, *as if* God can do all those things. Even if we know that God does not, we still ask God for these things because of our need. We need a God to hear us so that we can express our fervent hopes. We need our Tradition to show us how to have that conversation with God. We look into the rich past of Tradition, and out of that history is where we need to find God.

Positive Historical Judaism represents the passionate center of Judaism. I have attempted in these pages to explain what it means to me. Too often derided as a dry academic excuse for spirituality, I only know that it is nothing like that for me. In my first year of college, I went through a difficult time when my grandmother died of an awful illness. The rabbi with whom I spoke told me that each morning, when I would put on my tallit, I must think about what I see. When I returned to him he asked me what I saw. I could not understand, then, what he was trying to teach me. "Fabric, stripes, patterns," was my answer. "Look again," he said. Now I think I understand that it is not what we see with the eyes but what we feel that is most important. I still put on my tallit every morning, and I feel wrapped in the comfort of tradition, or, in other terms, God's embrace. I thank God for that which was posited for me through history. On that, I remain passionately centered.

APPENDIX 1
Women and the Minyan

Approved by the Committee on Jewish Law and Standards on June 12, 2002, by a vote of fifteen in favor, none opposed and two abstentions (15-0-2). Voting in favor: Rabbis Kassel Abelson, Ben Zion Bergman, Elliot N. Dorff, Robert E. Fine, Myron S. Geller, Susan Grossman, Vernon H. Kurtz, Aaron L. Mackler, Daniel S. Nevins, Paul Plotkin, Joseph Prouser, Joel Rembaum, Joel Roth, Paul Schneider, Elie Kaplan Spitz. Abstaining: Rabbis Baruch Frydman-Kohl, Avram Israel Reisner.

שאלה

May women count in the minyan and serve as שליחות ציבור [prayer leaders]?

תשובה

Since most Conservative congregations count women in the minyan, the answer to the question must by necessity turn to analysis of the proposed halakhaic bases for why women may count in the minyan and serve as שליחות ציבור, as well as address the question of whether women have an equal obligation to prayer with men.[1] Following the analysis, a new proposal is offered.

The Committee on Jewish Law and Standards permitted women to count in the minyan, and, by extension, to serve as שליחות ציבור, in 1973. However, the issue has continued to engender debate and halakhic positions have continued to crystallize since then as the Conservative movement has become more and more egalitarian in its profile. A brief overview of the various stages and positions in the

---

[1] This paper will focus on the question of minyan and שליחות ציבור, and assumes that these two issues are linked. Some might argue that they are not, but it seems to me that the only way one might argue that a woman may serve in a minyan but may not serve as a שליחת ציבור is כבוד הציבור. Since the Law Committee already decided in 1955 that כבוד הציבור was not sufficient reason to continue to forbid women from taking aliyot since a woman's education is no longer an insult to our honor (but rather does us honor), such an approach should apply as well to this potential objection to women serving as שליחות ציבור. Neither do I consider קול אישה as a significant objection. The question of women and tallit, tefillin and head covering/kippah will be addressed by separate papers which have been commissioned of other authors.

I thank the members of the Law Committee for their encouragement, advice and criticism that have helped form this paper. I am also indebted to Dr. Anne Lapidus Lerner and Rabbi Joel Meyers for their helpful critiques. I thankfully acknowledge the influence of my father, Rabbi Robert Fine, who argued the conclusion of this paper with me for many years until I became convinced of it.

halakhic discussion of women and minyan within the Conservative movement is necessary before an evaluation and new position can be proposed. Special attention will be devoted to the 1973 Law Committee decision since, in addition to its importance, not all of the papers relating to that decision are published, or even extant. The positions to date are, from the perspective of this paper, already precedented halakhic responsa. As such it is crucial that our discussion begin with these papers, and that we determine whether there is anything new to add to a question that has already been "asked and answered" for some time.[2]

There are three stages of discussion to be analyzed: 1972-1976, 1977-1992, and from 1993 to the present.

Stage One: 1972-1976

The halakhic discussion of the status of women with regard to the minyan began in 1972 when Ezrat Nashim, a group of Conservative Jewish women activists, brought its platform of halakhic reform of the status of women to the Rabbinical Assembly Convention.[3] On August 29, 1973, the Law Committee discussed the position papers of Rabbi Aaron Blumenthal and Rabbi Phillip Sigal (both in favor of women counting in the minyan) and of Rabbi David Feldman (opposed to women counting in the minyan).[4] It appears from the Minutes that the Law Committee began to hear a series of proposals on the status of women from Rabbi Blumenthal on January 25, 1973, and May 3, 1973, with the first substantial discussion held on June 27, 1973.[5] At that meeting Rabbi Blumenthal urged the

---

[2] On a personal note, I was but five months old when the Law Committee voted to permit women to count in the minyan. However, the issues continued to reverberate through my schooling and upbringing in the less-than-calm Conservative movement of the 1980s. It is with some trepidation, though, that I venture to take issue with some of the later positions which belong to my teachers: Rabbis Joel Roth, Mayer Rabinowitz and David Golinkin.

[3] For an overview of this "event" and its contextual significance in the American Jewry of the 1970s see Anne Lapidus Lerner, "Who Has Not Made Me a Man: The Movement for Equal Rights for Women in American Jewry" *American Jewish Year Book* 77 (1977): 3-38. For another and more recent account see Michael Panitz's chapter on the Rabbinical Assembly since 1970 in Robert E. Fierstein, ed., *A Century of Commitment: One Hundred Years of the Rabbinical Assembly* (New York: Rabbinical Assembly, 2000).

[4] Versions of the papers by Phillip Sigal and David Feldman are published in Seymour Siegel, ed., *Conservative Judaism and Jewish Law* (New York: Rabbinical Assembly, 1977), pp. 281-305. Unfortunately, the original papers by Rabbis Blumenthal, Sigal and Feldman do not appear to be extant in the archives and are preserved only in these later published forms and in the "excerpts" distributed by Seymour Siegel to the RA membership in a circular of October 5, 1973.

[5] Minutes of the CJLS. The Minutes of the August 29, 1973, meeting note, however, that "The May 3, 1973, meeting was declared inoperative due to lack of a quorum. Therefore, it has no status." Rabbi Blumenthal's comprehensive paper was eventually published as Aaron

circulation of Phillip Sigal's paper. The discussion from that point on took the form of a debate between the suggestions of Rabbi Sigal (supported by Rabbi Blumenthal) and Rabbi Feldman.[6] The discussion concluded on August 29, 1973, with approval of a motion, by a vote of nine in favor and four opposed, which read: "Men and women should be counted equally for a minyan."[7]

All that was approved was the ruling, since those voting in favor could not reach agreement on the argumentation. In an October 5, 1973, circular to the Rabbinical Assembly membership about the decision to count women in the minyan from Rabbi Seymour Siegel, then Chairman of the Law Committee, four "basic attitudes of the members" of the Law Committee are described. The circular also contains a digest of the August 29th meeting and summaries of the papers by Rabbis Blumenthal, Sigal and Feldman. Rabbi Siegel wrote that two attitudes represented those voting in favor of the resolution and two attitudes represented those voting against. Those voting in favor were split between those who supported the halakhic argumentation proposed by Rabbis Blumenthal and Sigal and those who were not convinced by the halakhic argumentation. Those voting against the resolution were split between those who supported the halakhic argumentation of Rabbi Feldman and those who dissented on other than strictly halakhic grounds, being concerned with the wisdom of the decision and its consequences regarding the life of the family, the synagogue and the Movement. Rabbi Siegel did not publicize who on the Law Committee fell into which group, if there was overlap, and which sides were stronger than the others. He did not even report the vote, but concluded his letter with the words: "I wish to call your attention to the fact that

---

Blumenthal, "The Status of Women in Jewish Law" *Conservative Judaism* 31 (1977): 24-40, but by then the focus was already turned beyond minyan. However, it does appear that Rabbi Blumenthal had presented an early form of this paper to the Law Committee in the spring and summer of 1973, although that form has not been preserved in the Law Committee archives. I wonder whether his paper, which addressed a comprehensive list of issues relating to women, was in direct response to Ezrat Nashim's platform brought to the RA Convention, whether the influence was more mutual, or even coincidental. Certainly, both reflected a *Zeitgeist* of change.

[6] This debate lived on in the pages of *Sh'ma* after the Law Committee concluded its deliberations. In late 1973 and early 1974 we see an ongoing exchange between Rabbis Sigal and Feldman (and involving other voices as well) with such titles as "Women in a Minyan: law rightly says no"; "Women in a Minyan: but law says yes"; "Women in a Minyan: no is still no"; "Rabbi Feldman's law is not living"; "Rabbi Sigal's Halakhah is Not Halakhah." See the bibliography in David Golinkin, *An Index of Conservative Responsa and Practical Halakhic Studies: 1917-1990* (New York: Rabbinical Assembly, 1992), p. 75.

[7] The CJLS Minutes report that those voting in favor were Rabbis Morris Goodblatt, Eli Bohnen, Phillip Sigal, Jacob Agus, Harold Kushner, Ephraim Bennett, Aaron Blumenthal, Seymour Siegel (chairman) and David Graubart. Those voting against were Rabbis Max Arzt, Isaac Klein, David Feldman and Edward Gershfield.

the text of the resolution was as follows: *Men and women should be counted equally for a minyan.* The vote did not refer to the adoption of any particular teshuvah [responsum], though, of course, the discussion was generated by the material presented by our colleagues, Aaron Blumenthal, Phillip Sigal and David Feldman."[8]

Rabbi Sigal's paper proposes that there is no essential halakhic objection to women counting in the minyan. He first posits that "it is clear that public worship is not a mere option in the halakhah but a mandatory requirement."[9] Rabbi Sigal then argues that public prayer is constituted in a minyan consisting of ten. Rabbi Sigal emphasizes that not until the Shulhan Arukh (OH 55:1) is it explicitly stated that the ten means ten males, עשרה זכרים. Earlier codifications, including the Mishnah (Megillah 4:3) and Maimonides (Mishneh Torah, Hilkhot Tefillah 8:4) are not so explicit, saying merely עשרה without specifying זכרים. That they meant to exclude women "may have been an assumption," Rabbi Sigal writes, "at first, in the light of women's exemption from certain mitzvot. But this cannot be stated unequivocally."[10] Rabbi Sigal then proceeds to argue that the halakhah is not essentially opposed to women's role in public prayer, in an attempt to interpret the codification of the Shulhan Arukh as מנהג [custom] rather than established law. He begins this section of his responsum with the perhaps astonishing words:

> We must establish that women are obligated to pray. For if they are not obligated to pray, we could neither urge their attendance nor expect them to participate. Furthermore, if they are not bona fide worshippers, there would be no grounds to count them in a quorum to legitimize worship for others, since if one is not obligated he cannot serve as the instrument that enables others to fulfill their obligation.

---

[8] Siegel to "Colleagues," p. 2.

[9] Phillip Sigal, "Women in a Prayer Quorum" in Siegel, ed., *Conservative Judaism and Jewish Law,* p. 284. See pp. 289, nn. 4-8 for his sources. Chief among them is B'rakhot 6a, which states that a person's תפילה is listened to only in the synagogue. One can argue, as I would, that such an extreme statement is of an aggadic rather than halakhic category. Nevertheless, the question of the obligatory status of public prayer is a matter of some dispute. It is interesting that Sigal takes the side of arguing that public prayer *is* mandatory, rather than arguing that women's obligatory status in relation to prayer is irrelevant since there is no obligation to public prayer. The boldness of Sigal's approach was recently noted by Orthodox Rabbi Michael Broyde. See Michael J. Broyde, "Communal Prayer and Women" *Judaism* 42 (1993): 390.

[10] Sigal, "Women in a Prayer Quorum," p. 285. Sigal does later note that Maimonides explicitly states that only males may be included in the minyan for reading the Torah (Hilkhot Tefillah 12:3). See p. 291, n. 16.

We will find, however, that the halakhah clearly established the obligation of women to participate in public worship.[11]

Rabbi Sigal refers to halakhic sources, including the beginning of Hilkhot Tefillah in the Mishneh Torah, which assert women's obligation to prayer. Rabbi Sigal notes the injunction of Mishnah Rosh HaShanah 3:8 that only one of similar or greater obligation can help fulfill the obligation of others. But from the fact that women are obligated to prayer Rabbi Sigal makes a significant jump in arguing that their obligation is to public prayer and equivalent to that of a man. Citing a series of talmudic and medieval rulings involving permission of women to participate in the Torah service, to blow the shofar, to read the Megillah, to perform ritual slaughter, and even to count as the tenth for a minyan of prayer,[12] Rabbi Sigal infers that women were present and expected to be present for public prayer. Therefore, a woman's obligation and status is the same as a man's. Therefore, the exclusion of women from the minyan as codified in the Shulhan Arukh is not based in halakhah but is rather a "מנהג" which has lost its reason and its appeal...which often runs counter to the best interests of Jewish communities."[13]

The classical source that permitted a woman to be counted as the tenth for a minyan belongs to R. Simhah and is reported in the Mordecai on B'rakhot 48a, note 173. While this point is underemphasized in the published version of Rabbi Sigal's paper, it receives greater prominence in the excerpt from the original paper which was included in Seymour Siegel's circular to the RA membership. There, Rabbi Sigal concludes:

> In the light of the Mordecai on B'rakhot 48a, and in view of all of these considerations, our Committee on Jewish Law and Standards ought to declare that women may equally with men constitute a community of worshippers in order to fulfill the great mitzvah of public worship....[and] we would not limit the ratio of women in a minyan.[14]

---

[11] Ibid., p. 286. I say "perhaps astonishing" because Professor Judith Hauptman, who argued in 1993 that a woman's obligation to prayer is the same as a man's (to be discussed below), wrote that "given this history of a consistently expanding obligation of women to pray, I find it hard to understand why the various responsa written recently on this topic fail to mention this trend at all." She mentions the papers by Joel Roth and Israel Francus, but nowhere does she refer to the 1973 responsum by Phillip Sigal, which already stated her thesis. Ironically, as mentioned in the previous note, Sigal's paper was noted by Michael Broyde in a critique of Hauptman's paper. Judith Hauptman, "Women and Prayer: An Attempt to Dispel Some Fallacies" *Judaism* 42 (1993): 98, and 102, n. 17.

[12] See Sigal, "Women in a Prayer Quorum," pp. 286-288, 291-292, nn. 16-25.

[13] Ibid., p. 288.

[14] Siegel to "Colleagues," p. 10.

The language of Rabbi Feldman's paper as presented in the "excerpt" in Seymour Siegel's circular is far stronger than the 1977 published version and speaks more directly to the arguments put forward by Rabbis Sigal and Blumenthal. Feldman is cited by Siegel as writing:

> Rabbi Sigal demonstrates the importance of public prayer as opposed to private, then demonstrates the obligation of women to pray at least privately, and then concludes that *therefore* they are to be counted in the minyan. That this logical leap is inadmissible is evident from the very existence of separate halakhot governing public as opposed to private prayer....As to explicit halakhah on the subject of women in the minyan, he acknowledges that Karo in the Shulhan Arukh OH 55:4 legally excludes women from the count, but then opposes to him the earlier permitting view of Mordecai...He overlooks the fact that Mordecai *questions* [R. Simhah]....The telling fact is that, according to Be'er HaGolah, Mordecai is the very source of Karo's prohibition. To this lone and questionable reference, Rabbi Sigal adds speculative material to prove that such a view is indeed in the halakhic tradition. Speculation of this sort might have been in order, were it not for a formidable body of *explicit* halakhah to the contrary.[15]

Rabbi Feldman, after providing ten sources which contradict Rabbi Sigal's proposal, concludes with a critique of Rabbi Sigal's conclusion, writing that "even if this lone and questionable source [i.e. R. Simhah in the Mordecai] were an adequate basis" for the first part of Rabbi Sigal's conclusion that the Law Committee should declare women equally part of the community of worshippers, it does not argue that we not "limit the ratio" of women in the minyan, since R. Simhah in the Mordecai limits the ratio himself to 1 to 9.

Rabbi Blumenthal's approach differed from that of Rabbi Sigal in that he did not argue on the basis of women's obligation in regard to prayer. He critiqued Rabbi Feldman's assertion that "equality of men and women is not at stake here, but equality of obligation."[16] Citing the talmudic source permitting a minor to count in the minyan for Birkat HaMazon [the Grace after Meals] (B'rakhot 48a), Rabbi Blumenthal argues that since in that case the minor is not equally obligated but counts, obligation is not of issue. Rather, Rabbi Blumenthal focuses on Rabbi Sigal's usage of R. Simhah as quoted in the Mordecai, and sees counting women equally with men in the minyan as a "logical extension of the opinion articulated by the Mordecai which originates with Rabbi Simhah of Spier and is shared by

---

[15] Ibid., p. 11.

[16] David Feldman, "Woman's Role and Jewish Law" in Siegel, ed., *Conservative Judaism and Jewish Law*, p. 300.

others" that women can count in order to help the community say the prayers which require a quorum. Rabbi Blumenthal argues that this is a conclusion that "Rabbi Feldman might have arrived at...but he refrains from taking that step."[17]

Rabbi Feldman responded to Rabbi Blumenthal in his paper, explaining why he refrained from "taking that step" and insisting that equality of obligation is indeed the issue. The statement of the Mordecai cannot be divorced from the question of exempting others from their obligations. In answer to Rabbi Blumenthal's argument of a minor permitted to be counted in the minyan for Birkat HaMazon, Rabbi Feldman cites a tosafot (to Rosh HaShanah 33a s.v. הא) on that very issue, which reads: ומקטן דמברך ברכת המזון אף על פי שהוא פטור אין ראיה לאשה דקטן בא בכלל חיוב, that is, the fact that a [male] minor can count in the minyan for Birkat HaMazon even though he is exempt from the obligation cannot be used as an inference that so may a woman count, because the minor will come into the category of obligation (when he reaches the age of majority) while a woman will not. Therefore, a minor has a higher status than a woman because, unlike a woman, a minor will eventually become obligated. Rabbi Feldman thus dismissed Rabbi Blumenthal's challenge that equality of obligation was not of issue and insisted that "no halakhic basis for counting women in the minyan is offered by the papers at hand."[18]

Rabbi Siegel reported to the Rabbinical Assembly membership that many on the Law Committee were not convinced by the attempt of Rabbi Blumenthal and Rabbi Sigal to permit women to count in the minyan on the basis of the statement of the Mordecai in the name of R. Simhah. Agreeing with Rabbi Feldman, many thought that relying on this particular source is questionable since it is clear that the mainstream of halakhah forbids the counting of women, that "to suggest that counting women is within the halakhic process, based on the Mordecai, is untenable."[19] However, others disagreed with that view. Even if we have the position of but one against the mainstream, if that position is preserved is that not a part of the halakhic process? Can we not lean on it for support if necessary? The necessity to go against the mainstream and depend on a minority view is perhaps created today because of the changing role of women in our society. That reality and the position of R. Simhah should justify the change. Others, while convinced that the societal change mandated a halakhic adjustment and the inclusion of women in the minyan, were unwilling to do so on the basis of the arguments put forward by Rabbis Blumenthal and Sigal. Perhaps agreeing with the halakhic

---

[17] Siegel to "Colleagues," p. 5.
[18] Ibid., p. 13. On Feldman's understanding of women and Birkat HaMazon, see Feldman, "Woman's Role in Jewish Law," p. 302.
[19] Siegel to "Colleagues," p. 3.

reasoning of Rabbi Feldman but determined to resolve according to Rabbis Blumenthal and Sigal, this (unidentified) group in the Law Committee sought another alternative.

Since the resolution proposed did not make reference to the reasoning of either Rabbi Blumenthal or Rabbi Sigal, the alternative for those unconvinced by their arguments was to consider the resolution a תקנה [enactment]. In his summary of the deliberations, Rabbi Siegel explained that the one group "of course, recognized that the weight of the tradition and traditional authorities were obviously opposed, but, in line with our philosophy of Jewish law it is possible to depend on even one authority when it is necessary to do so." Regarding the other group Siegel wrote:

> There were other proponents of the resolution who felt that halakhic considerations based on past authorities was too weak a standard upon which to depend. It was the view of these colleagues that the decision of the Committee should be viewed as a תקנה. The right to institute תקנות is vested in the authorities of each age when they see the need to correct an injustice or to improve the religious and ethical life of the community. It was felt that since we have given a greater role to women in synagogue life and education, and since we wish women to attend synagogue services, that it was appropriate now to recognize the equality of men and women in regard to minyan.[20]

Neither Rabbi Siegel nor the Minutes record how many of the nine rabbis voting in favor of the resolution voted for it as a תקנה rather than on the basis of the arguments put forth by Rabbis Blumenthal and Sigal. However, it is not for us to question the procedure of a court that came before us, even if we might not desire to pass a תקנה by concurrence of less than half of the majority of the Law Committee. The fact that this position was reported and disseminated by mail to the membership of the Assembly by the Chairman of the Law Committee implies that this was a procedurally official position and not just an "interpretation" of the resolution.

While the issue of women and the minyan continued to be debated within the Conservative movement on the central and local level, the various positions argued during the 1973 deliberations of the Law Committee establish a theoretical typology for all the positions to be later articulated. What we might call the "school" of Rabbis Blumenthal and Sigal believes that it is acceptable to depend on a single position, if necessary, even if the weight of precedent and tradition speaks to the contrary. The "school" of Rabbi Feldman disagrees with that view of the halakhic process. It is not enough to find one source and make it say what you

---

[20] Ibid., p. 1.

want it to say. On the contrary, the halakhah flows like a river and one cannot ignore the direction of the flow. There may be a point where the river can choose where it will go. But once that decision is made there is no going back.

Rabbi Sigal argued that an exclusion of women from the minyan was not a necessarily essential element of halakhah since women are indeed obligated to prayer as well as men. Therefore, he understands the codification of the Shulhan Arukh (and all who follow) as a מנהג and, as such, it can be modified with cause. But others disagreed. The fact that Karo codified the exclusion, and the fact that that codification is confirmed by all subsequent אחרונים [later authorities], means that we are not talking about a mere מנהג. But even if it were a "mere מנהג" that is not to say that it is not binding. The principles of מנהג מבטל הלכה, that a custom can even supersede a law, and הלכה כבתראי, that the law is according to the later authorities, should not be dismissed as the antics of a fundamentalist wing of an otherwise progressive rabbinate. A jealous loyalty to precedent and established custom is what puts the "Conservative" into Conservative Judaism. This was the position which distinguished Zacharias Frankel from the more liberal German reformers in the 1840s. His opponents argued that since halakhah does permit prayer in any language there is no halakhic impediment to praying in German. In fact, all of the early German reforms were based on carefully argued halakhic defenses. But Frankel argued that that is not enough. The conservative spirit of the people through history, the *Volksgeist,* is even more determinative than halakhic discourse. We all recognize that a gifted halakhist can argue for almost anything. But a Conservative rabbi must above all be loyal to the historical spirit of the people which the halakhah only attempts to describe. The law as it develops through history is the concretization of the spirit of the people, and, perhaps, of God's revelation. This is the key distinction between Conservative and Reform Judaism as they first developed. Reform Judaism sought to uncover the original pristine Prophetic Judaism before it became oppressed with talmudism and medieval rabbinisim which reflected the nature of an inward looking ghettoized Jewry. Conservative Judaism, on the other hand, argued that there is no pristine original essence of Judaism which can be uncovered by a careful reading of the Bible and ancient history. On the contrary, the essence of Judaism is the experience of the Jewish people through history. The essence of Judaism is fluid since it develops through time. What is crucial and often misunderstood is that this is an emphatically "Conservative" position crafted as a Romantic attachment to the experience of Jewish history in contradistinction to the liberal intellectualism of Reform Judaism. This too is what Solomon Schechter referred to as "Catholic

Israel," the totality of Jewish experience through history which argues for a religious conservatism.[21]

It may have been this sense of classical Conservatism that prevented the positions of Rabbis Blumenthal and Sigal from attaining a majority of the Law Committee. The centrists of 1973 could not but agree with Rabbi Feldman's arguments that there was no reasonable way to argue that the halakhic sources could be used to support women's inclusion in the minyan. Jewish law and practice developed so that it was indeed *the* law that women did not count in the minyan. However, they also believed that law can change. One cannot retroactively reroute a decision that was made upstream by the flow of the river. However, from where we stand the river continues on its journey. It has not emptied into a lake. While we cannot change what has already been determined upstream, we can direct the river from where we stand and influence where it will flow from us. For that reason, and because of the extraordinary circumstances of the changed societal nature of the role of women, these rabbis argued for a תקנה. The halakhic system, they claimed, gave them the authority to take an extraordinary measure against precedent if the situation warranted, and for the sake of the system itself. In order to save the river we are justified in redirecting it to avoid danger and provide for a safe course. In fact, such action would be praiseworthy. As such caretakers of the tradition, this group voted for the 1973 resolution as a תקנה, and their support insured its success.

Supporters of the halakhic changes in relation to the status of women in Jewish law in the Conservative rabbinate consistently argued that what distinguished us as a Movement was that we approached change *within* the halakhic system. We see from the 1973 discussion that there were three basic approaches to what it means to effect change within the system: through the use of classical minority positions, through extraordinary halakhic measures, and through loyalty to precedent and tradition. Even the third category, represented by Rabbi Feldman, was certainly not opposed to all change. There was a level of what Zacharias Frankel called "moderate reform" which was permitted and laudable within the precedented tradition. Tradition was never understood by Conservative rabbis to be a stagnant monolith.

---

[21] See my contribution in "The Open Forum: Positive-Historical Judaism" *Conservative Judaism* 47 (spring 1995): 71-81; and my "The Meaning of Catholic Israel" *Conservative Judaism* 50 (summer 1998): 29-47 [and Appendix 4 of this volume]. See also, on the importance of custom and tradition in Conservative Judaism, Elliot N. Dorff, "Custom Drives Jewish Law on Women" *Conservative Judaism* 49 (spring 1997): 3-21, and the discussion the following year in "The Open Forum: Custom, Halakhah and the Status of Women" *Conservative Judaism* 51 (fall 1998): 63-73.

Stage Two: 1977-1992

As analyzed above, the 1973 resolution of the Law Committee permitting women to count in the minyan could not have passed without the belief that the Conservative rabbinate held the authority to effect an extraordinary change within the community of the Conservative movement. For many rabbis, perhaps a majority of the Assembly, the authority of the Committee on Jewish Law and Standards to effect a תקנה on the status of women or to adjudicate questions of law even against the clear weight of precedent was unquestioned. However, the authority of the Law Committee was not sufficient in resolving the issues facing the Jewish Theological Seminary in its decision on whether or not to admit women to its Rabbinical School.[22] At the 1977 Rabbinical Assembly Convention a resolution was passed requesting that Rabbi Gerson Cohen, the Chancellor of the Seminary, address the issue of the ordination of women. Many in the Rabbinical Assembly felt it improper to dictate halakhah to their teachers at the Seminary, although they felt no qualms in sending a clear message of how they felt. From this point, the locus of the discussion shifted from the Law Committee and the Rabbinical Assembly to the Seminary.

In 1979 the Seminary Faculty prepared position papers on the question and all related questions, among which was the concern that a rabbi should be able to count in a minyan and serve as שליח ציבור. And so the question was reopened. Two of these papers, by Rabbis Joel Roth and Mayer Rabinowitz, were voted into the record of the Law Committee on November 7, 1984. These papers, along with the dissenting papers of Rabbis David Weiss Halivni and Israel Francus, are directly relevant for our discussion.

Of these four papers by Seminary Talmud professors, Rabbi Rabinowitz's was the only one which agreed with the 1973 Law Committee resolution in granting full equality to women in regard to counting them in the minyan. Although not referring to that discussion, Rabbi Rabinowitz agreed with Rabbi Blumenthal that "analysis of the sources dealing with minyan reveals that equality

---

[22] On the history of the decision to ordain women at the Seminary, see Beth S. Wenger, "The Politics of Women's Ordination: Jewish Law, Institutional Power, and the Debate over Women in the Rabbinate" in Jack Wertheimer, ed., *Tradition Renewed: A History of the Jewish Theological Seminary of America* (New York: Jewish Theological Seminary, 1997), vol. 2, pp. 483-523. See also Pamella S. Nadell, *Women Who Would Be Rabbis: A History of Women's Ordination, 1889-1985* (Boston: Beacon Press, 1998), specifically ch. 5. For the parallel story of ordination in the Christian world, see Mark Chaves, *Ordaining Women: Culture and Conflict in Religious Organizations* (Cambridge, Mass.: Harvard University Press, 1997). Unfortunately, Chaves focuses only on the Christian denominations.

of obligation is not a consideration for being counted in a minyan."[23] His analysis of the talmudic sources leads him to conclude that:

> The basic criteria qualifying one to be included in a minyan are: 1)גדולים—belonging to the class of adults, and 2) בני חורין—being free individuals. In the rabbinic period women were at a certain age classified as adults, but never as being completely free, because they started life as being legally subservient either to father or brother, and, when married, to their husbands. No one in our society today can reasonably argue that a woman is not as legally free as a man. Nor would any one today challenge her status as an adult. The criteria for eligibility to be counted in a minyan have therefore not changed. What has changed is the reality which now enlarges the number of those who meet the criteria.[24]

While acknowledging the ruling of the Shulhan Arukh (OH 55:1) that kaddish can only be recited with ten adult free males, Rabbi Rabinowitz questions that "Rabbi Joseph Caro does not explain why he felt it necessary to add the term 'males' when the Mishnah and the codifiers who preceded him did not deem it necessary to do so."[25] Here Rabbi Rabinowitz is echoing Rabbi Sigal's dismissal of the Shulhan Arukh in favor of the Mishnah which does not explicitly say that women are excluded from a minyan.

Rabbi Rabinowitz's paper has the advantage of being a clear and cogent argument for an egalitarian approach to women and prayer based on halakhic sources. Flowing from the school of Rabbis Blumenthal and Sigal, Rabbi Rabinowitz goes a step further in arguing that not only can we base our halakhic position on one voice from the tradition even though precedent developed otherwise, but that in this case that one voice was the true authentic halakhah, presented in the Mishnah, and only later "forgotten" by the time of the Shulhan Arukh. There is nothing essential about the exclusion of women from the minyan, evidenced by the failure of the Shulhan Arukh to explain it. Women are not excluded by the Mishnah, and they should not be excluded today. Those who did not accept Rabbi Rabinowitz's argument, on the other hand, were, among other things, unconvinced by the argument that the Shulhan Arukh fails to *explain* why women are excluded from the minyan. The Shulhan Arukh rarely explains anything. That is, law is just as often based upon practice and precedent than reason. Rabbi Rabinowitz may have illuminated what the criteria of the Rabbis

---

[23] Mayer E. Rabinowitz, "An Advocate's Halakhic Responses on the Ordination of Women" in Simon Greenberg, ed., *The Ordination of Women as Rabbis: Studies and Responsa* (New York: Jewish Theological Seminary, 1988), p. 112.

[24] Ibid., p. 115.

[25] Ibid., p. 114.

were for counting in a quorum, and we could certainly agree that were the Rabbis with us today they would consider women to fall within their criteria. However, at that time they did not. And that is how the law developed. Change in the societal nature of women should supply sufficient cause to reexamine the question, but that does not in and of itself overturn the precedent. We cannot ignore the fact that we are not the Rabbis determining the criteria of who counts in a minyan. Rather, we are the rabbis of our own time and have inherited a tradition which instructs us that women do not count in the minyan, and that is what we must address. That is, those flowing from the school of Rabbi Feldman were concerned primarily with precedent, which argued against counting women in the minyan, whereas those flowing from the school of Rabbis Blumenthal and Sigal were concerned primarily with the classical sources, which, at the least, could be used to argue either position with equal justification, and at the most, could be used to argue forcefully for women's inclusion in the minyan, as argued by Rabbi Rabinowitz.

The outstanding issue is the question of obligation. Rabbi Rabinowitz's opinion, following Rabbi Blumenthal, was found by many to be unconvincing in holding that equality of obligation is not the central question. The contentious element in the approaches of Rabbis Blumenthal and Rabinowitz is that they seem to accept that women's obligation is *not* equal, and that *even so* they should count equally in the minyan (a paradox that Rabbi Sigal was careful to avoid). Rabbi Rabinowitz extends his approach to the question of שליחת ציבור, arguing that the role today of the שליח ציבור has become eclipsed by the role of חזן [(hazzan) cantor]. The "reader" no longer fulfills the role of agency when all have their own סידורים [prayer books] from which to pray. Rabbi Rabinowitz cites a ruling of the Magen Avraham that מי שבקי אינו יוצא על ידי אחרים, that one who is knowledgeable cannot fulfill his obligation through others[26] However, while it might be the case that the repetition of the Amidah does not completely satisfy our individual obligations, the fact that we all hold סידורים does not mean that we have no need of a שליח. Often our כוונה [intention] is unfocused and we benefit, then, from the public repetition. Saying "amen" through the repetition could still be very important in the fulfillment of our obligation to prayer.[27] Additionally, while one can accept Rabbi Rabinowitz's argument that agency is only an issue in the repetition of the Amidah rather than kaddish,[28] in general our congregants do see their rabbis and cantors as their agents in reaching the divine. We should not be afraid to recognize that the major function of clergy is to help our people reconnect

---

[26] Ibid., p. 116. Magen Avraham to Orah Hayyim 53:19, note 20.
[27] For this reason I have always felt uncomfortable with the practice of a הכי קדושה [abbreviated repetition] as a regular standard of worship rather than restricted to special situations.
[28] Rabinowitz, "An Advocate's Halakhic Responses," p. 122, nn. 48, 53.

with the holy. That is the function of prayer, to which rabbi and cantor are agents if nothing else. This is not to say that Jewish worship is a sacrament in the formal sense. Any Jew can pray individually. But prayer is often easier (and preferable) in community.

Ultimately, those who take issue with Rabbi Rabinowitz's approach argue that that *even if* we could accept his argument that a שליח ציבור no longer performs the function of agency, he has still implied that at one time that function was performed. And if that function was performed, then how can we say that minyan has nothing to do with obligation! Even if practical agency is no longer relevant and vestigial, a vestigial organ is still part of the organism and tells us something about its history and development. It is impossible to divorce minyan from the issue of obligation. Throughout history minyan has provided a forum wherein Jewish men have gathered to fulfill their obligations to prayer. Whether or not one can fulfill such obligations in private is irrelevant since what is critical is that the minyan fulfills the obligations. A woman, then, cannot count in the minyan if her obligation is not equal.[29]

Rabbi Rabinowitz reflected elements of the positions of Rabbis Blumenthal and Sigal in his approach. He would argue, theoretically, that even if the weight of tradition argued to the contrary, as long as one can interpret the sources in a certain direction, that direction is available to the פוסק [halakhic decisor] when there is sufficient cause. Rabbis Roth, Halivni and Francus fall more under the "school" of Rabbi Feldman, that we must work with the weight of tradition and precedent rather than fight against it.

---

[29] In conversation, Rabbi Rabinowitz has argued that there are cases when obligation is not equal and that such does not effect counting in the minyan. For example, a מנודה, one who has been placed under a ban, is obligated but cannot be counted in the minyan, and, as another example, a man who has already davened has no obligation to daven a second time (in fact he should not do so). And yet, he counts in the minyan. I respond that such a case is not as clear as that of the אונן, one who has not yet become a mourner since burial has not yet taken place, where one has no obligation and does not count in the minyan. Here, in the case of one who has already davened, surely he can still benefit from saying amen to the repetition of the Amidah, especially in case he did not properly recite everything himself. However, Rabbi Rabinowitz would argue that he cannot fulfill his obligation through the repetition since the שליח ציבור no longer functions as a true שליח. In either case, the individual who already davened has an obligatory status that is equal to others even if it is already fulfilled. In the case of the מנודה, one could argue that there the exclusion from counting in the minyan is directly resultant of the ban, rather than the obligatory status. Rabbi Rabinowitz, on the other hand, sees these cases as further examples that obligation is not the essential qualifier for counting in the minyan, and would see the arguments to defend that explanation as strained. He rejects the contrary example of the אונן, where one is not obligated and not counted. See ibid., p. 121, n. 35.

As discussed above, there were a number of centrist rabbis who, while they sympathized with the "school" of Rabbi Feldman, supported the 1973 decision as a תקנה because of the extraordinary circumstances of the changed societal reality regarding the role of women which created an injustice in the life of the synagogue. After 1979 these rabbis no longer had to choose between Rabbi Feldman's position and a תקנה because Rabbi Roth's paper provided for them what appeared to be the perfect solution to the dilemma of being caught between tradition and change.

The first section of Rabbi Roth's paper argues that a woman may accept upon herself the equal obligation to perform various mitzvot and by such can aid in the fulfillment of that obligation by others, i.e. count in a minyan and serve as שליחת ציבור. Rabbi Roth never questioned what he understood to be the normative halakhah that in general women do not count in the minyan. Neither did he question Rabbi Feldman's explanation that the reason why women do not count in a minyan is because their obligation to prayer is not equal to that of a man. He attempted to argue, through the normative halakhic tradition, that there would be no objection to women *assuming* a greater obligation and hence qualifying for counting in the minyan.[30] Because of the importance of this responsum in our discussion, a brief summary is in order.

Rabbi Roth begins by asking, "May women perform those mitzvot from which they are exempt, and may they recite any blessings which may be appropriate to those mitzvot?"[31] Rabbi Roth demonstrates three positions in response to this question. The Ravad answers that women may not perform such mitzvot and they may not recite any blessings over them.[32] Maimonides answers that women may perform such mitzvot but they may not recite any blessings over them. Rabbi Roth explains that this may or may not be the view of Rashi, and that this was the view of Joseph Karo and the practice of the Sephardim. Finally, Rabbenu Tam, Rabbi Yitzhak HaLevi and later Askhenazic decisors held the view that women may perform and may recite the blessings for positive time-bound commandments.[33] Therefore, the majority Askhenazic tradition is that women may perform mitzvot from which they are exempt and may recite the blessings, even the words אשר קדשנו במצוותיו וציוונו. That is, once a woman takes upon herself the

---

[30] See Joel Roth, "On the Ordination of Women as Rabbis" in Greenberg, ed., *The Ordination of Women as Rabbis,* pp. 127-187.

[31] Ibid., p. 128.

[32] Ravad to Sifra, par. 2, Weiss ed., 4c. See Roth, "On the Ordination of Women," pp. 129-130.

[33] Maimonides, Mishneh Torah, Hilkhot Tzitzit 3:9; Shulkhan Arukh, Orah Hayim 589:6 and the Rama there who answers Karo: "Our custom is for women to recite the blessings on positive time-bound commandments." See Roth, "On the Ordination of Women," pp. 130-134, 174-176, nn. 17-37.

practice of a mitzvah she is as one commanded in its fulfillment. Rabbi Roth's second question is: "If women may observe mitzvot from which they are exempt, is their observance of these mitzvot governed by all the same rules as is the observance by men of those same mitzvot?" That is, are women entitled to violate a Sabbath prohibition in the observance of such mitzvot?[34] Rabbi Roth finds a "direct and unequivocal response" in the statement of Rabbi Lazar in the Yerushalmi (Kiddushin 1:7): "The paschal sacrifice by women is voluntary, but it takes precedence over Shabbat." Rabbi Roth finds a similar response of the Ravad.[35] The third question addressed by Rabbi Roth's paper is: "Can voluntary observance of a mitzvah ever become in some significant sense religiously obligated?"[36] Rabbi Roth finds an affirmative answer in the words of the Magen Avraham: נשים פטורות מספירת העומר דהוי מצוות עשה שהזמן גרמה, ומיהו כבר שווין עלייהו חובה, that is, that women are exempt from counting the Omer because it is a positive time-bound commandment, but they have made it an obligation upon themselves.[37] Rabbi Roth finds precedent for this statement of the Magen Avraham in the Halakhot Gedolot (attributing the view to the gemara), Eliezer ben Joel HaLevi (the Ravia, thirteenth century), Samson Bar Zadok (a student of Rabbi Meir of Rothenberg), and Isaac Di Molena (late sixteenth century).[38] At this point, Rabbi Roth has cogently argued for a woman's right to accept upon herself an obligation to a mitzvah she might not otherwise be obligated to perform. Up until this point, as we shall see below, Rabbi Halivni would agree with Rabbi Roth.

The final question which Rabbi Roth must ask is: "If it can, can that self-imposed obligation have the same legal status as the obligation of men which, legally speaking, is 'other-imposed' either by Torah or by rabbinic authority?"[39] The question revolves around the statement of Rabbi Haninah (Kiddushin 31a and parallels): גדול המצווה ועושה ממי שאינו מצווה ועושה, that is, that greater is the one who is commanded and complies than the one is who is not commanded and complies. This statement must be harmonized with the rule of the Mishnah (Rosh HaShanah 3:8): זה הכלל—כל שאינו מחויב בדבר אינו מוציא את הרבים ידי חובתן, that is, that one who is not "obligated" may not aid in the fulfillment of obligation of those who are so obligated. The question is whether, when a woman accepts upon herself, voluntarily, an halakhic obligation, can she be מחויבת [obligated] as one who "inherited" the obligation, or is she as one שאינו מצווה ועושה [who is not commanded and complies] and, hence, unable to perform agency for one המצווה

[34] Ibid., pp. 128-129.
[35] Ibid., pp. 134-135. The statement of the Ravad is the same as that referred to above, n. 32.
[36] Roth, "On the Ordination of Women," p. 129.
[37] Magen Avraham to OH 489, par. 1. See Roth, "On the Ordination of Women," p. 136.
[38] See Roth, "On the Ordination of Women," pp. 136-141, 177-179, nn. 45-68.
[39] Ibid., p. 129.

ועושה [who is commanded and complies]? Rabbi Roth grapples with this problem and concludes that Rabbi Hanina's statement refers to the שכר מצווה, the reward, rather than the obligation. That is, it is a theological, perhaps even aggadic statement and is irrelevant to the issue of equality of obligation. A woman may accept upon herself the practice or even the obligation of performing a mitzvah from time to time. Such a woman could not fulfill the obligations of others. But if the woman accepts upon herself the obligation to perform a mitzvah *equally with men,* and she understands that failure to comply is a "sin,"[40] then she is equally מחויבת and may perform agency.[41] Rabbi Roth clarified his conclusion that "women may be counted in a minyan and serve as ש"ץ only when they have accepted upon themselves the voluntary obligation to pray as required by the law, and at the times required by the law, and only when they recognize and affirm that failure to comply with the obligation is sin."[42]

Rabbi David Weiss Halivni agreed with almost all of the steps of Rabbi Roth's arguments. While he withdrew his paper after the Seminary decided to ordain women in 1983, and so his paper was not published in the 1988 volume edited by Simon Greenberg, he does in his 1996 autobiography make reference to his "responsum":

> I made some suggestions (among them, that women take upon themselves the observance of time-bound commandments from which, traditionally, they were exempted) which would symbolize submission to halakhah, to the divine writ, and hence to God, and which might have reflected precedents. I even wrote a responsum outlining this view, which I later withdrew. My proposal was rejected as insufficiently egalitarian, because it maintained some restrictions on women and because its effect would not have been felt until a new generation of women grew up whose mothers observed time-bound commandments, thus obligating their daughters halakhically to do the same, as an expression of *Torat imecha,* "the instruction of your mother" (Proverbs 1:8). But without antecedent support, I would not tamper with any law or custom.[43]

Rabbi Roth's responsum also "maintained some restrictions on women." The only difference, then, is that Rabbi Halivni held that women had to take upon themselves the obligation for certain mitzvot for a generation in order for their obligation to "hold" and be equal to that of a man's and only then could women

---

[40] See the discussion below on the meaning of sin in Conservative Judaism.
[41] Ibid., pp. 141-148, 179-185, nn. 69-90.
[42] Ibid., p. 168.
[43] David Weiss Halivni, *The Book and the Sword: A Life of Learning in the Shadow of Destruction* (Boulder: Westview Press, 1996), p. 105.

perform agency for men. Rabbi Halivni was bothered by the statement of Rabbi Hanina, the prospect that even a vow can be annulled, and the fact that he only expected but a few women to comply, then, with this voluntary acceptance of mitzvot. Until such observance becomes an established מנהג, he held, women cannot perform agency and the Seminary should not ordain women.[44]

Rabbi Francus strongly disagreed with both Rabbis Roth and Halivni. While he agreed that a woman may "acquire the status of a חיובית—of 'one obligated' in relation to mitzvot from which she is exempt," he categorically rejected the notion that "the quality of her 'obligation' be of such a nature as to qualify her to be מוציא—'to act as an agent to perform mitzvot' in behalf of men."[45] Through his examination of the sources he concludes that there is no way that a voluntarily assumed obligation can ever equal that which is otherly "imposed by the Torah or the sages."[46] Rabbi Francus makes clear his objection to the approach of Rabbi Halivni as well as Rabbi Roth when he writes: "A woman can never—not today, not tomorrow, not next year, and not next generation—acquire the status of a חיובית—of one 'obligated' in relation to a mitzvah from whose performance she is now halakhically exempt, which would qualify her to act as agent in the performance of those mitzvot in behalf of men."[47] If his intent was not clear enough, he explains in his footnote: "See also the paper of Dr. Roth...and the paper of Dr. Halivni...for different views. According to the former, it can be accomplished here and now, and according to the latter, only after a generation. I respectfully disagree with both."[48]

After a few years of debate, the Seminary Faculty decided to admit women to the Rabbinical School in 1983. The decision of the faculty was based upon the collective arguments of the faculty papers, but not officially accepting any particular approach. This was not unlike the decision of the Law Committee on women in the minyan in 1973. But in the case of the Seminary, Rabbi Roth's proposal did, at least to some extent, succeed in becoming Seminary policy. To this day the Seminary's *Academic Bulletin* lists as a requirement for admission to Rabbinical School that "women candidates are required to accept equality of

---

[44] David Weiss Halivni, "On Ordination of Women," manuscript pp. 9-16, included in the unpublished 1979 collection *On the Ordination of Women as Rabbis: Position Papers of the Faculty of the Jewish Theological Seminary of America* which was later published as the volume edited by Simon Greenberg, without Halivni's paper. The 1979 collection is available in the Jewish Theological Seminary Library, BM 726.J48 1983.

[45] Israel Francus, "On the Ordination of Women" in Greenberg, ed., *The Ordination of Women as Rabbis*, p. 36.

[46] Ibid., p. 43.

[47] Ibid., p. 36.

[48] Ibid., p. 43, n. 1.

obligation for the mitzvot from which women have been traditionally exempted, including tallit, tefillin and tefillah."[49] Similarly, a second minyan of the Seminary Synagogue was founded after the decision was made to ordain women, called at that time Schiff II,[50] where only women who accepted the equal obligation to תפילה could be counted in the minyan and serve as שליחות ציבור, a policy which remained in effect until 1994.

The ten years from 1983 to 1993 can be understood, in the context of women in the minyan, as a period of soul-searching within the Rabbinical Assembly and the Conservative movement. The decision of the Seminary to ordain women had a tremendous effect in bolstering the move toward greater egalitarianism in Conservative synagogues. "If the Seminary can ordain women rabbis," many Conservative Jews reasoned, "certainly we can count women in our minyan!" But the repercussions in the rabbinate were more complex. Rabbi Roth's responsum had served the purpose of not only legitimating the admission of women into the Seminary Rabbinical School but simultaneously of *delegitimating* the practice of counting women *equally* with men in the minyan, as authorized by the Law Committee in 1973. Not a few members of the Rabbinical Assembly were quite influenced by Rabbi Roth's arguments, not only because of his scholarship, which had played such an important role in the Seminary's admission of women into the Rabbinical School, but also because of his role within the Rabbinical Assembly as Chairman of the Law Committee from 1984 to 1992. Many rabbis who were committed to egalitarianism came to question the halakhic basis of the 1973 decision which did not reach the criteria of Rabbi Roth's responsum. Indeed, Rabbi Roth's position was much closer to Rabbi Feldman's than the other views from 1973. Committed teenagers and college students trained in those years at Camp Ramah and the Seminary were confused since outside of those central institutions there were few, if any, synagogues that followed Rabbi Roth's ruling.[51] But the sociological trend towards greater egalitarianism far outweighed the halakhic concerns of certain rabbis and other educated laypeople. A rabbi of an egalitarian synagogue would not consider "opening up old wounds." Also rare would be a rabbi of a synagogue moving towards greater egalitarianism who would seek to "rock the boat" of the political struggle by introducing the restrictions of Rabbi

---

[49] *Jewish Theological Seminary Academic Bulletin* (2001-2002): 73. In contrast, the Ziegler School of Rabbinic Studies at the University of Judaism [now, American Jewish University] maintains no such requirement.

[50] "Schiff II" refers to the second floor of the Schiff Building, that is, the Old Reading Room, where the minyan met, and still meets today as the Women's League Seminary Synagogue, directly above the Stein Chapel.

[51] Such was my experience, that I was taught at Camp Ramah and the Seminary *not* to be comfortable at my home synagogue.

Roth's responsum into the arena. Additionally, there were many who were bothered by Rabbi Roth's maintenance of a separate "subsidiary" category of women in relation to men in terms of classes of worshippers. Such more "orthodox" egalitarians were far more comfortable with Rabbi Rabinowitz's paper which sees women in the same primary class as male worshippers.

Some understanding of the historical and sociological context of the struggle for "egalitarianism" in Conservative synagogues is necessary in order to understand the ambivalence which Rabbi Roth's responsum engendered. What Jack Wertheimer has called "The Triumph of Egalitarianism" was achieved through this period up to the mid-1990s. "Perhaps the most dramatic and visible change in Conservative synagogues during the past quarter century," Professor Wertheimer writes, "has been the introduction of egalitarian practices in virtually every aspect of congregational life."[52] In the initial 1996 report of the survey which he coordinated of Conservative congregations, Professor Wertheimer describes the process towards greater egalitarianism:

> The introduction of...egalitarian practices often prompted heated debates within congregations. These sometimes dragged on for years and, in some instances, provoked dissatisfied members to leave their congregations because the pace of change was either too fast or too slow. On the national level, battles over women's equality focused on the advisability of admitting women to the Rabbinical School of the Jewish Theological Seminary, a question that was resolved affirmatively in 1983. Since the early 1970s, local congregations debated similar questions concerning the expansion of women's roles. Our surveys indicate that, by the mid-1990s, most of these conflicts have been resolved in favor of women's equality.[53]

Focusing only on the question of women counting in the minyan, studies have shown that while in 1962 only 6 percent of Conservative congregations counted women in the minyan, and that by the mid-1970s one-third to one-half of congregations counted women in the minyan, by the mid-1990s 83 percent of North American Conservative congregations counted women in the minyan.[54]

---

[52] Jack Wertheimer, ed., *Jews in the Center: Conservative Synagogues and Their Members* (New Brunswick: Rutgers University Press, 2000), p. 7. The term "The Triumph of Egalitarianism" is found on p. 10, n. 11, and refers to the initial report cited in the following note.

[53] Jack Wertheimer, ed., *Conservative Synagogues and Their Members* (New York: Jewish Theological Seminary, 1996), p. 14. The title of this chapter of the report is "The Triumph of Egalitarianism."

[54] For the figures from 1962 and the mid-1970s, see Jack Wertheimer, "The Conservative Synagogue" in Jack Wertheimer, ed., *The American Synagogue: A Sanctuary Transformed*

Egalitarianism came to be an essential and positive identifying characteristic of Conservative Judaism. As Steven M. Cohen writes:

> Certainly by the 1980s, the largely egalitarian stance of the Conservative movement served to mark a clear boundary with the Orthodox. In the past, most differences between the two could be chalked up to Conservative concessions to the demands of modernity. In contrast, the egalitarian stance constituted the first major distinction with Orthodoxy where Conservative leaders could point to a clear difference of principle, rather than a surrender to the pressures of a religiously lax constituency.[55]

Egalitarianism had become the standard of the new vitality of the Conservative movement. No longer seeing themselves as "mere compromisers and concessionists," Conservative rabbis were finally able to look upon their Judaism as a principled reading of Judaism into modernity. For many, the egalitarian mode of worship came to be, and is, a high religious ground.

Such an atmosphere provided little room for those sympathetic with Rabbi Roth's argument to do anything about it. To openly question the legitimacy of the 1973 Law Committee ruling would be to question the legitimacy of the whole enterprise of egalitarianism in the Movement. The ordination of women by the Seminary was seen as a confirmation of that enterprise; it could not be used as a critique. Intentional or not, the five long years that it took the Seminary to publish its faculty papers after the decision to ordain women probably served to quiet any unrest that the papers may have caused after receiving wider distribution. Nevertheless, the halakhic questions remained, especially at the Seminary where Rabbi Roth's responsum still governed the Rabbinical School and the Seminary Synagogue.

Stage Three: 1993 to the Present

A decade after the decision was reached to ordain women, many felt that it was time to establish the egalitarian principle on firm halakhic grounds. Rather than do so on the basis of Rabbi Roth's responsum which sprang from the "school" of Rabbi Feldman, the new attempts by Professor Judith Hauptman, Rabbi Ismar

---

(Cambridge: Cambridge University Press, 1987), p. 137. For the mid-1990s figures, see Wertheimer, ed., *Conservative Synagogues and Their Members,* p. 16, and Wertheimer, ed., *Jews in the Center,* p. 250. Restricting the survey to congregations within the United States would yield an even higher percentage (see Wertheimer, *Conservative Synagogues and Their Members,* p. 20).

[55] Steven M. Cohen, "Assessing the Vitality of Conservative Judaism in North America: Evidence from a Survey of Synagogue Members" in Wertheimer, ed., *Jews in the Center,* p. 27.

Schorsch and Rabbi David Golinkin appeared essentially as reformulations of the position of Rabbi Sigal.

Professor Judith Hauptman published an article in *Judaism* in the winter of 1993 which argued that according to the classical rabbinic sources women were indeed equally obligated with men in regard to prayer.[56] Her paper caused somewhat of an uproar both from the Orthodox world, which she criticized for not emphasizing the true teaching of the halakhah regarding women and prayer, and from within the Conservative world, for challenging the bases of the halakhic discussion from 1979. While she does not mention Rabbi Sigal, she formulates a similar argument, that women are obligated to pray, that women rightfully have a place in public worship, and that the exclusion of women from the minyan was the custom of a society where women had a lower status. Today, when women's societal status is equal to that of men, an exclusionary practice should be abolished and we should return to the essential halakhah which understood women and men as equals in regard to prayer.

Judaism published a response to Professor Hauptman by Michael J. Broyde, an academic and Orthodox rabbi.[57] His response is also remarkably similar to Rabbi Feldman's response to Rabbi Sigal. Rabbi Feldman had written: "Rabbi Sigal demonstrates the importance of public prayer as opposed to private, then demonstrates the obligation of women to pray at least privately, and then concludes that therefore they are to be counted in a minyan."[58] Similarly, Rabbi Broyde writes that Professor Hauptman "assumes that because women are generally obligated to pray, they can fulfill the role of shaliah tzibbbur/cantor in communal prayer."[59] That is, the demonstration that women have an obligation to pray does not mean that their obligation, according to classical halakhah as interpreted through the ages, is equal to a man's. On the contrary, there are ample halakhic sources which imply that it is not and state that women may not count in the minyan. Professor Hauptman's argument, which was articulated in her article and expanded in her rejoinder to Rabbi Broyde,[60] sought to separate minyan from שליחת ציבור. To count in a minyan one must be obligated to prayer, as women are. But to serve as a שליח ציבור one must also have social status. A woman lacked

---

[56] See Hauptman, "Women and Prayer: An Attempt to Dispel Some Fallacies" *Judaism* 42 (1993): 94-103. [This paper was written before Rabbi Hauptman received ordination, which is why she is referred to here as "Professor" and not Rabbi."]

[57] Michael J. Broyde, "Communal Prayer and Women" *Judaism* 42 (1993): 387-394.

[58] Feldman in Siegel to "Colleagues," p. 11.

[59] Broyde, "Communal Prayer and Women," p. 387.

[60] Judith Hauptman, "Some Thoughts on the Nature of Halakhic Adjudication: Women and Minyan" *Judaism* 42 (1993): 396-413.

social status in the same way as a beardless man.[61] Rabbi Broyde argues that the analogy of a woman to a beardless man is "an erroneous analogy as that person is fully obligated in communal prayer and counts in the quorum, unlike women."[62] But Professor Hauptman was attempting to separate the issue of שליח ציבור from minyan, much the way Rabbi Rabinowitz had done in his responsum. By arguing that the requirement for leading the minyan was social status above obligation, she sought to make a clear case for halakhic "adjudication" since today women are certainly not considered to be of a lower social status than men. But Rabbi Broyde could not accept the argument, insisting that "any discussion of women as prayer leaders, without a discussion of minyan/quorum and who counts in it is incomplete."[63]

Rabbi Broyde's critique is very convincing for those who have trouble accepting the logic of Professor Hauptman's argument. As she herself explains it, the structure of her argument is:

1) Because women were always obligated to pray, and their obligations have even increased over time, prayer for women need not and cannot be regarded as a self-imposed obligation; 2) however, obligation alone is not sufficient. For a woman to lead a congregation, the community must view her social standing as equal to a man's.[64]

We can agree with her that social status plays a role in the determination of legal categories. Therefore, it is difficult to understand how she can separate the two. The *reason* why women were excluded from the minyan is because they were not considered to be of full status as were the men. For that reason their obligation to perform mitzvot was of a lesser degree, that of the category of minors and slaves. As she explains elsewhere, "The reason women are exempt from positive time-bound mitzvot is that only the full-fledged members of society are obligated to perform the ritual acts that define Jewish practice."[65] The first part of her argument should have been enough, that women are equally obligated with men to pray. That was, in fact, the only part of her argument that was utilized by Rabbi Golinkin in his responsum, to be discussed below.

That assumption of Professor Hauptman, that women are equally obligated to pray, is what is most contentious. She cites B'rakhot 20b to explain that women are obligated to pray דרחמי נינהו, because they too are in need of petition. It is by no

---

[61] Hauptman, "Women and Prayer," p. 99, citing Hullin 24b: "When his beard grows in, he may serve as שליח ציבור and pass before the ark and lift his hands in the priestly blessing."
[62] Broyde, "Communal Prayer and Women," p. 388.
[63] Ibid.
[64] Hauptman, "Women and Prayer," p. 100.
[65] Judith Hauptman, *Rereading the Rabbis: A Woman's Voice* (Boulder: Westview Press, 1998), p. 237.

means clear whether the gemara was referring to the personal need to pray for mercy, or the need of the community as a whole to pray for the communal welfare, which is what a minyan does. As Professor Hauptman has explained, however, it makes sense that women would have been excluded from such a purpose since they were not considered full citizens of the community. While Professor Hauptman has demonstrated that the classical sources assert a woman's obligation to pray, many have not been convinced that a woman's obligation is equal to a man's, or relates to public prayer at all. Additionally, she must rely on the classical sources in opposition to the way they have been understood since at least the time of the Shulhan Arukh. It may be true that many later authorities have followed Nachmanides' position that women have the same time-bound obligations to prayer as men, at least for Shaharit and Minhah on weekdays (as opposed to the view of Maimonides, that the Toraitic prescription for prayer is a general obligation on all, but the specific time-bound liturgical requirements are rabbinic obligations solely upon men). But it is also the case that it is unclear whether that obligation extends to Maariv or to Shabbat and festivals, and that the halakhah was very lenient with classifying a woman for any number of reasons as a טרודה, busy or occupied, and hence exempt from the regular obligations for prayer.[66] And not all later authorities followed Nachmanides. According to Rabbi Aharon Ziegler, who has committed to writing many of the halakhic positions expressed orally by Rabbi Joseph Soloveitchik, Soloveitchik was concerned that only a full Amidah would satisfy the requirement of Maimonides rather than a simple Modeh Ani. He concludes that "Even women must say the entire *Shmoneh Esrei* every day, at least once a day. Once the children grow up and the women have more time available they should add to that basic requirement. But at no time can they be satisfied with less."[67] What is phrased as a *mahmir* [stringent] position from the premier rabbinic authority of American modern Orthodoxy still falls far short of the *equal obligation* to prayer with men that Professor Hauptman reads from the halakhah.

---

[66] See Menachem Nissel, *Rigshei Lev: Women and Tefillah: Perspectives, laws and customs* (Southfield, Michigan and Nanuet, New York: Targum and Feldheim, 2001), ch.1. See also ch. 7, regarding the various views on the extent of a woman's obligation to daven with a minyan. What is clear is that the obligation, while present, is less than a man's. Nissel's volume contains much polemical material defending the role of women in halakhah, and argues against the "Orthodox feminism" of women's prayer groups. But the polemics aside, the volume is useful in presenting the halakhic views. A less polemical presentation, but far more condensed, can be found in Getsel Ellinson, *Women and the Mitzvot,* vol. 1, *Serving the Creator* (Jerusalem: World Zionist Organization, 1986), chs. 9-10.

[67] Aharon Ziegler, *Halakhic Positions of Rabbi Joseph B. Soloveitchik,* vol. 2 (Northvale, N.J.: Jason Aronson, 2001), p. 87.

Professor Hauptman recognized that she was departing from the general trend of interpretation, extending "an invitation to the halakhic and scholarly community to re-examine contemporary synagogue practices in the light of classical Jewish texts." She admittedly was seeking "a different conclusion," examining "the texts in question from fresh perspectives, with the hope of finding alternate, yet valid ways of interpreting them."[68] In this way she falls within the "school" of Rabbis Blumenthal and Sigal, since she is willing to rely on new readings of classical sources even when tradition and precedent developed differently through the intervening centuries. Her position is distinct from that of Rabbi Rabinowitz in that she does understand the issue of obligation as critical. Professor Hauptman anticipates the objections to her position, and argues, along lines similar to Rabbi Sigal, that the exclusion of women from the minyan is not an essential conclusion of the classical sources but "has been the prevailing practice—minhag—for centuries."[69] She then proceeds to argue that there are times when מנהג can be overturned. But several objections remain. Firstly, it is questionable whether the exclusion of women from the minyan can be relegated to מנהג. But even if it is, we are still faced with the already mentioned aversion of classical Conservative Judaism from dismissing a custom just because it is a custom. On the contrary, Conservative rabbis by definition are supposed to protect the customs and traditions of our people as developed through its history. This objection to Professor Hauptman's views is made clear by her argument that we may disregard this particular מנהג because the exclusion of women from an equal role with men in society is חוקת הגויים, a practice of the non-Jews, and, hence, not binding.[70] But counting in the minyan is a particularly Jewish practice! To say that Judaism is by nature egalitarian were it not for outside influence is a difficult argument to accept. As students of the Historical School, we understand that Judaism was formed out of the various environments which have given it sustenance. If we were to question every practice which was influenced by the non-Jewish world we would be left with a very empty tradition. Neither patriarchy nor egalitarianism are exclusively Jewish concepts.

These difficulties aside, Professor Hauptman's paper was extremely influential in reconfiguring the debate on women in the minyan. Rabbi Schorsch, the [then] Chancellor of the Seminary, and Rabbi Golinkin, currently the President of the Schechter Institute, came to agree with her that women are indeed equally obligated to prayer, that their obligation is equal to a man's, that there is no need to

---

[68] Hauptman, "Some Thoughts on the Nature of Halakhic Adjudication," p. 396.
[69] Ibid., p. 404.
[70] Ibid., p. 405.

specifically accept an equal obligation, and that men and women therefore count equally in a minyan.

Rabbi Schorsch's endorsement of Professor Hauptman's arguments coincided with other major changes in the Seminary Synagogue. After ten years of using the Old Reading Room, the Women's League for Conservative Judaism decided to fund a project that would provide the "Schiff II" minyan with a more permanent synagogue space. The Old Reading Room was completely refurbished as a permanent synagogue, renamed "The Women's League Seminary Synagogue." While this project was underway, Rabbi Schorsch, as Rabbi of the Seminary Synagogue, agreed in the fall of 1994 to two major changes in the worship of that minyan: 1) the inclusion of the אמהות [the matriarchs along with the patriarchs in the opening benediction of the Amidah] would be permitted as an option for the שליח ציבור in compliance with Rabbi Joel Rembaum's responsum approved by the Law Committee in 1990; 2) women would be counted equally with men in the minyan. Regarding the first change, Rabbi Schorsch explained that he was bowing to pressure from the community even though he himself thought that such a liturgical innovation "does violence to the text." He endorsed the second change, however, quite enthusiastically as motivated by his deep commitment to egalitarianism, because of the overwhelming practice in Conservative synagogues, and because of the convincing scholarship recently published by Professor Hauptman.[71]

While Rabbi Schorsch's decisions in 1994 were popular, there was some dissent. The inclusion of the אמהות was justified by a Law Committee responsum,[72] but the basis by which Rabbi Schorsch chose to count women equally in the minyan was not even phrased in any responsum! Rabbi Schorsch's response was that he, as the Rabbi of the Seminary Synagogue, invoked his authority as מרא דאתרא [mara d'atra] to make a halakhic decision. His decision was informed by Professor Hauptman's paper. It was not necessary for him to write up as a responsum considering what she had already written. A halakhic decision does not have to be committed to writing in order to take effect. And the conclusion he had reached, that women should count equally in the minyan, in fact conformed with the 1973 decision of the Law Committee, whereas Rabbi Roth's paper, while voted

---

[71] Chancellor Schorsch announced his decision at the Rabbinical School/Cantorial School Kallah in Connecticut in the fall of 1994 as a surprise ending to his Friday evening דבר תורה. He explained that he chose that moment to make his ruling since we were "stuck with each other until after Shabbat." (I was there for what was one of the most dramatic moments of my rabbinical school years.)

[72] See Joel Rembaum, "The Inclusion of the Names of the Matriarchs in the Amidah," *Proceedings of the Committee on Jewish Law and Standards of the Conservative Movement 1986-1990* (New York: Rabbinical Assembly, 2001), pp. 485-490.

into the Law Committee record, was not discussed in that forum. Nevertheless, many in the Seminary community were bothered that there was no responsum written as such which justified the new practice of the Seminary Synagogue. Thus, the ambivalence caused by Rabbi Roth's responsum was renewed in a new form since we were still left to wonder what was in fact the halakhic grounding for the egalitarianism of Conservative Judaism.

In 1997 the Vaad Halakhah of the Rabbinical Assembly of Israel approved a responsum by Rabbi David Golinkin which argued, along lines similar to Professor Hauptman, that women are equally obligated with men in regard to prayer and can thus count in the minyan.[73] He lists the halakhic sources that argue for a woman's obligation, and posits that therefore her obligation is equal and she can fulfill the obligation of others. He recognizes that there is a vast halakhic literature forbidding women from counting in the minyan,[74] but emphasizes: איסור כזה אינו נזכר באף מקום בתלמוד או אצל הרמב"ם, that the prohibition is not explicit anywhere in the Talmud or Maimonides.[75] That is to say, of course, that the prohibition is quite explicit after Maimonides. Recognizing, then, that his conclusion, while based on the classical sources, does go against the אחרונים, Rabbi Golinkin argues that we are permitted to base ourselves on minority positions if necessary, and that we are permitted to rule against the prevailing custom and tradition if our situation varies from the situation of those who confirmed the inherited customs and tradition.[76] In

---

[73] David Golinkin, "תשובה בעניין נשים במנין וכשליחות ציבור" in תשובות ועד ההלכה של כנסת הרבנים בישראל, כרך ו': תשנ"ה-תשנ"ח (Jerusalem: Schechter Institute, 1998), pp. 59-80. The paper was accepted by a vote of six to one.

[74] See ibid., pp. 75-76, n. 20.

[75] Ibid., p. 68.

[76] Ibid., pp. 70-72. Golinkin cites a passage from Schechter which argues that the codes of Maimonides and Joseph Karo are not perfect and that rabbi and scholar ought to read them critically. Golinkin himself understands Schechter as saying that halakhah is not frozen in the codes, that the codes are important guides to halakhah but not necessarily the final word. There is a difference, though, between extending analysis beyond the Shulkhan Arukh on the one hand, and overturning an entire tradition of precedent expressed through the centuries on the basis of new reading of the classical sources, on the other. That is not to say that one may not at times overturn precedent and invoke classical sources before the precedent was established. But we must still recognize that such a decision is an overturning of precedent, and should only be done for great cause. Golinkin does believe that he has such cause when he argues at the top of p. 72 that our situation, namely the societal role of women, is different than that of the society of the Aharonim and the Shulkhan Arukh. However, he later claims on p. 72 that all women have always been obligated to pray as men, that אינני רואה דרך אחרת להבין את המקורות...המשנה, התלמוד והראשונים. But while we might offer a fresh interpretation of classical sources as a support in overturning a precedent, surely we should accept that the Aharonim had the systemic authority to interpret the classical sources as they saw fit, הלכה כבתראי. Schechter's very point was that a legal system rests upon judicial autonomy and

this way we see that Rabbi Golinkin combines elements from various approaches: he agrees with Rabbi Feldman, et al., that equality of obligation is key. But he also agrees with Professor Hauptman and Rabbi Schorsch that a woman is in fact equally obligated to prayer according to the classical sources. Finally, he agrees with Rabbis Blumenthal and Sigal that one can rely on classical sources, even on minority views, and can use such sources to override precedent and tradition if conditions warrant.

One must understand that where we stand on practical issues and how we approach halakhah in theory is not easily defined into a left and right wing. Rabbi Golinkin's approach to halakhah, as seen in this responsum and others, is that if a source can be found as a support then the change can be argued. But if no source can be found for support then no change can be argued. While he is "liberal" in permitting innovation and change of precedent, he insists that changes in halakhah be supported in previously existing halakhic sources. Rabbi Roth, on the other hand, is more flexible, since he argues that there are times when an authority can overturn precedent if there is sufficient cause and if the original reasons for the norm no longer exist, even if there is no specific source to support the change. The ultimate authority, for Rabbi Roth, is the rabbinate, which can even, theoretically, overturn matters מדאורייתא [from the Torah].[77] While Rabbi Golinkin's approach is more lenient in regard to the prevailing precedent, it is ultimately more stringent since it requires some kind of precedent on which to be based. In the case of women and the minyan, Rabbi Golinkin's approach is far more liberal than Rabbi Roth's since Rabbi Golinkin is able to free himself from precedent and tradition and rely on his (and Professor Hauptman's) reading of the classical sources, whereas Rabbi Roth must work with the prevailing precedent.

---

development of precedent rather than solely the codifications of law, be it classical or later. The context of Schechter's remark which Golinkin cites is a review of Isaac Hirsch Weiss's דור דור ודורשיו, an account of the development of Jewish law through history. History, for Schechter, as I have argued elsewhere (see above, n. 21), is a conservative influence on practice. (See Solomon Schechter, *Studies in Judaism,* First Series [Philadelphia, 1896], p. 211.)

[77] Rabbi Roth maintains strong distinctions between what is permitted in theory and what ought to be done in practice. At various discussions of the Law Committee Rabbi Roth has argued against decisions that approached an uprooting of a Torah law because he felt that the Law Committee would be too presumptuous to assume the ultimate authority of amending the Torah itself. Such should be reserved for extremely rare moments and should be invoked only by authorities who are recognized as preeminent throughout the Jewish world (what Rabbi Roth calls "self-validating authorities"). Nevertheless, Rabbi Roth has always affirmed the theoretical right of the rabbinate of any age to uproot matters from the Torah. See Joel Roth, *The Halakhic Process: A Systemic Analysis* (New York: Jewish Theological Seminary, 1986), ch. 7.

At the conclusion of his responsum Rabbi Golinkin takes issue with one point of Rabbi Roth's responsum. Rabbi Roth had argued against the general imposition of equal obligation upon women by a תקנה "because the imposition of legal obligation by תקנה would make noncompliance with the dictates of the תקנה sinful. That would result in the creation of a large class of sinners where none now exists."[78] Rabbi Golinkin, who through his responsum achieves a result similar to the imagined תקנה by Rabbi Roth, responds that he sees no other way to read the classical sources except to conclude that women are already obligated to pray the same as men.[79] That is, the "large class of sinners" already exists. Rabbi Roth had continued his theoretical objection that no "segment of the Conservative movement should seek to impose a set of obligations not already recognized by the tradition upon any woman who is satisfied with the status quo."[80] Rabbi Golinkin responds that the decisions of rabbis are not necessarily binding on those who do not choose to abide by them.[81] "Any woman who is satisfied by the status quo" will not be guided by a decision permitting women to count in the minyan. But while Rabbi Roth's concern might have been for traditionally trained women who did not consider themselves obligated equally with men for prayer, he was probably more concerned with the greater mass of women of "egalitarian" congregations who are counted in the minyan by virtue of the 1973 Law Committee decision which makes no demands on obligation. If we say that to count in the minyan women must be equally obligated to prayer and we then continue to count all women equally in a minyan we are then saying that a great mass of tens of thousands of women have suddenly become "sinners." We must consider what we mean by "sin" and then ask ourselves whether we see this as problematic. It is unlikely that women of the Conservative movement would consider their obligations and their shortcomings any differently than do the men of the Conservative movement. The "New Proposal" below discusses the halakhic and theoretical implications of this condition.

The preceding detailed account of the various positions on the question of women in the minyan to date was necessary because each stage of deliberation on the question has rested upon the arguments of the stage before. Such is indeed the natural flow of legal development, that each chapter directly follows the one that came before. We have seen that two basic schools of legal philosophy have been represented, one believing that new readings of halakhic sources and the

---

[78] Roth, "On the Ordination of Women," p. 166.
[79] Golinkin, p. 72.
[80] Roth, "On the Ordination of Women," pp. 166-167.
[81] Golinkin, p. 72.

introduction of alternative halakhic sources can be used to overturn a precedent, the other believing that precedent will stand unless new compelling circumstances warrant a reexamination of the law, and that a new position can be justified within the historical body of tradition. The approaches of both schools can and have been used to justify the counting of women in the minyan. The arguments from the first school permitting women to count in the minyan (and serve as שליחות ציבור) that flow from the arguments of Aaron Blumenthal and Philip Sigal, Mayer Rabinowitz, Judith Hauptman and David Golinkin, claim that the halakhah in its pristine form recognizes the equality of men and women. The practice of excluding women from counting in the minyan and from active participation in the liturgy developed due to societal influences rather than from the law itself. Women should now be counted in the minyan, either because in fact their obligation is equal to men's and we must restore the original egalitarian intent of the halakhah (as argued by Rabbi Sigal, Professor Hauptman and Rabbi Golinkin), or because obligation is not a relevant issue here at all (as argued by Rabbis Blumenthal and Rabinowitz), but rather the fact that women are today the societal equals of men, and that this reality must be reflected in liturgical practice just as in the past the condition (perceived or real) of women's inequality with men was reflected in the liturgical practice of the past.

A New Proposal

The other "school" of approach to Jewish law is divided between those who would permit women to count in the minyan, those who forbid, and those who are ambivalent. The author of this paper, wishing to permit women to count in the minyan, falls into this other school. He has expressed reservations with the positions of Rabbis Sigal and Blumenthal, Rabbi Rabinowitz and Professor Hauptman and Rabbis Schorsch and Golinkin at each stage of the discussion. The author of this paper would have supported the תקנה in 1973 as the only way to justify the change since his halakhic sensibilities would have sympathized with the arguments of Rabbi Feldman even if his desire to change the law would have agreed with Rabbis Blumenthal and Sigal. For this reason he had believed that Rabbi Roth's responsum was the perfect solution to the dilemma, if anything because it grew directly from the perspective of Rabbi Feldman which in its turn grew from precedent and tradition. But the technicalities of Rabbi Roth's solution proved difficult to execute in practice. How can one, in the few minutes that one has as a minyan is gathering, determine if a woman considers herself obligated to prayer equally with men if she has never thought of the issue that way and yet she is offended if we would suggest that she might not be equal to a man? Many Conservative rabbis have been moved by the arguments of the more egalitarian position, recognizing new halakhic interpretations as worthy of consideration in light of an overwhelming change in sociological reality, in this case, the role of women in public life, and, specifically, in Conservative synagogues. If we believe that such a reality is proper, that is, that egalitarian worship is a high ground, that it is God's will, then we must be able to ground it in precedent and tradition as well. The following proposal attempts do so on the basis of Rabbi Roth's and even Rabbi Halivni's responsa, which flow from the "school" of Rabbi Feldman.

Through the history of its incorporation at the Seminary and the Ramah camps there have been two major misconceptions surrounding Rabbi Roth's responsum. One was that a woman had to wear tallit and tefillin in order to count in a minyan. Another was that a woman had to pray three times a day to count in a minyan. The source for the first misconception is that Seminary policy has been that candidates for Rabbinical School accept equal obligation to all mitzvot including tallit, tefillin and tefillah. The source for the second misconception was the reasoning that if a woman did not pray three times a day then how can we say that she has accepted the equal obligation to pray? That these are misconceptions is clear from Rabbi Roth's paper when he writes: "Women may be counted in a minyan or serve as ש"ץ only when they have accepted upon themselves the voluntary obligation to pray as required by the law, and at the times required by law, and only when they recognize and affirm that failure to comply with the obligation is a sin."[82] According to Rabbi Roth, then, a woman does not have to accept the obligation of tallit and tefillin (where no agency is involved) in order to count in the minyan and serve as שליחת ציבור (where agency is involved).[83]

More crucially, according to Rabbi Roth, women do not have to comply with the obligation, but rather they have to understand that failure to comply is a sin. Women need not demonstrate any special observance beyond that of men, but rather an equal obligation. Just as men are obligated to prayer and hence count in a minyan regardless of how often they pray, so too would a woman equally obligated to prayer with a man count in a minyan regardless of how often she prayed. That is, we need to recognize the authority of the law over ourselves, whether we observe it or not. The law holds by virtue of our acceptance of its authority, not by virtue of our lawful behavior. An analogy is speeding: the fact that I speed does not mean that I do not recognize that I am in violation of the law. I may always break the law but I also always recognize that I am in violation of the law, whether or not I will be asked to account for that.

[82] Roth, "On the Ordination of Women," p. 168.
[83] When I once served as Rosh Tefillah at Camp Ramah in the Berkshires (summer of 1992) the Rashei Edot did not believe me that girls who did not wear tallit and tefillin could count in the minyan (if they accepted equal obligation to prayer) until I had Rabbi Roth personally confirm with them that it was permissible.

This paper proposes an acceptance of the reality that *women in the Conservative movement have, as a general class, accepted upon themselves the equal obligation to prayer with men*. Such an assumption is precedented in the statement of the Magen Avraham discussed in Rabbi Roth's responsum, that נשים פטורות מספירת העומר דהוי מצוות עשה שהזמן גרמה, ומיהו שווין עלייהו חובה, that women are exempt from counting the Omer but they have accepted the obligation upon themselves.[84] Rabbi Roth invokes this statement in his responsum, and invokes support from a number of subsequent halakhic authorities, as discussed above. The Magen Avraham does not say that a woman must individually accept the obligation to counting the Omer. Rather, he says that "women" as a general class, have accepted this obligation. We should say so today regarding prayer, that because of the context of co-education and egalitarian worship in our synagogues, women as a class have accepted upon themselves the equal obligation for prayer. By recognizing this reality we achieve the challenge of Rabbi Rabinowitz's paper, to consider women as a part of the primary class of worshippers rather than of a subsidiary class.

Several objections can be raised against this proposal, and are now addressed individually:

1) How can we say that women as a class have accepted the equal obligation to prayer when it is clear that the majority of women in Conservative synagogues, just as the majority of men, do not pray three times a day? We respond that, based upon Rabbi Roth's responsum, observance is not of issue but rather acceptance of obligation and understanding that failure to comply is a sin. Therefore, the question is not whether Conservative women pray three times a day, but rather whether they understand their obligation to pray to be equal to that of men, and whether they understand that the failure to comply is a sin. We are comfortable in responding affirmatively to both questions. We must not be too dismissive of our constituency. There is a substantial ideological difference, if not a practical difference, between Conservative and other Jews. Conservative Jews, as individuals, believe that Jewish law is binding even if they fail in compliance. They believe that tradition should remain authoritative even if they do not always have a personal stake in its preservation. They believe in the concept of obligation, even if they would not phrase it as such. Professor Hauptman is correct when she argues that obligation is tied to issues of social status. Now that women have equal social status it is absurd to imagine that they would not recognize for themselves an equal obligation next to men.

---

[84] Magen Avraham to OH 489, par. 1.

These assumptions can be confirmed by recent sociological research. Samuel Heilman writes that "in effect, egalitarianism may be defined most simply as a willingness to afford equal rights *and obligations* to men and women in the synagogue."[85] Nancy Ammerman writes that "strong majorities agree that Conservative Jews are obligated to be observant, but equally strong majorities claim that they are able to choose how to be so and that they can be 'religious' without being observant. On the surface, these appear to be contradictory or hypocritical statements. Surely one must either obey the law or simply bargain it away. Those are the alternatives posed by the modernist frame. But Conservative Jews appear to be doing something different, neither obeying in full nor absolving themselves of that obligation."[86] That is, the unique religiosity of the Conservative Jew is one who believes in the authority of tradition even if behavior does not always conform to that authority. While there is certainly much work to be done in terms of religious *behavioral* education in the Conservative movement, the basic mindset of respect for tradition is already there, is firmly there, and is the defining characteristic of the Conservative Jew.

The fact that Conservative Jews do not observe all the laws does not mean that they do not recognize the law as the law. Rather, they are, by self definition, already the "large group of sinners" that Rabbi Roth is hesitant to establish. But this need not be read as such a negative appraisal. We should not be afraid of the word "sin." Some would prefer that we use only the Hebrew terms עבירה or חטא, since the English word "sin" is too much encumbered by its associative role in Christian theology. Others would insist that we recognize the religious act for what it is, that it is our obligation as rabbis to "translate" our theology. "Sin" means an act of noncompliance with God's will. The theology of sin means that there is no behavior that is outside the prescription of the Torah. We either act according to God's ways, or otherwise. "Sin is conceived as an act of rebellion," Solomon Schechter wrote, "denying the root, that is the existence of God, or his providence, or his authority, indeed, excluding him from the world."[87] To act in a way other

---

[85] Samuel C. Heilman, "Holding Firmly with an Open Hand: Life in Two Conservative Synagogues" in Wertheimer, ed., *Jews in the Center*, p. 190. Emphasis added.

[86] Nancy T. Ammerman, "Conservative Jews within the Landscape of American Religion" in Wertheimer, ed., *Jews in the Center*, p. 371. The 1996 interim report (Wertheimer, *Conservative Synagogues and Their Members*, p. 10) records that 62 percent of Conservative Jews responded that they "are obligated to obey Halakha (Jewish law)" while 76 percent responded that "a Jew can be religious even if he/she isn't particularly observant." Obviously, this is the same group of people responding affirmatively to two supposedly contradictory statements. But apparently they are not contradictory for our constituency, and it is that situation, defined by the data, that Ammerman is explaining.

[87] Solomon Schechter, *Some Aspects of Rabbinic Theology* (1909; reprint, New York: Schocken, 1961), p. 233.

than that prescribed by the Torah and Tradition is to exclude God from the world. But that is not as unusual an act as it might at first seem. Whenever one behaves in a way other than that prescribed, one is living a life in the "secular" world guided by concerns, personal or others, but leaving God and Judaism out of it. We all do that quite often. We strive to do so less often. The expectation to bring God further and further into our lives is the challenge of Rosh HaShanah and Yom Kippur. We meet the challenge by, first of all, recognizing where we have fallen short. That recognition is the first step towards improvement, sometimes called תשובה [teshuvah]. Mitzvah and sin are two poles of religious life that go together. As Abraham Joshua Heschel explained: "Both poles, mitsvah and sin, are real. We are taught to be *mitsvah-conscious* in regard to the present moment, to be mindful of the constant opportunity to do the good. We are also taught to be *sin-conscious* in regard to the past, to realize and to remember our failures and transgressions. The power of both mitsvah and sin must be fully appreciated."[88] Therefore, while sin is surely a negative, the *recognition* of sin is a positive religious attribute. The fact that Conservative Jews recognize that they fall short of tradition is a sign of their inner piety. We should all recognize that we fall short of expectations.[89]

Crucial to this theological perspective is the understanding that "sin" means falling short of religious expectations, rather than committing an offense for which real punishment awaits. Mordecai Kaplan questions the use of the term "sin" in contemporary religious vocabulary:

> Traditionally, "sin" implied: (1) that the commission of an act, or its omission, as the case might be, was an infraction of a law commanded by God, and (2) that such an infraction carried with it a penalty to be inflicted by man, by God or by both. That notion of sin is clearly *incompatible* with a spiritual conception of God, free from anthropomorphisms. To be compatible with a spiritual conception of God, "sin" would have to be the commission of an act, or the omission of one, that runs counter to the self-fulfillment of the individual as an integrated personality, or of mankind as a fraternal cooperative society. As long as people still associate the term "sin" with the old meaning, as is often the case at the present time, it would be wrong to characterize a breach of ritual observance as "sin," since

[88] Abraham Joshua Heschel, *God in Search of Man: A Philosophy of Judaism* (1955, reprint; Cleveland and Philadelphia: Meridian Books and Jewish Publication Society, 1963), p. 363.

[89] The philosophical grounding for a popular sense of "commandedness" not necessarily connected with observance can be found in the writings of Franz Rosenzweig. For a recent discussion of such and its potential application to the religiosity of American Jews see Arnold M. Eisen, *Rethinking Modern Judaism: Ritual, Commandment, Community* (Chicago: University of Chicago Press, 1998).

that would imply that the observance was divinely commanded, in a literal and not in a figurative sense, and that the breach of it was a punishable offense. That, however does not mean that we have no obligation to maintain religious observances and strengthen our faith and resolution in the pursuit of Jewish ideals.[90]

Kaplan is correct that the valence of the word "sin" is crucial to its appropriateness in contemporary religion, yet we might both differ with his presentation of the "old meaning" and propose that we are ready for the "new meaning." Even in pre-modern times the punishment that followed from failing to observe Jewish law was more often theoretical than real. In ancient times, when the halakhah was being crafted, the authority of the Rabbis over the people as a whole was minimal if existent at all.[91] Only in the medieval period did rabbis have real coercive power over the Jewish people, and even then the extent of that power varied in different communities. Usually *persuasion* has served as the means of "enforcing" Jewish law. There is, of course, the ancient concept that punishment is meted out by the hands of heaven for certain offenses. In general, Jews beg forgiveness for their sins before God even though they may never be brought to real account. We bring the accounting on ourselves. Yes, God commands, even if in the figurative sense. Belief that God commands means, for many today, to feel commanded by God. The commandedness of Jewish law is independent of its enforceability. Rather, commandedness depends on our conception of God's will, and our performance thereby. "Sin" should not depend on a literal commander and punisher. But even if it did, and even if we agreed with Kaplan that the term "sin" can no longer be used, we would still conclude with Kaplan that we are obligated "to maintain religious observances." One either fulfills or fails to fulfill an obligation. The failure to fulfill the obligation has religious meaning, even if the word "sin" is not the first that comes to mind.

2) Even if we accept the fact that Conservative Jews feel obligated towards mitzvot that they do not as a whole observe, on what basis can we assume that women feel *equally obligated* to the mitzvah of prayer? In fact, we cannot make a similar assumption regarding tallit and tefillin. While many of us believe that women *should* wear tallit and tefillin and accept such practice as obligatory, we cannot yet say that women as a class have assumed such an obligation. Recent

[90] Mordecai M. Kaplan, *Questions Jews Ask: Reconstructionist Answers* (New York: Reconstructionist Press, 1956), pp. 233-234.

[91] For an excellent survey of contemporary scholarship, see Catherine Hezser, *The Social Structure of the Rabbinic Movement in Roman Palestine* (Tübingen: Mohr Siebeck, 1997). See also Seth Schwartz, *Imperialism in Jewish Society, 200 B.C.E. to 640 C.E.* (Princeton: Princeton University Press, 2001), esp. ch. 3.

sociological research has shown that while 83 percent of Conservative synagogues count women in the minyan, only 36 percent of girls of the Bat Mitzvah class of 5755 "reported that they were taught to put on tefillin, compared with 76 percent of the boys."[92] Nevertheless, Barry Kosmin concludes that "there is little conflict over gender roles between home and synagogue. For most of these teenagers and their parents, both environments are now egalitarian."[93] In a follow-up study on the attitudes of this same Bar/Bat Mitzvah class of 5755 four years later, Barry Kosmin and Ariela Keysar found that "the gender differences were again statistically insignificant." If anything, the few very minor differences show a greater commitment on the part of the girls.[94] Tallit and tefillin and kippah are not good indices of egalitarianism since many regard them (perhaps erroneously) as "male clothing." A woman does not have to dress or appear as a man in order to be equal with a man. Minyan, however, is the best index of the new egalitarian society because counting in the minyan is understood as being a full citizen of the community. While girls educated in a Conservative synagogue might not think to don tallit and tefillin if not encouraged to do so, it would unlikely ever occur to them that their obligation to pray was any different from that of the boys.

Much educational work needs to be done to "convince" women to wear tallit and tefillin and to cover their heads for worship. But in regard to worship in general, women do not see themselves as separate from the men in any religious sense. Both are subject to Jewish law and tradition, and both fall short. Both say ולקיים את כל דברי תלמוד תורתך באהבה (and to fulfill with love all the things taught in Your Torah) and both say סלח לנו אבינו כי חטאנו (forgive us Our Father for we have sinned).[95] Both are voting members of the synagogue, and both are responsible for "minyan duty" where such is the custom.

This natural development of a popular sense of equal obligation is not new today, at the beginning of the twenty-first century. It can be traced back as early as 1855. In that year the Jewish women of Mannheim in Baden, Germany, wrote a petition protesting against the maintenance of the benediction thanking God "Who has not made me a woman" in their new liturgy. In the course of this petition the women wrote:

---

[92] Barry A. Kosmin, "Coming of Age in the Conservative Synagogue: The Bar/Bat Mitzvah Class of 5755" in Wertheimer, ed., *Jews in the Center,* p. 250.

[93] Ibid., p. 253.

[94] 35% of the girls reported themselves as less observant than they were four years ago, and 27% as more observant, compared with 39% of the boys as less observant and 19% as more observant. Barry Kosmin and Ariela Keysar, *"Four Up": The High School Years, 1995-1999: The Jewish Identity Development of the B'nai Mitzvah Class of 5755* (New York: Jewish Theological Seminary, 2000), p. 35.

[95] I thank Rabbi Joel Rembaum for this thought.

Dank den weisen Anordnungen der hohen Behörden geniessen die israelitischen Mädchen in den Schulen von der frühesten Kindheit denselben Religionsunterricht, sie werden von den Lehrern und Rabbinen zur Schulentlassung mid den Knaben unter völlig gleichen Religionsgrundsätzen ausgestattet, finden in denselben nur Liebe, aber keine Ausscheidung bei der Gottesverrehrung, zu welcher *wir uns ebenso verpflichtet erachten wie unsere Männer und Brüder.*

That is: "Thanks to the wise directives of the venerable authorities benefiting Jewish women through schools from their earliest childhood with the same religious education from teachers and rabbis as boys, leaving school with fully equal religious grounding, finding in the same only love and no separation from the honor due to God, towards which *we consider ourselves just as obligated as our husbands and brothers.*"[96] Michael Meyer, in referencing this source, notes that this was "an exceptional example of female religious activism."[97] The protest was exceptional, but the change of religious attitude was not. These women were exceptional in articulating what many women must have felt, and how most Conservative Jewish women must feel today. Religious education breeds devotion to religious tradition. The result of co-education is that women will feel the same devotion *and obligation* towards the tradition as men. The most direct expression of religious devotion is prayer. How could modern educated Jewish women feel any less bound to pray to God than men? This is the argument of the women of Mannheim, and we can comfortably reason that if women could reach such a conclusion in 1855, that co-education yields a sense of equal obligation to prayer, all the more so would they in the Conservative Judaism of today.

Rabbi Halivni, in his responsum, argued that only when enough women take upon themselves equal obligation so that there is "assurance of the continuity of their observance" can "meaningful equality" be enacted. "That may take a generation or so," he writes.[98] But while Rabbi Halivni is insistent that a generation of practicing observing women establish the מנהג of women's obligation to prayer, Rabbi Roth is content with the understanding that failure to comply is a sin. If we combine that standard of Rabbi Roth with Rabbi Halivni's standard of "a generation," then we stand on solid ground. A generation has indeed passed since 1979.[99]

---

[96] Cited in Adolf Lewin, *Geschichte der badischen Juden* (Karlsruhe, 1909), p. 331. Emphasis added. Translation my own.

[97] Michael A. Meyer, ed., *German Jewish History in Modern Times* (New York: Columbia University Press, 1997), vol. 2, p. 324.

[98] Halivni, "On the Ordination of Women," manuscript, p. 15.

[99] One might argue that since Halivni withdrew his responsum it cannot be used as a halakhic source. However, in his autobiography, *The Book and the Sword,* Halivni restates the

Some have proposed that we need merely argue that since the מנהג of counting women in the minyan has been clearly established in the overwhelming majority of Conservative synagogues, the halakhah must now reflect this change of practice notwithstanding any lingering halakhic issues, for מנהג מבטל הלכה, custom can supersede law. While such a proposal has some merits, its weakness is that the fact that rabbis and synagogue ritual committees have decided to count women in the minyan establishes more a change of policy than of ritual practice, or מנהג. Conservative Jewish women have not massively begun to pray thrice daily. The proposal put forward in this paper is based not upon a change in practice, but rather a change in perception. It is not that women observe more than they did--though perhaps many do--but rather that they, and the community as whole, perceive that they *ought* now observe the same as men. The distinction between permitted and obligated was the essential concern of Rabbi Roth's paper. The argument is put forward here that that distinction exists, and has now existed for about a generation.

3) Even if we accept that women in egalitarian synagogues assume an equal obligation to prayer, how can we apply that to women as a general class, since not all of our synagogues are egalitarian? We respond that in making general assumptions it is a precedented procedure to "follow the majority," אחרי רבים להטות. And, as Rabbi Golinkin noted, not all responsa are binding on all Jews. Obviously, this paper would not be used as guidance in synagogues not counting women in the minyan. But in general we can assume that since at least 85 percent of Conservative synagogues count women in the minyan, women as a general class in the Conservative movement have accepted an equal obligation to prayer.

We can reconcile the conclusions of this paper with the pluralism of our Movement and the Jewish world through the concept of מנהג המקום [the custom of the place]. If a woman from an egalitarian congregation or otherwise guided by this responsum were to attend a synagogue where women did not count in the minyan, she would not by virtue of her presence there suddenly lose her obligation to prayer equally with men. While she would not count in the minyan in such a community because of מנהג המקום, she would still retain her personal level of obligations as the חומרי מקום שיצא משם, the stringencies of the place from where she

---

argument of his responsum (as discussed above) and gives no explanation for his withdrawal of the paper besides his political disenchantment with Chancellor Cohen and the Seminary. He was upset, and perhaps for good reason, that his halakhic efforts were not appreciated. But that is politics, not halakhah. Perhaps he felt that his halakhic arguments could not be applied to a community that did not want to hear them. (See Halivni, *The Book and the Sword,* pp. 103-114). That may be so, but this is a different situation here. I see no reason why we cannot use his responsum as support.

came. And by joining with the congregation she still fulfills her obligation to prayer, even if the congregation does not count her in the minyan. Similarly, if a woman from a congregation where women did not count in the minyan or otherwise not guided by this responsum were to attend a synagogue where women did count in the minyan, she would not by virtue of her presence there suddenly gain an obligation to prayer equally with men. She herself would retain her personal level of obligations as קולי מקום שיצא משם, the leniencies of the place from where she came. However, the congregation would still count her in the minyan since by their reckoning women have as a general class accepted the equal obligation to prayer with men, and the individual should respect that position of the community as חומרי מקום שהלך לשם, the stringencies of the place in which she has arrived.[100]

It is possible that a woman raised and educated in an egalitarian synagogue (and all the more so one not so raised but belonging to such a community) might wish to not consider herself obligated to regular prayer equally with men, a decision reached through study of the halakhic development of the issue and concern not to transgress that which might otherwise be transgressed.[101] Such a woman would fall under the category of women belonging to congregations where women to do not count in the minyan, as discussed in the previous paragraph. While at some point we might be able to say that *all* women are so obligated, as the Magen Avraham does with the counting of the Omer, at this point we recognize the plurality of practice and interpretation within our greater community. As long as such options exist, individual Jews could opt for them. The local rabbi is not always *the* authority for all personal halakhic issues. This paper does not argue that all women everywhere are obligated to regular prayer. Rather, the argument is that within egalitarian Conservative congregations we may legitimately *assume* such obligation. A woman may personally exempt herself from liability for the mitzvah of regular prayer, תפילה בזמנה. However, for public purposes she is still counted in the minyan in egalitarian contexts, as explained in the preceding paragraph.

4) How can we base halakhah on a practice when we have said that the practice itself may not have rested on solid halakhic grounding? While some reservations have been expressed about some of the arguments in favor of counting women in the minyan, solid ground rested with those who voted for the Law Committee resolution as a תקנה in 1973. At that time a תקנה was required. Now, a generation later, we no longer need to rely solely on a תקנה.

---

[100] This terminology is found in Mishnah Pesahim 4:1.

[101] I thank my teacher Rabbi Joel Roth for raising the question of this possibility.

5) Why should an approach based upon sociological argument be preferable to arguments based upon the classical halakhic sources themselves? This paper is not the place for a defense of the use of sociological and other extralegal data in halakhic decision making. Such has already been well demonstrated in the theoretical writing of Rabbi Roth.[102] Sociological data can play a role in demonstrating a change in reality which can impinge on the appropriateness of a certain law in the eyes of the decisor. Sociological data is especially important for those of the school of Jewish law who are most concerned with the perseverance of precedent. Arguing that a law needs to evolve because of changed circumstances preserves the organic unity of the law's evolution from its inception through its various implementations. Rather than choose to reread classical sources and thereby annul whole centuries of halakhic development, this approach has the advantage of accepting precedent and development and continuing that process, but this time in the direction of inclusion of women. The weakness of this approach is that it is not as purely "egalitarian" as the approach employed in this case by the school of Rabbis Blumenthal and Sigal, et al. According to that approach, the law itself was always essentially egalitarian in regard to women, men and prayer. According to that school, the Rabbis of the Mishnah intended for women to count equally in the minyan. The new proposal presented here, flowing from the school of Rabbi Feldman, can make no such claim. Rather, there was never an intent to count women equally with men in the minyan until now. This is a new development of Jewish law, albeit a development that is fitting and proper. According to the opposing position, the equality of men and women in prayer is essential to halakhah and Judaism. According to this new proposal, the counting of women equally with men in the minyan and permitting women to serve as שליחות ציבור is a result of historical and sociological development.[103]

Summary

---

[102] See Roth, *The Halakhic Process*, ch. 9.

[103] It is for this reason that the approach argued here cannot necessarily be used to obligate women to wear tallit, tefillin or head covering/kippah. Since these practices have not yet spread universally among women in the Conservative movement, we cannot argue that women have accepted these obligations upon themselves. Perhaps women ought to be obligated to these mitzvot, and perhaps an adherent of the school of Rabbis Blumenthal and Sigal, et al., will make the argument that in fact the halakhah always intended women to be so obligated. But that argument has not to date been made. While I do encourage women to cover their heads and wear tallit and tefillin, I would not consider such practices to be obligatory until I could be satisfied that women have taken the practice upon themselves as an obligation.

Conservative rabbis who permit women to count in the minyan and serve as שליחות
ציבור argue such by various and opposing argumentations, either by reading the
classicial halakhic sources as obligating women to prayer equally with men and
thereby permitting them to have equal liturgical status, or by understanding the
classical halakhic sources as not mandating the liturgical inequality of women, or
by accepting the legislative authority of the 1973 תקנה, or by recognizing that
women in the Conservative movement have, as a general class, accepted upon
themselves the equal obligation to prayer with men.

Conclusion

Women may count in a minyan and may serve as שליחות ציבור.

APPENDIX 2
The Halakhah of Same-Sex Relations in a New Context

Rabbis Myron S. Geller, Robert E. Fine and David J. Fine

The following paper was submitted as a dissent to the decisions of the Committee on Jewish Law and Standards on December 6, 2006. Concurring and dissenting opinions are not official positions of the Committee on Jewish Law and Standards. Note: This paper was declared a takkanah by a vote of twelve in favor, nine opposed, and four abstaining (12-9-4) which is a majority of those present and voting. It failed by a vote of six in favor, seventeen opposed and two abstaining (6-17-2).

שאלה

Are intimate relations permitted between two men or two women? May members of the Rabbinical Assembly or the Cantors Assembly officiate at same-sex unions? May openly gay or lesbian Jews who are otherwise qualified be ordained and serve as rabbis or cantors?

תשובה

We will address the questions in the following sections:
1. Introduction
2. Essential Halakhic Sources
3. The CJLS on Homosexuality
4. Reading Parashat Arayot
5. The Term תועבה
6. Our Changed Societal Context
7. The Systemic Question
8. Responding to an Alternative Approach
9. The Requirement of Consecration
10. פסק דין – Conclusion

Section One: Introduction

The present reopening of formal discussion on homosexuals and their sexuality in Conservative Judaism does not vitiate the importance of our earlier teshuvot on this subject. In a series of responsa by Conservative writers in 1992 and since, some approved by the Committee on Jewish Law and Standards, others rejected, some submitted in reaction to approved teshuvot [responsa] and others never having come before the CJLS at all, traditional halakhic sources about those who engage in same-gender sex relations have been fully identified and explored, recorded and debated. These sources are already in plain view and there is little that new teshuvot will uncover in the halakhic canon to impact the outcome of our current effort.

There is not much disagreement about what the halakhah was, only whether it is now possible and necessary to decriminalize gay sexuality and allow homosexuals equal participation in our religious life from the present time forward. Some of us are restrained by the assumption that the halakhah is immutable. They see Scripture's sexual ethic as unchallenged by the passage of time and sufficient for the contemporary Jewish community. Others, in response to a shift in their own and society's perception of homosexuality, would reinterpret the halakhah. Given the transformation in our understanding of the subject in recent decades, that is, widespread agreement that "sexual orientation is most likely the result of a complex interaction of environmental, cognitive and biological factors...shaped at an early age,"[1] and its "enduring" character, they no longer view homosexuality as a choice or gay sexual behavior as deviant or unnatural and would remove some or all restraints to which homosexuals have been subjected heretofore.

As we deliberate on this matter we must in our view balance our obligation to the halakhic record and its method against the uncertain but insistent claim of contemporary sexual ethics. The posek [halakhic decisor] should consider the impact of social, ethical and scientific change in the interpretation and development of halakhah. A teshuvah should be more than a look at sources and precedents, it must reread them in light of current circumstances, perceptions, and realities. The historical and evolutionary character of halakhah is not unique to Judaism, it is a significant element in any vital legal system. It presupposes a creative role for the posek as well as an archeological one. This has been true since the earliest days of halakhic debate and decision making.

The tension between past and present has created an open flexibility in the Jewish legal system that has sometimes encouraged the emergence of diametrically

---

[1] Judith Glassgold, "Summary of Research on Select Issues in Lesbian, Gay and Bisexual Psychology," appendix to Elliott Dorff, Daniel S. Nevins and Avram Israel Reisner, "Homosexuality, Human Dignity and Halakhah" approved by the CJLS, December 6, 2006. http://www.rabbinicalassembly.org/sites/default/files/assets/public/halakhah/teshuvot/20052010/dorff_nevins_reisner_dignity.pdf _

opposed views of halakhah. This will no doubt be a feature of our present undertaking and will demonstrate once again that Jewish law does not express the unambiguous thundering voice of God, only the limited attempts of limited human beings to discover God's will and to express it in their own formulations.

Section Two: Essential Halakhic Sources

The Torah prohibits a male from engaging in sexual relations with another male, as he might with a female, and criminalizes it. ואת זכר לא תשכב משכבי אשה תועבה היא "Do not lie with a male as one lies with a woman; it is an abhorrence" (Lev. 18:22). This act along with some twenty other sexual relationships plus infanticide are prohibited as תועבות [abhorrences].

The chapter in which this passage is found opens with a general admonition against mimicking behavior common in the lands of Egypt and Canaan, that is, in the past and future lands of residence and historical experience of the Israelites then attending to God's voice. כמעשה ארץ מצרים אשר ישבתם בה לא תעשו וכמעשה ארץ כנען אשר אני מביא אתכם שמה לא תעשו ובחוקתיהם לא תלכו. "Do not follow the practices of the land of Egypt in which you have dwelt, do not follow the practices of the land of Canaan to which I bring you, and do not observe their laws" (Lev. 18:3).

The term תועבות is repeated four times in the chapter's summary statement which again urges Israelites to imitate the deeds of neither Egyptians nor Canaanites among whom the specified abhorrent behaviors were considered to be common practice. A punishment of כרת [karet] is imposed for violations (Lev. 18:24-30).

The prohibition and criminalization of משכב זכר [male-male relations] is repeated in a second list of proscribed acts, mainly sexual, where emphasis is placed on creating distinctions between טהר [pure] and טמא [impure] in order to achieve a life of sanctity. ואיש אשר ישכב את זכר משכבי אשה תועבה עשו שניהם מות יומתו דמיהם בם "If a man lies with a male as one lies with a woman, the two of them have done an abhorrent thing; they shall be put to death—their blood guilt is upon them" (Lev. 20:13).

Here the term תועבה appears only a single time, to describe משכב זכר, and while the Egyptians are overlooked, the identification of the entire list of prohibited acts with the practices of the unnamed nation inhabiting Eretz Yisrael before the arrival of the Israelites is repeated (Lev. 20:22-24). Moreover, both lists include the threat of expulsion of the Israelite nation from its anticipated territorial patrimony, should it engage in the prohibited practices (Lev. 18:28, 20:22).

Although Scripture refers only to משכב זכר, the Sifra expands the biblical prohibition to forbid female homosexual relations also. The point of departure is the prohibition against mimicking Egyptian practices: ומה היו עושים האיש נושא לאיש והאישה לאישה,"What did they do? A man would marry a man and a woman a woman" (Sifra, Aharei Mot 9:5).

The Mishnah rules: הבא על הזכור ועל הבהמה והאישה המביאה את הבהמה בסקילה. "He who commits sodomy with a male or a beast and the woman who commits bestiality are stoned" (M. Sanhedrin 7:4). The Gemara identifies Leviticus 18:22 and 20:13 as the source of the prohibition and its punishment while elaborating on the mishnah:

ת"ר: "איש" (ויקרא כ:יג) פרט לקטן. "אשר ישכב את זכר" בין גדול בין קטן. "משכבי אשה" מגיד לך הכתוב ששני משכבות באשה. א"ר ישמעאל הרי זה בא ללמד ונמצא למד. מות יומתו בסקילה.

Our sages teach: "[If a] man [lies with a male] (Lev. 20:13), to exclude a minor. [That is, since the word "man" is used rather than "male" we learn that a minor is exempt from culpability if he is the active partner. The Torah continues:] "Lies with a male" [teaching that, since here the word "male" is used rather than "man," there is no difference] whether [the passive partner is] an adult or a minor. [That is, even if the passive partner is a minor, the active partner is still culpable assuming that he is an adult. The Torah continues:] "As one lies with a woman." Scripture teaches that there are two types of sexual intercourse with a woman [i.e., vaginal and anal]. Rabbi Yishmael says: Behold this comes to teach [regarding male-male relations] and goes to teach [a general rule that is applied in other cases, that anal intercourse is equivalent to vaginal intercourse in all cases of sexual infractions. The Torah continues:] "They shall sure be put to death" by stoning (B. Sanhedrin 54a).

Elsewhere the Gemara, like the Sifra, adds sexual relations between women to the list of prohibitions in the following discussion: דא"ר הונא נשים המסוללת זו בזו פסולת לכהונה. "Rav Huna said: Women who engage in sexual practices with one another are forbidden in marriage to a kohen." That is to say, the stigma of זונה, a prostitute, is invoked upon these women and a kohen is forbidden to marry them. Rashi explains the term מסוללת to mean a very specific form of lesbian sexual relations, דרך תשמיש זכר ונקבה משפשפות נקבתן זו לזו, "the way that a male and a female, while engaging in intercourse, rub their genitalia against each other" (B. Yevamot 76a). The opposing opinion of Rabbi Elazar is also cited. He distinguishes between the unmarried male and female who engage in promiscuous sexual relations without an intention of marriage, where the male is not culpable or stigmatized but the woman becomes a very much stigmatized זונה, and two women who engage in sexual relations which is considered פריצותא בעלמא, mere licentiousness, because there has been no actual intercourse, hence no prostitute status and the women are not prohibited from marrying a kohen. The Rabbis disagree only about invoking the זונה designation when women are sexually active together but not about the forbidden nature of what they are engaged in. And that has been defined very precisely by Rashi.

Maimonides codified the criminalization of משכב זכר in these words:

הבא על הזכר או הביא זכר עליו כיון שהערה אם היו שניהם גדולים נסקלים שנאמר
ואת זכר לא תשכב בין בועל או נבעל.

A male who penetrates another male or who causes a male to penetrate him, from the moment of penetration, if they are both adults they are both subject to stoning. As the Torah says, "Do not lie with a male..." neither as the penetrator nor as the penetrated" (Hilkhot Issurei Biah 1:14).

Maimonides also codified the prohibition against female sexual relations:

נשים המסוללת זו בזו אסור וממעשה מצרים הוא שהוזהרנו עליו שנאמר כמעשה ארץ
מצרים לא תעשו אמרו חכמים מה היו עושים איש נושא איש ואישה נושאת אשה
ואישה נושאת לשני אנשים אע"פ שמעשה זה אסור אין מלקין עליו שאין לו לאו מיוחד
והרי אין שם ביאה כלל לפיכך אין נאסרת לכהונה משום זנות ולא תיאסר אשה על
בעלה בזה שאין כאן זנות וראוי להכותן מכת מרדות הואיל ועשו איסור.

Women are forbidden to engage in sexual relations with one another and it is among the Egyptian practices about which we were warned, as the Torah says, "Do not imitate the practices of the land of Egypt." The Rabbis said: "What did they do? A man would marry a man, a woman would marry a woman, or a woman would marry two men." Although this act is forbidden, lashes are not imposed because there is no specific prohibition and there is no actual intercourse. For that reason women who do this are not prohibited in marriage to a kohen as harlots and are not forbidden to their husbands because there is no

Rationales for the prohibitions of same gender sexual relations are varied. The Talmud offers the opinion of Bar Kappara that the biblical term תועבה is a contraction of תועה אתה בה, "You are lost because of her/this" (B. Nedarim 51a). Some believed that the word בה "her" referred to the entire list of sexual violations with various women enumerated in the Bible text rather than משכב זכר alone.[2] However, Tosafot, Rosh and Ran viewed the antecedent of בה translated as "this" to be משכב זכר, using almost identical phrases to explain the scriptural prohibition. In the words of Tosafot, שמניחין נשותיהן והולכין אצל משכב זכור, "They abandon their wives to pursue sex with men." This somewhat ambiguous concern may possibly have been about the preservation of family and the tragedy of an abandoned wife. Or the Torah's prohibition of משכב זכר could have been over a rejection of the mitzvah of procreation and that is what Tosafot and other Rishonim pointed to.

This much is clear, Bar Kappara was understood by the Rishonim to read the Torah verse to apply to married males and it was about the neglect of two specific mitzvot that devolve upon them, rather than any abhorrence with homosexual activity as a despicable, repugnant or unnatural act. If the concern was indeed about procreation, one may well wonder if the prohibition of משכב זכר should include married men whose wives are pregnant or who have already fulfilled the mitzvah of procreation. The prohibition would hardly seem applicable to those unmarried males who, because of their homosexuality, are unlikely and possibly unable ever to take wives in marriage to procreate. And Bar Kappara was silent about sexual relationships between women, who are not bound by the mitzvah of פרו ורבו [procreation].[3]

Section Three: The CJLS on Homosexuality

In 1992, the CJLS adopted the following Consensus Statement on Homosexuality:

---

[2] A lengthy analysis of the Bar Kappara passage can be found in Joel Roth, "Homosexuality," in Kassel Abelson and David J. Fine, eds., *Responsa 1991-2000* (New York: Rabbinical Assembly, 2002), pp. 623ff.
[3] See Hilkhot Ishut 5:2.

The Committee on Jewish Law and Standards of the Rabbinical Assembly affirms the following policies:
(A) We will not perform commitment ceremonies for gays and lesbians.
(B) We will not knowingly admit avowed homosexuals to our rabbinical or cantorial schools or the Rabbinical Assembly or the Cantors Assembly. At the same time, we will not instigate witch hunts against those who are already members or students.
(C) Whether homosexuals may function as teachers or youth leaders in our congregations and schools is left to the rabbi authorized to make halakhic decisions for a given institution within the Conservative Movement. Presumably, in this as in all other matters, the rabbi will make such decisions taking into account the sensitivities of the people of his or her particular congregation or school. The rabbi's own reading of Jewish law on these issues, informed by the responsa written by the Committee on Jewish Law and Standards to date, will also be a determinative factor in these decisions.
(D) Similarly, the rabbi of each Conservative institution, in consultation with its lay leaders, will be entrusted to formulate policies regarding the eligibility of homosexuals for honors within worship and for lay leadership positions.
(E) In any case, in accordance with the Rabbinical Assembly and United Synagogue resolutions, we hereby affirm gays and lesbians are welcome in our congregations, youth groups, camps and schools.[4]

It is possible that the anomalous last paragraph of the CJLS statement was an accommodation to two resolutions, one adopted in 1991 by the United Synagogue, the other a year earlier by the Rabbinical Assembly. The latter read:

THEREFORE BE IT RESOLVED that we, the Rabbinical Assembly, while affirming our tradition's prescription for heterosexuality,
(A) Support full civil equality for gays and lesbians in our national life, and
(B) Deplore the violence against gays and lesbians in our society, and
(C) Reiterate that, as are all Jews, gay men and lesbians are welcome as members in our congregations, and

---

[4] "Consensus Statement on Homosexuality," *Responsa 1991-2000,* p. 612.

(D) Call upon our synagogues and the arms of our movement to increase our awareness, understanding and concern for our fellow Jews who are gay and lesbian.[5]

The CJLS Consensus Statement opposed gay participation in community life far more strongly than the two resolutions would have warranted, only its last paragraph reflecting their welcoming tone, the rest at odds with them. The consensus that was achieved was contradictory. It was not possible to welcome gays and lesbians to Conservative synagogues at the same time that gay and lesbian rabbis and cantors were excluded from employment and synagogue honors were withheld from lay people. The Consensus Statement exposed a fault line of disagreement within the CJLS between those who would restrict gays and those who preferred their full inclusion. Consensus was reached to prevent what Rabbi Elliot Dorff saw as "a disaster for the Movement if the Committee on Jewish Law and Standards approved opposing papers on a topic as central to people's lives as their sexuality; it would mean that we are totally incoherent."[6] Instead, the incoherence was formalized in a contradictory Consensus Statement.

It seems to us that homosexuality as a general condition, or "orientation," need not be a halakhic problem. While certain sexual types such as the castrated male or the *androginos* [hermaphrodite] are identified as unique categories in halakhic parlance, the homosexual or the lesbian is not. There exists, in fact, no Hebrew word for "homosexual" other than the transliteration, evidence that such a category never existed in Jewish law. It is conceivable that a kohen gadol [high priest] who met all other requirements and was willing to participate in a heterosexual marriage but was by our contemporary understanding homosexual, could nevertheless enter the Holy of Holies on Yom Kippur to seek absolution for his own sins and those of his people.

It seems wrong to us, therefore, that the Consensus Statement on Homosexuality adopted by the CJLS in 1992 which remains our Movement's policy to this day [that is, until 2006], should far exceed what the halakhah required. The statement not only bars commitment ceremonies for homosexuals, it also opposes the admission of "avowed" homosexuals to Conservative rabbinical and cantorial schools and to the Rabbinical Assembly. It urges congregational rabbis to use policies set down by the CJLS in considering employment of gays as

---

[5] *Proceedings of the Rabbinical Assembly* 52 (1990): 275.
[6] Elliott Dorff, "Jewish Norms for Sexual Behavior: A Responsum Embodying a Proposal," in *Responsa 1991-2000*, p. 710.

teachers or youth leaders and even in the formulation of policy regarding synagogue honors. In these latter concerns, no distinction is made between "avowed" and other homosexuals. Therefore, the Consensus Statement reads as restricting the participation of gays and lesbians in general within Conservative Judaism, and that restriction went beyond the requirement of halakhah. The Statement should have clarified that these restrictions do not apply to all gay and lesbian Jews, but rather only to those who are known to engage in same-sex intimate relations.[7] Furthermore, it is generally the case that beyond greater expectations of clergy, the Conservative movement hardly limits the participation of lay public sinners of any type. It is inconceivable that restrictions on the study or teaching of Torah or receiving synagogue honors would be imposed by those who would enforce the halakhic ban on gay sexual activity upon gays who should enjoy a presumption of innocence that they do not violate the law at all and if they are in violation of halakhah are doing so only in private.

The CJLS also considered the use of placement services by a homosexual rabbi already a member of the RA and ruled, "In accord with the apparent intent of the consensus statement, the Joint Placement Commission should not recommend 'avowed homosexuals' for placement in congregations."[8] An opposite conclusion was also accepted thanks to an argument based not on halakhic but organizational grounds.[9] It seems to us that the decisions reached by both sides in this discussion were extra-halakhic, disregarding the actual limits placed by tradition on homosexual behavior. These have nothing at all to say about gays as rabbis and cantors or their placement in congregations. We recognize that the adjective "avowed" may have indicated that the reference is only to gays and lesbians who avowedly engage in activities that violate halakhah as per the CJLS's determination.[10] We further recognize that there might be a general assumption

---

[7] Rabbi Joel Roth's 1992 responsum on homosexuality made this distinction quite clear: "We have asserted that halakhah does not prohibit homosexual attractions or arousals. Its exclusive concern is with homosexual behavior, primarily homosexual intercourse. As a result, it follows that one who is of homosexual orientation, but affirms that the lifestyle that usually accompanies that orientation is halakhically unacceptable and therefore chooses to live a celibate life, suffers no halakhic restriction of any kind whatsoever. Such a person could serve in any position of religious leadership, professional or lay, including the rabbinate and the cantorate" (Joel Roth, "Homosexuality," in *Responsa 1991-2000*, p. 667).

[8] Kassel Abelson, "Placing Homosexual Rabbis in Congregations," *Responsa 1991-2000*, p. 723.

[9] Arnold M. Goodman, "Placing Homosexual Rabbis in Congregations," *Responsa 1991-2000*, pp. 724-725.

[10] This is a charitable reading. The 1993 responsa on placement of avowed homosexual rabbis (*Responsa 1991-2000*, pp. 722-729) consistently refer to avowal of "homosexuality," not of any form of behavior. Additionally, one of the papers specifically identifies the case that brought

that someone who is avowedly gay or lesbian would be engaged in intimate same-sex relations. And yet, we are perplexed why the CJLS would assume that all gays and lesbians are engaging in intimate relations. Would we automatically assume that all heterosexual rabbis are sexually active, even if they are not married? Does "avowal of homosexuality" apply only to gays and lesbians in committed relationships? What about a rabbi who is openly gay but single? The precedents appear to be discriminatory against gays and lesbians because of their sexual orientation and with no regard to the context of their personal relationships. This perception of broad discrimination is unfortunate.

Regardless of whether the *issur* [prohibition] is defined broadly or narrowly, the prohibition of משכב זכר ought not to become the basis for the exclusion of homosexuals from Jewish life and leadership. The enforcement of the biblical prohibition in our day, if it is to be enforced, should not justify the elevation by the Conservative movement of משכב זכר above every other issur and its violators should not be singled out for restrictions and exclusions never imposed on those who do not live in accord with other demands of halakhah.

In addition to the Consensus Statement, four teshuvot were also adopted in 1992 that provided differing philosophical and legal rationales for it.

1) Rabbi Elliot Dorff proposed a delaying posture because he did not believe that the Conservative movement was prepared to embrace total parity between gay and straight sexual activity and unions despite the RA and United Synagogue resolutions supporting full civil equality for gays. Rabbi Dorff distinguished between homosexual sex and anal sex, the former he believed was not under prohibition at all, the latter banned by a decree of the Torah that might eventually be eased. He hoped that the Bible text would not be the sole authority in determining the halakhah but that contemporary views on homosexuality, that it is neither a disease nor reversible, could counterweigh the halakhic record in future CJLS deliberations. Rabbi Dorff, feeling that there was not sufficient evidence then available for the Conservative movement to come to a definitive conclusion about homosexuality, sought the creation of a commission to study all aspects of the issue.

---

about the שאלה: "A colleague, having been 'outed,' has avowed his homosexuality" (Arnold M. Goodman, "Placing Homosexual Rabbis in Congregations" ibid., p. 725). While the facts of the case may have been otherwise, the presentation in the responsa refer to avowal of sexual orientation, not to forbidden behavior.

2) Rabbi Reuven Kimelman was satisfied that halakhic issues were being dealt with in other teshuvot so he addressed only the public policy aspects of homosexuality. He was fearful that "the approval of a priori non-procreative marriages as a class could tend to devalue the type of sexuality that leads to procreation" and "to equalize the status of the two especially in the eyes of children."[11] He was also concerned that "same sex activity has the potential of undermining the whole idea of sexual prohibitions." He therefore favored retaining traditional restraints on homosexuality, rejected homosexuals as suitable Jewish role models and supported the imposition of additional limits on their acceptance in public life.

Rabbi Kimelman was anxious about the very problem perceived by the Rishonim who applied Bar Kappara's exegesis of the term תועבה to a married man engaging in gay anal sex to avoid procreativity with his wife. But Rabbi Kimelman also perceived a threat to the procreative ideal in marriage when unmarried gays engage in non-procreative sex. In fact, procreative potential is not an entry requirement for Jewish marriage and its absence is no hindrance to heterosexual unions. Non-procreative marriages and non-procreative sexual relations within marriage are not prohibited in Jewish law and are not deemed a threat to equalize procreative and non-procreative marriages in children's eyes. Nevertheless, Rabbi Kimmelman feared negative effects upon heterosexual procreativity if homosexual non-procreative unions were not stigmatized. He asserted, without proof, that gay sex undermines the idea of sexual limits in human behavior.

While the Jewish community is certainly dependent for its continuity on heterosexual marriage and procreative sexual unions, Rabbi Kimelman offered no prooftext at all that the Jewish tradition prohibits non-procreative sex except in the specific circumstance described by Tosafot and he provided no sociological evidence for his assertion that a Gresham's Law of human sexuality exists, the bad, which he defined as homosexual, driving out the good, which he defined as heterosexual.

Rabbi Kimelman's public policy concern for encouraging procreative sex and the danger to it that he senses if gay non-procreative sex were permitted seems to us to be overstated. We cannot imagine any heterosexual couple refusing to have children because their next door neighbors are childless homosexuals. That is too preposterous a scenario to be the basis for determining the status of gays in our

---

[11] Reuven Kimelman, "Homosexuality and the Policy Decisions of the CJLS" in *Responsa 1991-2000*, pp. 676-685.

community. Rather, we believe that the public policy issue is a different one entirely. Firstly, contemporary reproductive technologies, as well as adoption, provide same-sex couples with options to raise children that they never had before. But more importantly, we do not condemn the infertile heterosexual couple, nor do we insist that they take advantage of contemporary reproductive technologies.[12] Moreover, the prophet Isaiah was mindful of the pain experienced by the childless eunuch who might be feeling like an עץ יבש, a dried out stick, and was sympathetic. He reassured those without offspring, ונתתי להם בביתי ובחומתי יד ושם טוב מבנים ומבנות שם עולם אתן לו אשר לא יכרת, that the keeping of the Sabbath, choosing what God wishes and affirming the covenant may bring rewards better and more lasting than sons and daughters. What Isaiah seems to us to be saying is that because God has a house for all, it is good public policy to include the minority who are physically unable to engage in procreative sex in the ברית [covenant]. It is reasonable to speculate about the position Isaiah might take on gays who for reasons beyond their control may be childless.

3) Rabbi Mayer Rabinowitz determined that עקירת דבר מן התורה, abrogating biblical law, would be the only way to change the halakhah on homosexuality, that abrogation "had to be done for the betterment of the Jewish people as a whole, not simply for the benefit of a minority of the people," and that therefore, it was inapplicable in this instance. He ruled that homosexuals who advocate homosexuality as an acceptable alternative Jewish lifestyle are prohibited from holding leadership positions in our synagogues, institutions and schools.[13]

Rabbi Rabinowitz did not allow that any alternative way to address the biblical prohibition of משכב זכר may be available and he imposed an additional prohibition to exclude gays from leadership in the Jewish community. Since the CJLS has ruled that we do not accept testimony about illegitimacy,[14] Rabbi Rabinowitz's teshuvah and others lead to the ironic circumstance that a *mamzer*, biblically excluded from the Jewish community, may become a rabbi while a gay person may not.

Rabbi Rabinowitz, aware of the proportional distribution of the largely heterosexual majority and the small homosexual minority, did not allow redress of the biblical criminalization of gay sex. He believed that only a minority would

---

[12] See Elliott Dorff, "Artificial Insemination, Egg Donation and Adoption," *Responsa 1991-2000*, p. 509: "Infertile couples are not required to engage in these procedures to have children."

[13] Mayer Rabinowitz, "On Homosexuality," *Responsa 1991-2000*, p. 689.

[14] See Elie Kaplan Spitz, "Mamzerut," *Responsa 1991-2000*, p. 558.

benefit from doing so. He did not consider that there was another way to define the majority, that is the majority of Conservative Jews who, as demonstrated by approved resolutions of the Rabbinical Assembly and United Synagogue, had rejected limits on the participation of homosexuals in our religious and communal life. Those resolutions seemed to indicate that changes in the halakhah regarding homosexuals would in fact address the ethical and sociological needs of the majority of the Conservative community and reflect their wishes.

Nor did Rabbi Rabinowitz explain why only homosexuals advocating homosexuality as an acceptable alternative Jewish lifestyle should be subject to censure. According to his reasoning, heterosexuals who do so should also be excluded from our seminaries, from the rabbinate and from teaching in our schools because they too project undesirable behavior as licit, if not by example then by advocacy. Moreover, they cannot make the mitigating claim that they are אנוסים, acting under compulsion, as gays might. Should members of the CJLS who support them be censured? We do not believe that Rabbi Rabinowitz would support such action against heterosexuals and we cannot agree with the conclusions reached in his teshuvah.

4) Rabbi Joel Roth read Leviticus 18:22 and 20:13 to "posit some type of prohibition against homosexuality."[15] That was a surprisingly loose reading of the texts because they actually refer only to משכב זכר but not to homosexuality.[16] He asserted that "the Torah defines homosexuality as תועבה," a too broad and, we believe, inaccurate reading of Scripture. Rabbi Roth claimed that lesbianism is forbidden based on the Sifra's understanding of Leviticus 18:3. While his assertion was accurate that the prohibition against נשים מסוללות is דאורייתא [Toraitic], he translated the phrase to mean "lesbianism" when Rashi had a decidedly narrower and very precise understanding of it. Rabbi Roth may have used the terms homosexuality and lesbianism to refer to gay sexual relations, but that was inaccurate, unfortunate and misleading. His use of these terms was confusing and unnecessary particularly since he acknowledged "that the Torah does not prohibit homosexual attraction-orientation."

Rabbi Roth's conclusions were based on the Bible text and many halakhic sources that ban משכב זכר as תועבה and he included other physical expressions of

---

[15] Joel Roth, "Homosexuality," *Responsa 1991-2000,* p. 624.
[16] Some claim that the Torah's prohibition is specific to anal sex between men. See the paper approved by the CJLS by our colleagues Rabbis Dorff, Nevins and Reisner for an elaboration of this.

gay sex in the prohibition. Although this expansive understanding of the halakhah was not the only way in which it might be understood or applied, it would be very hard, we think, to refute the fact that the entire weight of halakhic evidence to this point takes this view. But when he evaluated various rationales for the Torah's attribution of תועבה to homosexuality (actually, only to משכב זכר and possibly to other gay sexual acts as well), Rabbi Roth acknowledged that there may not be a single adequate explanation for it but used that as an argument to determine that the prohibition was irreversible. Had there been a clear rationale it might be refuted to permit or compel a change in the law, as we will suggest below. But when there is only the unexplained and unambiguous Bible text, Rabbi Roth concluded and has continued to argue that nothing could overturn that text or the halakhic pattern that followed in its wake. It seems strange to us that Rabbi Roth empowered the text with unalterable control over our practice when text interpretation is the very basis of Jewish law and the halakhic system. Our own view of halakhah as a historically based religious/legal system that reflects the values, ethics and circumstances of the Jewish people at any particular period and whose evolving judgments, including those recorded in Scripture, are expressions of Jewish ideals in a given place and time, compels us to disagree.

We recognize that positions taken in these teshuvot do not result from any animus toward or fear of gays or lesbians, what is generally called "homophobia," but rather out of theological or halakhic concerns. Nevertheless, we reject their conclusions that oppose the normalization of Jewish gays and lesbians in the community, for reasons articulated below.

Section Four: Reading Parashat Arayot

The prohibition of homosexual behavior originates in the Rabbinic understanding of the term משכבי אשה in Leviticus 18:22 and 20:13. As is evident from the gemara in Sanhedrin (54a-b),[17] the phrase משכבי אשה teaches us that anal sex is legally considered to be real sex, and that it is so when it is performed either with a man or a woman. What the phrase means is that anal intercourse with a man has the legal status of intercourse with a woman. One might have thought that the gender of the passive partner makes a difference. The Torah tells us that it does not, as far as constituting sexual relations.[18]

---

[17] As discussed above.

[18] Jacob Milgrom goes even further in arguing that "it may be plausibly suggested" that the term משכבי אשה is only used in relation to *forbidden* sexual relations, specifically those enumerated in

It might be argued that the prohibition of homosexual behavior derives from Deuteronomy 23:18 (the prohibition of the קדש, usually understood as cult prostitute) or from Genesis 19 (the story of the men of Sodom, and its parallel in Judges 19). But the Genesis and Judges sources are clearly concerned more with rape than homosexuality per se.[19] The Deuteronomy source is concerned more with what is permitted in the Temple rather than with purity of sexual life in general. Some scholars argue that the concern with the cult prostitute was an issue throughout the First Temple period (see 1 Kings 14:24; 1 Kings 15:12; 1 Kings 22:47; 2 Kings 23:7), perhaps only eradicated with the Deuteronomic reforms under King Josiah. Only later did Leviticus address itself beyond cultic concerns.[20]

Lev. 18, and that "sexual relations occurring with males outside these relations would not be forbidden" (Jacob Milgrom, *Leviticus 17-22: A New Translation with Introduction and Commentary* [New York: The Anchor Bible, Doubleday, 2000], p. 1569, s.v. "as one lies with a woman"). While Milgrom offers this interpretation as a mere "plausible suggestion" and does not follow through with it in his general interpretation of the verse (as we discuss below in this section), his argument here on the meaning of the phrase is important. He claims that the context of the verse is not homosexuality per se, but rather that male-male sexual relations are just as much forbidden as male-female sexual relations when the relationship is incestuous or adulterous as enumerated in Lev. 18 and 20.

[19] Interestingly, there is no known prohibition against homosexual behavior from the ancient Mesopotamian cultures. However, there are Assyrian laws against homosexual rape. See David F. Greenberg, *The Construction of Homosexuality* (Chicago: University of Chicago Press, 1988), p. 126; James B. Pritchard, ed., *Ancient Near Eastern Texts Relating to the Old Testament* (Princeton: Princeton University Press, 1969), p. 181; G.R. Driver and John C. Miles, eds., *The Assyrian Laws* (New York: Oxford University Press, 1935), pp. 71, 391. Some interpret Genesis 9:21-24 as narrating a homosexual encounter between Ham and Noah when Noah was drunk. But the text frowns upon Ham because he was inappropriate towards his father, not because of homosexual behavior per se. If it was just that he uncovered his father's nakedness, then the crime is that he uncovered *his father's* nakedness. If it really means incest, then the essence of the crime is that it was incest, not the sexual act itself. Interestingly, the only Hittite prohibitions of homosexual behavior are incestuous ones. See Pritchard, *ANET,* p. 196; Greenberg, *Construction of Homosexuality,* pp. 124-125.

[20] Louis Epstein writes: "Sodomy in the Temple was not eradicated until the vigorous reforms of the righteous King Josiah. It was then followed up by the deuteronomic legislator, who set down the specific prohibition, 'There shall be no *kedeshah* among the daughters of Israel nor shall there by any *kadesh* among the sons of Israel.' This prohibition, it should be noted, differed from the later levitical law in two ways. First, it stressed the crime of sodomy not as a sexual crime but as a form of idolatry, saying nothing concerning secular sodomy. Second, it prohibited it on the same level as prostitution but did not consider it a capital crime. The levitical law went the whole way" (Louis Epstein, *Sex Laws and Customs in Judaism* [New York: Bloch, 1948], p. 136. See also, on the homosexual cult in the ancient world in general, Greenberg, *Construction of Homosexuality,* pp. 94ff.).

Whether or not this can be accepted as a historical sketch, the halakhah sees the Leviticus verses as the heart of the prohibition. Since the halakhah is rooted in those verses, it is upon those verses we focus.

Recent efforts have attempted to understand Leviticus 18:22 and 20:13 in ways that limit or exclude their applicability in our time. For example, it has been suggested that the issur applies only to cultic, coercive or exploitative sex.[21] We find these efforts unconvincing because they do not fit the context of פרשת עריות [Leviticus 18]. We believe that context is the sanctity and purity of sexual relations.

According to פרשת עריות, real sex requires sanctification, codified later by halakhah as קידושין [kiddushin]. There is strong opposition in halakhic literature to sexual relations outside of marriage. According to most views it is forbidden.[22] The Torah, in פרשת עריות, lists a series of forbidden relations that include incest, adultery, homosexual acts and bestiality. They are forbidden because there is not any chance of them becoming "sanctified" through קידושין. Even though it was the Rabbis and not the Torah who fully developed the concept of betrothal, the Torah surely had a sense of marriage, and recognized marriage as sacred.[23] Adultery is a

---

[21] See Bradley S. Artson, "Gay and Lesbian Jews: An Innovative Jewish Legal Position," *Jewish Spectator* (winter 1990).

[22] The prohibition against nonmarital relations is not entirely clear from the halakhic literature, although Maimonides does state clearly in his introduction to Hilkhot Ishut in the Mishneh Torah that it is forbidden for a man to engage in relations with a woman without ketubbah and kiddushin. While there is no specific verse in the Torah forbidding nonmarital relations in general, one could argue that such a verse was unnecessary since the prohibition was surely known. In any case the category of a פילגש was developed in the Middle Ages to permit a man to engage in relations with a woman without kiddushin. The halakhic controversy, and the fact that the category is no longer invoked, shows that the tradition surely frowned on nonmarital relations in general. On the halakhic controversy, see Eliakim Ellinson, נשואין שלא כדת משה וישראל (Tel Aviv, 1982), pp. 25-79. See also Robert Gordis, *Love and Sex: A Modern Jewish Perspective* (New York: Women's League for Conservative Judaism, 1978), pp. 167-168; and Robert Gordis, *Sex and the Family in Jewish Tradition* (New York: Burning Bush Press, 1967), pp. 54-55, n. 56. He concludes: "Judaism maintains the principle that sexual relations are proper only within the marriage bond" (ibid., p. 41). The Rabbinical Assembly has clearly taken the position that "Judaism would have us refrain from sexual intercourse outside of marriage." See Elliot Dorff, *This Is My Beloved, This Is My Friend: A Rabbinic Letter on Intimate Relations* (New York: Rabbinical Assembly, 1996), p. 31. See also the responsum by Pesach Schindler in *Responsa of the Vaad Halakhah of the Rabbinical Assembly of Israel,* vol. 4, *5750-5752* (Jerusalem: Rabbinical Assembly of Israel and the Masorti Movement, 1992), pp. 81-90.

[23] See now Michael L. Satlow, *Jewish Marriage in Antiquity* (Princeton: Princeton University Press, 2001), for the Rabbinic construction of "Jewish marriage."

capital offense since it offends the sanctity of marriage and the union cannot be sanctified as a marriage because society would not permit it (hence the halakhah: אסור לבעל אסור לבועל [the adulteress is forbidden to both the husband and the adulterer]). Incestuous relationships could not be sanctified through marriage since society would not permit close relatives to marry. Of course, one could not marry an animal. And a man could not marry another man. It would seem that the sexual transgressions of פרשת עריות are primary transgressions because they lack even the possibility of marriage. However, non-marital sex, while prohibited, is not an ערווה since it can lead to marriage. The punishment, therefore, would be much less severe. What is noteworthy is that all the עריות lack the possibility of fulfillment because of societal standards. Sometimes societal standards change, as we are seeing today with same-sex domestic partnership and marriage. But from the perspective of the Torah and the Rabbis, there was clearly no possibility for same-sex marriage. From that perspective, same-sex relations meant only sex. And the Torah teaches, then, that gay sex is real sex and is forbidden as are the other עריות.

Jacob Milgrom as well, in his recent comprehensive commentary on Leviticus, argues that Leviticus 18:22 and 20:13 must be understood within the context of the list of forbidden relations, the עריות. However, he understands the concern of the chapter(s) to be procreation rather than marriage. "The common denominator of all the prohibitions, I submit," he writes, "is that they involve the emission of semen for the purpose of copulation, resulting in either incest and illicit progeny or, as in this case, lack of progeny (or its destruction in the case of Molek worship, v. 21). In a word, the theme (with Ramban) is procreation."[24] Milgrom goes on to explain that nocturnal emissions require purificatory rites (Lev. 15:16-18) because of the wasting of seed, but that the Torah nowhere explicitly forbids masturbation and, Milgrom infers, would permit birth control "as long as the couple reproduced itself."[25] Female-female sexual relations are ignored by the Torah, Milgrom argues, since there is no exchange of seminal fluids and hence no destruction of seed. What is extraordinary about the lists of forbidden relations in chapters 18 and 20 is that they can only hope to produce illicit children (through incest or adultery), no children (through male-male relations and bestiality), or dead children (through Molek worship). While Milgrom's approach is slightly different from our suggestion in focusing on procreation and the emission of semen rather than on marriage, he agrees that it is the licit or illicit nature of the relationship that permits or forbids the exchange of fluids. A non-marital heterosexual union would not be an ערווה because unlike incest or adultery,

---

[24] Milgrom, *Leviticus 17-22*, p. 1567.

[25] Ibid., p. 1568.

the potential progeny would not be illegitimate, and unlike male-male relations and bestiality, the potential for procreation does exist.

We are now in a position to consider the underlying rationale of פרשת עריות. The Torah's concern is the sanctity of marriage, as we formulate it; Jacob Milgrom understands the concern as the importance of procreation. These two views are, in fact, the two understandings among the Rishonim of Bar Kappara's statement in Nedarim 51a (discussed above) on the meaning of "abomination." Bar Kappara said: מאי תועבה: תועה אתה בה, what is *to'evah*? You go astray through it (a Hebrew play on words). The Rishonim understand this as meaning either destructive to the family or non-procreative.[26] The *meaning* of the Torah was to prohibit male-male anal intercourse. Its *rationale,* however, was to protect against non-procreative relations or non-marriageable unions.

The intent of the Torah, we have argued, was to teach that gay sex is real sex. This is not a lesson with which many today would disagree. But whereas the context of the Torah was to forbid such an activity to Israelite men lest they think that sex with a man was not real sex and hence permitted, today we are faced with a very different context. Our שאלה relates to committed Jews who wish to form marital bonds, the very bonds that the Torah and the Rabbis were so concerned to preserve and keep pure through the sexual purity rules of Leviticus. In the past, same-sex unions were not a societal option.[27] They are today. If the concern is procreation, then our times also offer new options.

---

[26]See the discussion of these sources in Joel Roth, "Homosexuality," *Responsa 1991-2000,* pp. 627, 635.

[27] This is clearly true despite the statement of the Sifra (Aharei Mot 9:5) cited above that in ancient Egypt men married men and women married women. The Sifra is polemical. The Rabbis are projecting onto ancient Egypt practices they wish to prohibit. There is no evidence for same-sex marriage in ancient Egypt. If there were, it would certainly be trumpeted by the many studies of homosexuality in the ancient world that have been written in recent decades. Any real example from the ancient world of same-sex *marriage* (as opposed to general homosexual behavior), such as the emperor Nero's marriage to his young male lover, is clearly aberrational and does not represent societal acceptance. (Caligula made his horse a senator. Does that mean that Roman society accepted animals as senators?) The effort to interpret the wall paintings discovered in the necropolis of Saqqara outside Cairo in 1964 as a gay couple has certainly not achieved scholarly consensus. "Over the years, the tomb's wall art has been subjected to learned analysis, inspiring considerable speculation. One interpretation is that the two men are brothers, probably identical twins, and this may be the earliest known depiction of twins. Another is that the men had a homosexual relationship, a more recent view that has gained support among gay advocates... Most Egyptologists accept the normal-twins interpretation advanced most prominently by John Baines, an archaeologist at the University of Oxford in

Today, both male and female same-sex couples have various means of raising children, including adoption.[28] We need only point to recent CJLS decisions on adoption, artificial insemination, in vitro fertilization and surrogate motherhood to indicate the many options available to couples who wish to raise children.[29] What should be clear is that both primary concerns of the Torah, marriage and procreation, can be fulfilled today by same-sex couples in ways that did not exist in earlier times. This is a clear case of שינוי העיתים, of changing times and contexts.

Section Five: The Term תועבה

Any discussion of שינוי העיתים in this context must address the meaning of the term תועבה. We are convinced that the term תועבה as used in the Torah was not absolute but relative to society, to culture, to individuals and to time. It was attributed to same gender sexual relations in the distant and recent past but generally no longer reflects the attitude of most members of the Jewish community. The halakhah is now at odds with the legal status of gays and their sexual habits in Jewish society both in Israel and in the United States because gay sex is no longer considered תועבה or criminal by most Jews and by others.

We begin by examining the meaning of the term תועבה in the Torah, where it appears a number of times and is generally translated as "abhorrent." The translation implies an aesthetic or moral judgment although that is not how תועבה was viewed by some Rabbis in the prohibition of anal sex among males. It was understood to be a rationale for prohibiting a husband from violating his sexual responsibility to his wife or his obligation to have children.

England" (John Noble Wilford, "A Mystery Locked in Timeless Embrace" *The New York Times*, December 20, 2005. Cf. John Baines, "Egyptian Twins" *Orientalia* 54(4) [1985]: 461-482).

[28] As Milgrom writes following his elucidation of the meaning of Leviticus 18:22: "Finally, it is imperative to draw the logical conclusion of this discussion for our time. If my basic thesis is correct that the common denominator of the entire list of sexual prohibitions, including homosexuality, is procreation within a stable family, then a consolatory and compensatory remedy is at hand for Jewish gays....If gay partners adopt children, they do not violate the *intent* of the prohibition. The question can be asked: Why didn't the biblical legist propose this remedy? The answer simply is that this option was not available, since ancient Israel did not practice adoption" (Milgrom, *Leviticus 17-22*, pp. 1568-1569).

[29] See the papers by Elliot Dorff, Aaron Mackler and Elie Kaplan Spitz in *Responsa 1991-2000*, pp. 461-557.

The word תועבה is also used in the Torah to describe objects that Israelites are urged to abhor, such as idols[30] and non-kosher food[31] or actions such as idolatry[32] or the use of false weights and measures in business transactions.[33] The Torah generally deems only the object or action a תועבה but not the sinner. While an idol or non-kosher meat are identified as abhorrent, the idolater, the consumer of treif meat and one who engages in משכב זכר are not. Not so the unscrupulous merchant who is personally abhorrent to God.

Rabbi Joel Roth correctly claims that תועבה as used in the Torah is an attributed quality rather than an inherent one. One people's תועבה may be another's means of gaining a livelihood or celebrating its deliverance. Sheep herding[34] and lamb[35] are תועבות מצרים but they are favorably considered by Hebrews, the former as a desirable occupation, the latter for an offering to God. Egyptians may not sit at a dining table with Hebrews, they call it a תועבה,[36] while the Torah forbids משכב זכר, from the perspective of the Torah an acceptable and widespread practice among Egyptians, as תועבה. The term is not used to describe the inherent or universal quality of an item or human action, it expresses its culturally or religiously determined value in a given society and identifies specific material objects or behaviors that are denied to its members.

Scripture views some תועבות, however, as abhorrent not only to a given society but to God. The falsifying of weights and measures is an inequity that places the violator in this category although other forms of commercial cheating do not. Most often the phrase is used to describe idols and idolatry as abhorrent to God[37] but so is cross-dressing,[38] while homosexual intercourse is not identified in this way. And even when an object or action is designated in the Torah as a תועבת יי, there is the recognition that non-Israelite societies may not react with the abhorrence felt by Israelites or their God.

---

[30] Deut. 7:26: ולא תביא תועבה אל ביתך והיית חרם כמהו שקץ תשקצמו ותעב תתעבנו כי חרם הוא.
[31] Deut. 14:3: לא תאכל כל תועבה.
[32] Deut. 13:15, communal, and Deut. 17:4, individual idolatry.
[33] Deut. 25:16: כי תועבת יי א-להיך כל עשה אלה כל עשה עול.
[34] Gen. 46:34.
[35] Exod. 8:22.
[36] Gen. 43:32.
[37] Idols in Deut. 7:25 and 27:15; infanticide in Deut. 12:31 and 18:9-12 where auguring, hidden sorcery, divining, enchanting, magical knot tying, seeking ghosts and spirits and inquiries of the dead are added; the wages of female and male prostitutes, probably in connection with a cult in Deut. 23:19.
[38] Deut. 22:5.

Abhorrence is not only relative to society and its values. The Torah believes that individuals may experience תעוב based on their historical experience. Israelites are warned against abhorring Edomites or Egyptians despite any cultural or personal inclination that may impel them in that direction.[39] Abhorrence it seems is something that the Torah believes can be controlled and there are occasions when it ought to be.

Behavior that is not deemed תועבה in one generation may be so in another. The Torah includes among the sexual practices enumerated as תועבות in Leviticus 18 marriage to one's half sister[40] or to two sisters[41] yet a few generations earlier, the Patriarchs Abraham[42] and Jacob[43] had consummated such marriages. Of course the Torah was not yet promulgated and the Patriarchs were not obligated to observe its sexual prohibitions. But does this mean that in the biblical view they engaged in sexual relations that God deemed abhorrent at the time but God, remaining silent, without a word of admonition to the Patriarchs, established the covenant with them and with the descendants born out of these abhorrent relations nevertheless? Or does the Bible mean that God did not consider their marriages abhorrent at all before the Torah was given at Sinai? These Leviticus prohibitions are not identified as תועבת יי and perhaps they are not to be perceived in that way at all.

These are instances in which permitted actions were subsequently banned as תועבות. An example of something prohibited as תועבה being permitted at a later time is to be found in the Talmudic discussion about the permissibility of meat from stabbed animals brought to Eretz Yisrael during the period of the Israelite conquest. Rabbi Jeremiah b. Abba cites Rav that based on the biblical promise that the conquerors would discover בתים מלאים כל טוב, "houses full of all good things," even כתלי דחזירי that Rashi helpfully explains are חזירים יבישים שקורין בקיני"ש, "dried pigs that are called bacons," were permitted at that time and surely בשר נחירה, "stabbed meat."[44] The assertion that pig meat, a forbidden תועבה, was permitted for a time goes unchallenged because in the view of the Rabbis, the תועבה designation was subject to suspension. Even more remarkable, perhaps, is that something considered תועבה by Scripture should be located by Rav under the rubric of "all

[39] Deut. 23:8.
[40] Lev. 18:9 and repeated in 20:17.
[41] Lev. 18:19.
[42] Gen. 20:12.
[43] Gen. 29:18-28.
[44] B. Hullin 17a. Stabbed meat refers to the flesh of kosher animals not dispatched according to the requirements of kosher slaughter.

good things." Most remarkable is that he was prepared to accept the consumption of meat that is תועבה by our ancestors through text interpretation alone, without concluding that it was one of the takkanot ascribed by tradition to Joshua.

What is clear to us is that the use of the תועבה term in the Bible may apply only to a specific society and within that society to a specific and limited period of time in its history, and the rabbinic tradition was at peace with that. Moreover, the transition from licit to abhorrent could take place in the Torah's telling, over a very short span of time.

Since תועבה is an attributed characteristic rather than an inherent one, it is proper to ask if the attribution, once made, is unalterable. Is the biblical prohibition of משכב זכר along with the halakhic record in its wake fixed for all time or is change possible? The Torah does not suggest that homosexual relations are תועבת יי so they would not seem to fall into the permanent category that would include idolatry. We believe that the Torah's תועבה attribution to same gender sexual relations is entirely accurate to the biological facts and sexual morality as understood and practiced in ancient and even in more modern times but not as they are today. The general state of scientific knowledge about homosexuality does not sustain that perception nor does the Jewish community in the Diaspora or in Israel still consider same-gender sex relations תועבה or subject to capital punishment.

It may be an incidental but not insignificant point that contemporary sexual morality is egalitarian in ways never contemplated in the Torah. Engaging in promiscuous premarital heterosexual intercourse has no subsequent social implications for a male but according to halakhah transforms a Jewish women into a זונה, a prostitute. Because our sexual ethic has evolved from patriarchal to more nearly egalitarian, this is a morally unacceptable distinction for us and we dare say to very many Jews today. One cannot fault the Torah or the halakhic tradition for not being aware of contemporary sensibilities. But we are not and need not be limited by ancient sensibilities.

Section Six: Our Changed Societal Context

At the present time, it is almost universally accepted in the scientific community that homosexuality occurs naturally in a given percentage of the population, is neither a sickness nor a personal choice and is irreversible. In 1974, the American Psychiatric Association removed homosexuality from its list of mental disorders, followed closely by the American Psychological Association and the

National Association of Social Workers. At the 2004 CJLS retreat in Baltimore, where the issue was addressed by several psychiatrists and psychologists, it became clear that modern scientific thinking does not consider a homosexual orientation as one of choice. It certainly is not a "lifestyle" chosen from a shopping list of alternatives.

Particularly telling was the statement by Dr. Abba Borowich, a psychiatrist who has worked for more than two decades to reverse homosexuality in the Orthodox community where he is affiliated. He reported that although intensive therapies may be able to exert some movement on the Kinsey scale to make it possible for some gays to marry and have children, he has abandoned all efforts toward that end. Despite his religious commitment and professional history of some success, Dr. Borowich's experience with reversion and the creation of unhappy individuals and families has moved him to terminate his efforts to make it possible for homosexuals to live as heterosexuals. This is consonant with what we believe is the broader scientific consensus that not only do homosexuals not choose their sexual orientation but that it is essentially irreversible.[45]

In Israel the treatment of homosexuals has been transformed by legislation that decriminalizes homosexual intercourse, prevents discrimination based on sexual orientation in employment or the military and provides eligibility to same sex partners for various social and monetary benefits. The Knesset also passed the Prevention of Sexual Harassment Law that includes provision for civil and criminal relief to victims.[46] This transformation in the conservative social environment of Jewish society in Israel, despite its setting in the Middle East, its population's roots and the influence of Orthodox rabbinic authority, has resulted in a gap between the halakhah and public law that invites attention. How much more so should Conservative Jews in the United States and other parts of the West attempt to bring halakhah, their sexual morality and the law into agreement!

The changes that have occurred and continue to occur in public law in Western societies as more and more jurisdictions are acknowledging same-sex

---

[45] These arguments are presented forcefully and compellingly, with all the supporting scientific evidence, by Rabbis Dorff, Nevins and Reisner in their paper, "Homosexuality, Human Dignity and Halakhah."
[46] Alon Harel, "The Rise and Fall of the Israeli Gay Legal Revolution," *Columbia Human Rights Law Review* (spring 2000). The author's conclusion that the liberalization of the law has provoked a reaction in an essentially conservative society that will make further changes more difficult seems obvious. It does not alter the fact that discrimination in Israeli society against gay sexuality is no longer tolerated according to the law.

couples are the result of a process undertaken by legal authority. In Israel the amelioration of the legal standing of gays is reflected in the law as written by Jews and under which they live of their own choice. That is a powerful message to us that the halakhah, if it is not merely to be a frozen historical record but offer direction for contemporary Jews wherever they reside, must be impacted by this transformation in public law. This has been true in the past and efforts to block considered (due process) change in halakhah at this time only diminish its authority and render it irrelevant. To maintain in this day that gays who engage in same gender sex are criminals who deserve to be executed by stoning will in our view bring no glory to God, Torah or כלל ישראל [kelal Yisrael].

It seems to us that a remarkable change has taken place in the attitude of the Jewish community towards gays in recent times and this must cause an evolution in the halakhah. We are left, therefore, with the burden of finding a resolution within the Conservative movement that is theologically and morally consistent with a reasonable and acceptable concept of Jewish law.

More than a decade has passed since the Conservative movement through the United Synagogue and the Rabbinical Assembly has expressed its opposition to restrictions on homosexuals and welcomed them to the community. Despite that, the consensus reached by the CJLS in 1992 imposed limits on the roles gays may play in our community. That should be corrected at this time.

Why? What has changed since the 1992 CJLS deliberations? While "commitment ceremonies" were a part of the discussion, they were not the central focus. Since then, the movement for recognition of same-sex unions has been waged across the globe and political efforts to achieve rights for gay and lesbian partners, be it through actual marriage, health care, inheritance, etc., have flourished. Recently, courts in Canada, as well as California, Connecticut, Massachusetts, Hawaii, Maine, New Jersey, Vermont, and the District of Columbia, and a growing number of governments including Andora, Argentina, Belgium, Brazil, Croatia, the Czech Republic, Denmark, Finland, France, Germany, Iceland, Israel, Luxembourg, the Netherlands, New Zealand, Norway, Portugal, Slovenia, South Africa, Spain, Sweden, Switzerland and the United Kingdom have ruled that either same-sex unions or marriages must be civilly recognized. Some American municipalities have begun to offer same-sex marriages, although this is an ongoing legal debate. The category of "domestic partnership" has become widely accepted. A proposed constitutional amendment in the United States banning same-sex marriage acknowledges this changed reality. Opposition to same-sex marriage has been surprisingly combined with acceptance of domestic partnerships. And in a landmark case, the United States Supreme Court's 2003 decision in *Lawrence v. Texas,*[47] overturning *Bowers v. Hardwick,* struck down the "sodomy laws." This is a profound transformation of society, and much of it has taken place after 1992. Again, this is what halakhists call שינוי העיתים.

The idea of a same-sex couple living comfortably in society and having the option of raising children was not as pervasive in 1992 as it is today. Through the popular media of television and film the general culture has become accustomed to same-sex couples and their families in ways that were not imagined only a decade ago. Many newspapers now regularly include same-sex couples with the marriage announcements in the society pages. Additionally, we know much more about the viability of same-sex family life and child-rearing. Gays and lesbians have, in the last decade, been more active in suing for custody of children and the courts have examined (and commissioned) social-scientific studies concerning family relationships of gays and lesbians. These studies have shown that lesbians and gays are at least as successful as heterosexuals in forming stable relationships, that they are as interested in forming strong unions and raising children as heterosexuals, and that the children born to or raised by gay or lesbian parents are no less "normal" that those born to or raised by heterosexual parents.[48]

In summary, the CJLS could not envision in 1992 that the *ideal* of the Jewish family could be fulfilled in a gay or lesbian context. Rather, it struggled with exempting those who could not fulfill that ideal from the responsibilities of our general expectations. The CJLS decided that concerns for marriage and children outweighed the needs of gay and lesbian Jews. The Consensus Statement itself was only intended to be temporary until further study could take place, as argued strongly by Rabbi Dorff at the time. It no longer reflects the needs of our community, nor our reading of halakhah and God's will.

In our view, the Torah prohibitions of same-gender male or female sexual relations as תועבה, abhorrent acts, are not consistent with current knowledge almost universally accepted in the scientific community about the origins of

[47] 539 U.S. 558 (2003).

[48] Some argue that gay and lesbian families are statistically *safer* environments for children since there is a lower reported incidence of domestic abuse in same-sex families. See, for example, Charlotte J. Patterson, "Family Relationships of Lesbians and Gay Men," *Journal of Marriage and the Family* 62 (November 2000): 1052-1069, for a thorough overview of recent studies through 2000, including an extensive bibliography. See also, though now dated, Laura Benkov, *Families We Choose: Lesbians, Gays, Kinship* (New York: Columbia University Press, 1991).

homosexuality, its natural occurrence in a given proportion of the population, its essential irreversibility and that it is neither a sickness nor a choice. The תועבה designation and subsequent halakhic prohibitions no longer reflect the legal treatment of gays in Israel or in most other Western countries and do not represent the perception of them in most of the Jewish community. This disparity between what the law allows and what halakhah has heretofore denied, between the halakhah and general perceptions about same gender sexuality, should be a cause for concern to everyone who would live according to a code of Jewish religious law.

Section Seven: The Systemic Question

We have suggested a way of reading פרשת עריות where the reasons for the prohibition would no longer apply today. We have argued that the context of same-sex relations in our time is not the same as that known by the Torah and the Rabbis, and that the criminalization that the Rabbis codified can no longer be maintained. This conviction is driven by the overwhelming consensus of scientific and sociological findings on homosexuality. And yet we recognize that the precedented view of the Rabbis has been that the Torah meant to prohibit all acts of משכב זכר, and that it is a bold step to suggest a limitation or the non-applicability of what the Rabbis understood to be דאורייתא.

We agree that the text of the Torah is unchangeable, but the meaning that the text holds, that is, its halakhic meaning, is explained by the rabbis. An analogy from American constitutional law is that while the judiciary cannot amend the Constitution, it can reinterpret its meaning. The duty of the judiciary to determine the legal meaning of the Constitution is as basic to American constitutional law as is the duty of the rabbis to determine the meaning of the Torah. We fully understand that a change in understanding of the Torah's halakhic meaning is a major change in precedented rabbinic law. Only a significant difference in historical circumstances, such as the case before us, could merit such a change. We believe, however, that in this case the change in historical circumstance is adequate to justify a change in the halakhah.

The systemic question arises whether we, as modern-day rabbis, have the authority to offer our own readings or limitations of the Torah if they are at variance with the precedented interpretations of the Sages. One must usually follow precedent in order to retain the integrity of the legal system. But there are circumstances when precedent can be overturned. Rabbi Joel Roth defines those circumstances as "compelling reason," that is, when, in the judgment of the decisor, there is sufficient justification for overturning precedent.[49] We feel there is ample compelling reason in this case.

Throughout the history of Jewish law, rabbis have found it necessary over and over again to limit or exclude the applicability of ancient legislation when faced with changed circumstance or "compelling reason." A classic example is the limitation of the law of the rebellious son (Deut. 21:18-21) by means of interpretive exclusion. The *mi'utim* offered by the Rabbis in this discussion go so far as to depart from the obvious *pshat* of the text. Specifically, the Rabbis argue that the phrase איננו שמע בקלנו (he does not listen to our voice), since קל is singular rather than plural, excludes any child whose mother and father do not have voices identical in tone and timber. The Rabbis themselves recognize that this virtually eliminates the law when they say immediately after: בן סורר ומורה לא היה ולא עתיד להיות, the stubborn and rebellious son never was and never will be.[50]

The Rabbinic treatment of the law of the apostate city (Deut. 13:13-19) similarly renders it inoperative through the process of *mi'ut*.[51] Yet another example is the mishnaic treatment of the man who had suffered a seminal emission, a *zav* (Lev. 15:1-18). Rabbi Akiva rules that if a man has eaten or drunk anything prior to seeing the signs of *zivah*, the flow can be attributed to that and exempt him from the necessary purification rites. He maintains his view even when challenged that this eliminates the possibility of anyone ever being considered a zav.[52]

An example of rabbinic limitation of an explicit Toraitic law due to cultural change is the treatment of the proscription of the Canaanites (Deut. 20:15-18). The Torah says: "Thus [referring to the previous legislation about offering terms of surrender] you shall deal with all the towns that do not belong to nations hereabout. In the towns of the latter peoples, however, which the Lord your God is giving you

---

[49] See Joel Roth, *The Halakhic Process: A Systemic Analysis* (New York: Jewish Theological Seminary, 1986), ch. 4.

[50] Sanhedrin 71a. The statement of Rabbi Jonathan in the gemara that disagrees with this conclusion stating that he saw a בן סורר ומורה and sat on his grave does not mitigate the gemara's conclusion. R. Jonathan's statement is appended as a minority voice against the gemara's bold conclusion. Alternatively, it is a way of saying that although we do not adjudicate this law, there are indeed people who deserve the punishment of בן סורר ומורה. And even assuming that R. Jonathan is referring to an actual adjudicated case, subsequent Jewish law has completely disregarded this legislation.

[51] Sanhedrin 71a.

[52] Mishnah Zavim 2:2.

as a heritage, you shall not let a soul remain alive. No, you must proscribe them—the Hittites and the Amorites, the Canaanites and the Perizzites, the Hivites and the Jebusites—as the Lord your God has commanded you, lest they lead you into doing all the abhorrent things (תועבתם) that they have done for their gods and you stand guilty before the Lord your God." The Rabbis limited the application of this law because they could not believe that God would have commanded genocide of the native populations. And so the Sifrei teaches: אם עושים תשובה אין נהרגים, if they repent, we do not kill them.[53] That is, only unrepentant Canaanite idolaters are to be killed. The Torah's legislation is quite clear. But the Rabbis looked at the context of the law, and saw that the concern of Deuteronomy was with the danger of idolatry in the midst of ancient Israel. They reasoned that if that concern were mitigated by repentance on the part of the Canaanites, then the Torah's command of proscription would not apply. That is, if circumstances changed so that the practices of the Canaanites were no longer considered תועבה, and therefore their continued existence no longer posed a threat to the spiritual security of ancient Israel, then the legislation would no longer apply.[54]

This is precisely the type of mi'ut, based on a changed cultural context, that we are proposing here. Casual or promiscuous sex, whether heterosexual or homosexual, does indeed threaten the values of the Torah. However, consecrated societally recognized same-sex unions, which did not exist in the ancient world but do in ours, are not a threat to the Torah's values; on the contrary, such unions support them.

These mi'utim cited above were not considered to be takkanot in the framework of the halakhic system.[55] They derived their authenticity from the interpretive powers of the Rabbis to reread and rework an earlier understanding of

---

[53] Sifrei Deuteronomy to ch. 20, siman 102. For a discussion of the modern critical approach as well as that of rabbinic literature, see Excursus 18 in Jeffrey Tigay, *The JPS Torah Commentary: Deuteronomy* (Philadelphia: Jewish Publication Society, 1996), pp. 470-472.

[54] Cf. also the discussion on Hullin 17a of stabbed meat that had been considered תועבה, discussed above.

[55] See התקנות בישראל, שציפנסקי, ישראל (Jerusalem, Mosad Harav Kook, תשנ"א) for a fuller discussion of the subject. For example, the abandonment of the מים המאררים by Rabbi Yohanan b. Zakkai is not considered a takkanah because his decision was based on a verse from Scripture (p. שסז). The examples cited here are not included in Schepansky's comprehensive list of takkanot. See also Menachem Elon, "Takkanot," (*Enclyclopaedia Judaica* 15:714) and "Interpretation," (*Encyclopaedia Judaica* 8:1414) where he distinguishes between legislation derived from exegesis or midrash and takkanot.

the text in their effort to hear God's voice in their time.[56] The mi'ut that we offer in this paper is far less bold.

Two further examples of rabbinic limitation (mi'ut) of an explicit Toraitic law due to cultural/societal change (shinui ha'itim) are presented in Mishnah Sotah 9:9:

> משרבו הרצחנים בטלה עגלה ערופה--משבא אלעזר בן דינאי ותחינה בן
> פרישה היה נקרא, חזרו לקרותו בן הרצחן. משרבו המנאפים פסקו המים המרים.
> When murderers increased they cancelled the breaking of the heifer's neck. This was when Elazar ben Dinai came, who was at first called Tehinah ben Perishah but was then called ben Harazhan (son of the murderer). When adulterers increased they stopped the [ritual of the] bitter waters.

Deuteronomy 21:1-9 commands the breaking of a heifer's neck [eglah arufah] in a ceremony to relieve a town of blood-guilt when the identity of a murderer is unknown. The Mishnah limits the applicability of the command so that it does not apply in a society, such as the Rabbis knew, where the number of murderers has increased. The Torah envisioned a circumstance where there was no one in the world who knew who the murderer was. The Rabbis recognized that their world was a different world from that of the Torah. They even date the sociological change to the time of Elazar ben Dinai, who they note became known as Son of the Murderer. Elazar ben Dinai is remembered by Josephus as an active first century Zealot.[57] The Rabbis reflected on the experience of the Great Revolt as a period of great bloodshed that changed the nature of society. In their world, the mitzvah of the Torah could not apply. It was limited to a different historical circumstance.

The second example from the mishnah in Sotah addresses the ritual of the sotah itself, the bitter waters that an accused adulterous had to drink, as commanded by Numbers 5:11-31. The Mishnah teaches that the ritual of the bitter waters applies in a societal circumstance where adulterers were rare. As explained in the Gemara (Sotah 47b), the efficacy of the ritual could only apply where men were free from guilt, based on a non-contextual interpretation of Numbers 5:31: "The man shall be clear of guilt." The Rabbis argued that in their day men

---

[56] As Rabbi Roth has explained: "The scope of rabbinic authority is, in theory, unbounded. The meaning of the Torah in every generation, and with it the determination of the will of God for that generation, is entrusted to the hands of that generation. Rabbinic interpretation of the law is, as it were, the never-ending revelation of the will of God" (Roth, Halakhic Process, p. 133).

[57] Ant. 20:2-4,121,161; Wars 2:235, 253.

committed adultery in greater numbers, and in such a changed societal context the Torah's law of the Ordeal could not apply. This example is particularly interesting because the assumption that in their day adultery was more common than in the Torah's day is a difficult claim to prove, since adultery, by nature, is usually concealed. An increase in violence, as in the first case in the Mishnah, should be more readily apparent. Nevertheless, the Rabbis still assumed the discretion to make a sociological judgment, both about their own times, as well as the Torah's time. That judgment is an extra-legal factor, which they chose to consider in order to limit the application of Torah commands in their time.

Two rabbinic "legal fictions" that limit the applicability of biblical laws because of changed societal circumstances are the *prosbul* and the *heter iska*. Deuteronomy 15:2 orders the remission of loans in the sabbatical year. The basic principle behind the law is relief of the poor. However, by the time of the Rabbis, society was no longer barter-based but currency-based. In a currency-based economy, automatic remission of debts every seven years had an adverse effect on the poor, since no one would grant them credit in the sixth year of the cycle. The prosbul, instituted by Hillel, is a device whereby the court is a party to the loan, and the court's action is not cancelled by the sabbatical year. The intent of the Torah's command to remit debt was to protect the poor. In order to preserve the Torah's intent, the prosbul limits, indeed defeats, the Torah's law.

Similarly, the Torah forbids lending (at least to other Israelites) at interest (Exodus 22:24, Leviticus 25:35-37, Deuteronomy 23:20-21). Again, the basic principle is protection of the poor, that lenders not bleed them for interest in their time of need. However, in a barter-based economy like the Torah's, where lending was only practiced when there was a need, but not as a business of its own, the charging of interest could be considered an oppression of the poor. However, in a currency-based economy such as that known by the Rabbis, money itself was a commodity, bought and sold. Various halakhic solutions were developed over time to limit the applicability of the prohibition of lending at interest, since in such a world, lending at interest was not considered "usury." The most famous of these solutions is the heter iska, which establishes a partnership between lender and borrower so that the interest is considered as common profits. The application of the heter iska was extended by the CJLS in 1988, by a vote of eleven to one, so that a constructive heter iska was considered as operative in all transactions between Jews, and a specific document to that effect is no longer required.[58] Here

---

[58] Ben Zion Bergman, "A Question of Great Interest: May a Synagogue Issue Interest-Bearing Bonds?" *Responsa 1980-1990*, pp. 319-323.

we have a case of *lo ta'aseh,* a biblical prohibition, limited so completely as to have no practical application.

Two broad examples which might be deemed more philosophical are sacrifices (*korbanot*) and slavery. The Torah commands an elaborate system of sacrificial worship. Maimonides famously states in the Guide that sacrifices served a more primitive stage in relation to the Divine, but would not be appropriate in an age of philosophical thinking. While we do not know if that would be Maimonides' halakhic position were a Third Temple established, and while it is true that he treated the sacrificial code in full detail in the Mishneh Torah, nevertheless, we cannot but respect Maimonides' appreciation that the Torah addressed a particular time and society, even while it transmits eternal truths.

A major change in societal values was experienced in the nineteenth century when slavery was abolished in most of the civilized world. Although the Torah allows for slavery, Rabbi Sabato Morais, the founding president of the Jewish Theological Seminary, was a leading abolitionist voice in Philadelphia before and during the American Civil War. His absolute rejection of slavery was not inconsistent with his loyalty to the sanctity of the Torah. Rabbi Morais understood that the Torah's regulations regarding slavery were driven by the principle of the recognition of all human beings as images of the Divine. The Torah sought to regulate slavery, which was a societal given. No one living in the time of the Torah could envision a society without slavery. However, in Morais' time, the surrounding society was rejecting slavery. Therefore, the regulations permitting slavery ought not apply.

Just as the ancient Israelites could not envision a world without slavery, so could they not imagine a society where two men or two women could live together in a recognizable consecrated relationship and raise children. Just as the Rabbis understood that monetary interest could no longer be considered usury in a currency-based economy, so do we understand that same-sex relationships can no longer be considered תועבה. And just as the Rabbis limited the application of biblical laws (such as the proscription of the Canaanites, the eglah arufah and the sotah ordeal) because of changed societal circumstances, so are the rabbis of today able to limit the prohibition of משכב זכר and related laws in a society such as ours where same-sex couples are able to fulfill the intentions of the Torah, that is, to strive to achieve holiness in their relationships and to build families.

We have discussed the halakhah of משכב זכר and the grounds for excluding its applicability. An alternative approach to the question, argued by our colleagues Rabbis Dorff, Nevins and Reisner, makes a distinction between משכב זכר, understood strictly as anal intercourse between men, and other means of homosexual intimacy. They argue that only anal intercourse is forbidden by the Torah, while other forms of homosexual intimacy, while forbidden דרבנן, by the Rabbis, should be permitted today.[59]

The Talmud itself, in a fascinating gemara, discusses different forms of homosexual behavior. The Rabbis lived in the Greco-Roman world, and in that world anal intercourse was not the generally preferred means of male-to-male sexual contact. The more preferred, or more "honorable" means was what K.J. Dover describes as "intercrural intercourse," that is, through the thighs.[60] The Rabbis clearly recognized intercrural intercourse, as seen in the following passage from Niddah 13b:

ת"ר: הגרים והמשחקין בתינוקות מעכבין את המשיח..."משחקין בתינוקות" מאי היא?
אילימא משכב זכר--בני סקילה נינהו. אלא דרך אברים--בני מבול נינהו. אלא דנסיבי
קטנות דלאו אולודי נינהו.

Our Rabbi taught: Converts and those who make sport with children delay the coming of the Messiah.... "Those who make sport with children"—who does that refer to? If you wish to say that it refers to *mishkav zakhur* (male-male anal intercourse), [then you would be incorrect since] they are included among those who are executed by stoning [and therefore they cannot fall in the category of those who merely delay the coming of the Messiah]. If rather [you wish to say that it refers to those men who engage in sexual acts] between the limbs, [then you would also be incorrect since] they are included

---

[59] See Dorff, Nevins and Reisner, "Homosexuality, Human Dignity and Halakhah." This view was earlier presented by our colleague Rabbi Simchah Roth in "Dear David: Homosexual Relationships—A Halakhic Investigation." Though not formally submitted to the CJLS, this responsum was distributed to its members for informational purposes. Dated 2003, it can be accessed on the internet at: http://www.bmv.org.il/ab/dd.asp.

[60] Dover writes: "When courtship has been successful, the erastes [active partner] and the eromenos [passive partner] stand facing each one another; the erastes grasps the eromenos round the torso, bows his head onto or even below the shoulder of the eromenos, bends his knees and thrusts his penis between the eromenos's thighs just below the scrotum" (K.J. Dover, *Greek Homosexuality* [Cambridge: Harvard University Press, 2004], p. 98).

among those [who merit destruction] in the Flood [since, as R. Eliezer said above (Niddah 13a), whoever takes hold of his penis and makes water is as if he brings a Flood upon the world]. Rather, [the phrase] includes those who marry minors who cannot bear children [because they are too young].

This gemara presents here a hierarchy of actions which are frowned upon, but by decreasing levels of legislative control. Anal intercourse is a capital offense. Sexual acts that do not constitute sexual intercourse but involve spilling of seed (which is the ultimate effect of "between the limbs") are forbidden because they involve spilling of seed, an offense but not a capital offense. Reference is made to a statement of Rabbi Eliezer from the previous page in the Talmud: כל האוחז באמתו ומשתין כאילו מביא מבול לעולם, that one who takes hold of his penis and emits fluid/urinates is as though he had brought a flood upon the world. Rabbi Eliezer may have been simply referring to one who touches his penis during urination, but he is probably referring to masturbation, or is concerned that touching the penis during urination might lead to masturbation, and he is, thus, ultimately concerned with the spilling of seed. Finally, marrying young girls who will not be capable of having children for some time is not illegal, but discouraged as something that will delay the advent of the Messiah. That is not an actual spilling of seed, but it is still a waste of potential seed. The phrase דרך אברים is particularly interesting. It refers to what Dover describes as intercrural intercourse, a type of male-male sexual interaction that was not anal intercourse and includes the spilling of seed. This was not prohibited by the Torah, according to this gemara, but is prohibited by the Rabbis because of שכבת זרע, the spilling of seed.[61] One cannot imagine that the Rabbis would have made any real distinction between the prohibited nature of anal intercourse and intercrural intercourse. From the plain sense of the gemara, one knows that sexual activity, of any type, between men is forbidden. What is unclear is the source of the prohibition.

---

[61] The gemara in Niddah is concerned, in part, with the obligation to procreate. We understand the prohibition of שכבת זרע as driven by that concern. There are traditions in the halakhic literature that relax the concern for שכבת זרע when the man is not avoiding thereby a marital union where there is at least the possibility of procreation. See Tosafot to Yevamot 34b, s.v. ולא, for the opinion of the Ri, that when there is no intention to desist from the mitzvah of פרו ורבו, then any kind of seminal emission within marital relations is permitted. The decisions that same-sex couples make with respect to having children are not so dissimilar from the decisions that heterosexual couples make, especially infertile ones who also need to avail themselves of various modern technologies. We do not see שכבת זרע as a barrier to same-sex intimacy, especially within consecrated unions.

Female-female relations are not forbidden under the definition of משכב זכר as anal sex. The Talmud prohibits it as מסוללות, "lewdness," although, as we have seen, the Sifra suggests that this may also be a דאורייתא prohibition.[62] However, what constitutes מסוללות, lewd and licentious behavior, is a cultural judgment that is subject to change as culture and society evolve. Forms of male homosexual behavior other than anal sex should be understood in the same way. The Torah forbids משכב זכר because it saw it as a תועבה. Since we no longer see homosexual behavior as a תועבה, and since today same-sex couples may form legally recognized unions, the application of the Torah's prohibition should be limited. Since the basic prohibition does not apply, other forms of homosexual intimacy are no longer prohibited. The debate among our learned colleagues about whether or not female homosexual behavior and other forms of male homosexual behavior besides anal sex is אסור מדאורייתא or אסור מדרבנן becomes academic because the mi'ut of the chief prohibition applies to the other forms of intimate behavior as well.[63] Unlike our colleagues Rabbis Dorff, Nevins and Reisner, we are not compelled to waive certain prohibitions because of the concern for human dignity, כבוד הבריות. The prohibition itself does not apply.

We agree with the arguments put forward by our colleagues that homosexuality should not exclude Jews from full participation and acceptance in the Jewish community and the synagogue. However, we do not concur with their judgment that the prohibition of משכב זכר, narrowly defined as anal sex, ought to be preserved. We are troubled by the proposed limitation on the forms of intimacy in a couple's private life. Since Rabbis Dorff, Nevins and Reisner are prepared to accept the legitimacy of same-sex couples, we do not see how they can limit their forms of intimate expression. This approach seems to go against the precedented halakhic view that all is permitted between husband and wife. The Talmud, on Nedarim 20b, specifically rejects the view that anal sex is prohibited, concluding that, כל מה שאדם רוצה לעשות באשתו עושה. משל לבשר הבא מבית הטבח רצה לאכלו במלח אוכלו צלי אוכלו מבושל אוכלו שלוק אוכלו וכן דג הבא מבית הצייד--"A man may do whatever he pleases with his wife [at intercourse]. A parable: Meat, which comes from the abattoir may be eaten salted, roasted, cooked or seethed, so with fish from the fishmonger."[64]

---

[62] Yevamot 76a. See Mishneh Torah, Hilkhot Issurei Biah 21:8, and S.A. Even HaEzer 20:2.

[63] Rabbis Dorff, Nevins and Reisner argue that these forms of intimacy are all rabbinic prohibitions; Rabbi Roth argues that they may be Toraitic. See their respective responsa approved by the CJLS.

[64] Nedarim 20b, translation from Michael Gold, *Does God Belong in the Bedroom?* (Philadelphia: Jewish Publication Society, 1992), p. 81.

Maimonides applies logic where the gemara applied pithy parable: אשתו של אדם מותרת היא לו. לפיכך כל מה שאדם רוצה לעשות באשתו עושה, "A wife is permitted to her husband. Therefore, whatever a man wishes to do with his wife he may do" (Hilkhot Issurei Bi'ah 21:9). Maimonides is doing more than simply quoting the gemara. He offers a logical argument for the law, as indicated by the word לפיכך, "therefore." Unrestricted intimacy is a logical consequence of the permittedness of the relationship of husband and wife. If their intimacy is restricted, then they are not fully permitted to each other. Maimonides did not neglect to offer his own views, many from the gemara as well, about recommended and non-recommended forms of intimacy. But from the perspective of halakhah alone, there were no restrictions on intimate behavior.[65] Logic did not permit any other view.

The argument suggested by Rabbis Dorff, Nevins and Reisner, that heterosexual intimacy is restricted by the observance of *niddah*, is not convincing. The whole basis of *taharat hamishpahah* [family purity] is the temporary restriction of what is usually permitted. That cannot be compared to the permanent restriction of one form of intimacy as suggested by our colleagues. We fear, as well, that a judgment involving a restriction of intimacy will not only be derided by the public as hypocritical, but will ultimately fail to answer the needs of our people that the Torah be explained in a way that is consistent with our understanding of God's will.

The practical difference between our approach and that of our colleagues Rabbis Dorff, Nevins and Reisner, is not restricted to the question of the permissibility of anal sex between men. We also differ on the question of the permission of intimate relations between Jews of the same-sex without a Jewish ceremony. Our colleagues specifically avoid ruling on the halakhic status of gay and lesbian relationships. We find, however, that one cannot consider the permissibility of a sexual act without reference to its context. Therefore, on the specific question of anal sex between men, Rabbis Dorff, Nevins and Reisner forbid in all circumstances whereas we permit in some circumstances. But on the more general question of intimate relations between Jews of the same sex, Rabbis Dorff, Nevins and Reisner permit without a ceremony whereas we require a sanctifying act. We elaborate on this requirement in the following section.

---

[65] Maimonides does restrict this permission to circumstances where there is no wasteful ejaculation. See above, n. 61, for our discussion of שכבת זרע. In our view, where there is no willful avoidance of procreation, there is no wasting of seed. However, whether or not ejaculation is permitted, it is clear that Maimonides and most of the major halakhic authorities permit all intimate contact between husband and wife.

Section Nine: The Requirement of Consecration

What determines the permissibility of a sexual act, in our view, is not the nature of the act but its context. For a heterosexual couple who are married בקידושין, in a Jewish marriage ceremony, all sexual acts are permissible in traditional Jewish sexual ethics. Absent consecration, sexual intimacy is forbidden by most halakhic authorities. Acccording to the Rabbinical Assembly's 1996 *This Is My Beloved, This is My Friend: A Rabbinic Letter on Intimate Relations* edited by Rabbi Dorff, "Judaism posits marriage as the appropriate context for sexual intercourse....Only marriages can attain the holiness and communal sanction of *kiddushin* because it is the marital context which holds out the most promise that people can live by those views and values [previously articulated in the document] in their intimate relationships. Judaism would therefore have us refrain from sexual intercourse outside marriage."[66]

At the same time, the Rabbinic Letter acknowledges "that many Jews are engaging in sexual relations outside of marriage." Section C of the Letter addresses nonmarital intimate relations that are loving and committed. While nonmarital intimate relations are not given halakhic sanction, the individuals in such relationships are still bound by the sexual ethics and values, among them modesty, honesty, fidelity, concern for health and safety, that were already stated in the Letter in relation to married couples. In our view, this was the most important and controversial part of the document, that halakhic guidance was being offered for relations that were not halakhically validated. "Jewish norms in sexual matters, like Jewish norms in other areas," the Letter argues, "are not an 'all or nothing' thing. Certainly, failing to abide by Judaism's command that we restrict sexual relations to marriage does not excuse one from trying to live by the concepts and values that Judaism would have us use in all of our relationships, including our intimate ones."[67]

These same values are incumbent on same-sex couples according to the Rabbinic Letter on Intimate Relations. "Gays and lesbians," it says in conclusion to its discussion of homosexuality, "like heterosexuals, have the duty to strive to live by the values articulated in Section A [of the Letter] in all of their relationships, including their sexual ones."[68] Jewish sexual ethics require that both same-sex and

---

[66] Dorff, *This Is My Beloved,* p. 31.
[67] Ibid., p. 31.
[68] Ibid., p. 42.

heterosexual couples be subject to the same behavioral standard. Like adulterous, incestuous and coercive relations among heterosexuals, gay promiscuity and casual sexual encounters are to be condemned "since they involve little or no love or commitment."[69] Committed and long-term intimate relationships among gays and lesbians should be subject to the same values and principles that are incumbent upon heterosexual couples.

We further recognize, as guided by the Rabbinic Letter, that marriage is the halakhically valid context for intimate relations. The Letter acknowledges that unmarried couples "may care deeply for each other, especially in a long-term relationship, but their unwillingness to get married usually signifies that they are not ready to make a life-long commitment to each other."[70] In this view, *it is precisely the consecration of a long-term commitment that establishes the context for permitted intimate relations.* We call, therefore, for appropriate rituals of sanctification when same-sex individuals wish to live in an intimate relationship in accordance with halakhah.

At this point in time [2006], the possibility of same-sex marriage is available in some jurisdictions, but not in others. Civil unions, however, are increasingly available as a way to recognize the legal, spiritual and intimate relationships of same-sex couples. Because of דינא דמלכותא דינא, the respect given to the law of the land, we cannot authorize rabbis and cantors to solemnize same-sex marriages where the civil jurisdiction forbids. But we do authorize ritual celebration as far as civil law permits. Some form of Jewish ceremony will always be available.[71] The concept of שותפות (partnership) in Jewish law, on which there is an extensive literature, is available to structure same-sex unions and the responsibilities of contracting partners. The substance of the rites associated with same-sex commitment ceremonies and their dissolution is evolving. However, a Jewish ceremony is required to establish the consecration of the union. Without any consecration, the context to permit intimate relations has not been created.[72]

---

[69] Ibid., p. 30.

[70] Ibid., p. 31.

[71] Whether the resultant union is called a "marriage" or something else is a matter that we defer to the civil jurisdictions.

[72] The Mishnaic law of the androginos, one with both male and female genitalia, states that the androginos marries a woman but does not marry a man (Bikkurim 4:2 and Yevamot 8:6). This is because the androginos is ספק איש ספק אישה, possibly a man and possibly a woman. The possibility of a woman marrying another woman was preferable to the possibility of a man marrying another man, since in the latter case there would be a violation of משכב זכר while the prohibitions of female-female relations are, at worst, less severe. We learn from this that not

Same-sex couples should be encouraged to enter recognizable consecrated relationships and should be treated as married couples in Jewish law. Intimate relations are permitted in such contexts. Same-sex couples not in recognizable consecrated relationships are duty-bound to observe the many other requirements of Jewish sexual ethics as enumerated in the Rabbinic Letter on Intimate Relations of 1996.

Section Ten:
פסק דין --CONCLUSION

Jewish law has prohibited intimate relations between two men or two women because intimate relations are traditionally permitted only within the context of marriage, and a societally recognized same-sex union was never an option before our time. It is now, because homosexual relations are no longer considered an abomination. The term תועבה as used in the Torah to describe many proscribed actions, including gay sex, was not absolute but relative to society and time. The halakhic system recognizes that certain realities change through time. The new contemporary reality of a same-sex couple in a recognizable consecrated relationship should be excluded from the Torah's and subsequent halakhic prohibitions. This "exclusion" is called a mi'ut in halakhic parlance. There are a number of examples where the Rabbis limit, through mi'ut, the application of legislation from the Torah, which we cite in our responsum. However, like heterosexual relations, same-sex relations are permitted in the context of a recognizable consecrated union. Not only does this reflect a changed reality; it also accords with traditional Jewish sexual ethics, especially as articulated by the Rabbinical Assembly in its 1996 Letter on Intimate Relations. Consecrated unions establish the context where sexual intimacy can achieve holiness and be permitted by halakhah. The Torah's prohibition, then, does not apply in our new context.

In traditional midrashic parlance we might express our argument as follows: את זכר לא תשכב...תועבה היא. מתי לא תשכב? בזמן שתועבה היא. "Do not lie with a man...it is an abomination." When does the prohibition apply? When it is considered an abomination. However, when societal perceptions have changed

---

only did the Mishnah not consider the possibility of celibacy for the androginos, but also that this constituted a circumstance where two people of the same gender, specifically women, could marry one another (נשא). The concept of "marriage" then, was not absolutely restricted to the unions of men with women by the Mishnah.

and homosexual relations are no longer considered abominations, the prohibition disappears.

Therefore:

1. Intimate relations between two men or two women are permitted within the context of a recognizable consecrated relationship.
2. Members of the Rabbinical Assembly and the Cantors Assembly may officiate at same-sex unions to the extent permitted by civil law.
3. Gay or lesbian Jews who are otherwise qualified may be ordained and serve as rabbis or cantors.

APPENDIX 3
Solomon Schechter and the Ambivalence of Jewish Wissenschaft

SOLOMON SCHECHTER WAS THE LEADING JEWISH SCHOLAR of his day. Born in 1850 in the small Rumanian town of Focsani, Schechter studied rabbinics in Vienna and Berlin with   the central figures of the *Wissenschaft* movement in Jewish scholarship. His teachers included Isaac Hirsch Weiss and Meir Ish Shalom (Friedmann) in Vienna and Mortiz Steinschneider in Berlin[1]. Finding himself very uncomfortable in Germany due to the prevailing anti-Semitism of its scholarly world, Schechter immigrated to England. There, in 1890, he became the resident scholar in rabbinics at the University of Cambridge. His numerous publications, popular and technical, his discovery of the Cairo Genizah in 1896, and his appointment to the presidency of the Jewish Theological Seminary of America in 1902 all testify to his scholarly preeminence. Schechter's biography illustrates the drama of modern Jewry from its beginnings in small village life, through a bittersweet education in Germany, to settlement in the New World.[2]

Though he was one of the most influential he was also one of the most enigmatic figures in turn-of-the-century Jewry. His greatest legacy was the formation of an institution where Jewish scholarship would flourish in the context of a rabbinic seminary. Yet this double focus engaged him in the ambiguities and contradictions of modern life. The German-educated Cambridge professor once confessed that "the old Adam still asserts itself in me,"[3] the Adam of a young boy growing up among Habad Hasidim in Rumania. While Schechter embraced *Wissenschaft des Judentums*, the new academic study of Judaism, he furiously opposed the "higher criticism" of the Bible. He struggled against both anti-Jewish bias in the secular academic world, and the Reform movement in the Jewish world, which accepted many of the non-Jewish accusations against traditional Judaism. And the task of defending Jewish tradition along with his traditional loyalties prevented him from fully endorsing the critical inquiry central to *Wissenschaft des Judentums*.

1. Rabbinic Scholar and Polemicist
Isaac Hirsch Weiss and Meir Friedmann, Schechter's primary teachers in Vienna, were pioneers in the creation of critical editions of rabbinic texts. Applying the discipline of philology, they turned the study of Judaism into an academic "science." A text now demanded comparision to extant manuscripts and different versions; context was determined by literary and historical background which explained why the text was written, by whom, and what role was played by its society and history; meaning resulted from comparative linguistic analysis. This program of *Wissenschaft des Judentums* set forth by Leopold Zunz and his associates in the early nineteenth century defined the

work of Weiss and Freidmann and much of Schechter's scholarship, which were devoted chiefly to the establishment of the correct reading of classic texts.

Schechter's scholarly writings emphasized philologic analysis to determine the correct readings of texts, while much of his popular English writing was a polemic against the higher criticism of the Bible. "Lower" and "higher" criticism, terms used by Christian biblical scholars, with "lower" referring to the determination of the correct readings and meanings, and "higher" referring to the establishment of context and authorship, were the divisions of this scholarly practice. The "lower" criticism was the fundamental work upon which the theories of "higher" criticism were built. The adjective "higher" also hints at the belief in the conclusiveness of historical analysis. That Schechter's popular writings were a polemic against the conclusions of higher biblical criticism is most evident in his two most famous books, the first volume of the *Studies in Judaism*, and *Some Aspects of Rabbinic Theology*, both consisting of previously published articles in the English *Jewish Quarterly Review* around the turn of the century. [4]

Most religious Jews had difficulty in accepting the higher criticism of the Bible which in the late nineteenth century produced the Documentary Hypothesis of Pentateuchal origins. The Five Books of Moses, it was proposed, were not a unitary document, but a collection of several different writings divided into the strands J, E, P, and D according to philological analysis of sources, and only brought together in its present form perhaps an entire millennium after the traditional reckoning. This theory was not openly accepted by the community of Jewish studies until the latter half of the twentieth century. [5] In Schechter's day the theory was generally rejected even by those who, like Schechter, were steeped in the philological study of rabbinic texts. But rather than defend the Mosaic authenticity of the Pentateuch, Schechter devoted his popular English writings to a defense of rabbinic Judaism, which was most threatened by the "higher critics." Julius Wellhausen, in his 1878 treatise on the Documentary Hypothesis, explained how the priestly and later rabbinic concept of the "law thrusts itself in everywhere; it commands and blocks up the access to heaven; it regulates and sets limits to the understanding of the divine working on earth. As far as it can, it takes the soul out of religion and spoils morality." [6]

While there is nothing new in this judgment against rabbinic Judaism, which was often articulated by Christian polemicists, its restatement by Wellhausen was particularly painful for traditional Jews like Schechter who had been trained as scientific philologists. Wellhausen's views coincided with the decline of tolerance among the educated and the increasing influence of racist doctrines. The word "anti-Semitism" was created by Wilhelm Marr in 1879 in an attempt to give racialism an "element of the pseudoscientific," as Peter Pulzer explains, "the up-to-date, the apparently objective, and the dialectal in this six penny version of Darwin." [7] Heinrich von Treitschke and Houston Stewart Chamberlain, both respected academics, added historical arguments to the "problem of the Jews." [8] The 1870s and 1880s had shown a surprising resurgence of anti-Semitism in Germany which was not condemned by the government or the educated classes. The anti-Jewish feeling carried into general academic discourse. As Ismar Schorsch describes, "Generally Protestant scholarship portrayed Rabbinic Judaism in terms of the unbearable yoke of the Law, the transcendence of God, the abandonment of prophetic religion, national particularism, and soulless piety."[9] The "transcendence of God" was seen as a negative characteristic in the latter half of the nineteenth century when the immanence of God in Christianity (through Jesus) was seen as superior to the perceived coldness of God's transcendence in Judaism.[10] For them, Christian love was preferable to Jewish law.

Wellhausen's negative appraisal of religious law was echoed by the Reform movement which had accepted much of his critique. Emil G. Hirsch, a leading American Reform rabbi at the turn of the century, writes concerning the influence of higher criticism on Reform Judaism: "The Pentateuch is not the work of one period....The original content of Judaism does not consist in the law and its institutions, but in the ethical monotheism of the prophets. Legalism is foreign to Judaism."[11] Traditional Jews more committed to the legal aspects of the Pentateuch than their Reform counterparts were troubled by Wellhausen's conclusions. His views of Pentateuchal legalism were central to his understanding of the composition of the Pentateuch. While the early J and E sources provided the world with its loftiest ideals, he claimed, the late D source and even later P source imposed an oppressive cultic legalism upon the Pentateuch and the religion of Israel. The conclusion of this thesis, as read by Jews and Christians alike, was that after the constant struggles of the prophets this cultic legalism was finally overcome by Jesus, who restored the original purity which had been lost. Thus Wellhausen not only attacked Judaism but the Torah itself. His theories, which challenged the foundations of Judaism, claiming it was an aberration, had the authority of science. The scientific force of this religious message was very powerful, convincing both Jews and Christians. The response of Reform Jews was to develop a strategy of rejecting the redemptive role of Jesus while seeking to restore true prophetic idealism.

Schechter, a traditionally observant Jew and a distinguished scholar, was profoundly agitated by Wellhausen's conclusions. His writings testify to his need to show that Wellhausen was wrong. For Schechter, the Law is not stifling but the highest form of religion. "The motive of love," argued Schechter, "the privilege of bearing witness to God's relationship to the world, the attainment of holiness in which the Law educated Israel, as well as...the joy felt by the Rabbis in the performance of the Law and the harmony which the Rabbis perceived in the life lived according to the Torah, were the true sources of Israel's enthusiasm for the law."[12] "Whatever meaning the words of the Apostle may have, when he speaks of the curse of the Law," writes Schechter, referring just as much to his Christian contemporaries as to Paul, "it is certain that those who lived and died for it considered it as a blessing. To them it was the effluence of God's mercy and love."[13] In an even more obviously polemical passage, Schechter writes:

On the one side, we hear the opinions of so many learned professors, proclaiming *ex cathedra*, that the Law was a most terrible burden, and the life under it the most unbearable slavery, deadening body and soul. On the other side we have the testimony of a literature extending over about twenty-five centuries, and including all sorts and conditions of men, scholars, poets, mystics, lawyers, casuists, schoolmen, tradesmen, workmen, women [*sic*], simpletons, who all, from the author of the 119th Psalm to the last pre-Mendelssohnian writer — with a small exception which does not even deserve the name of a vanishing minority — give unanimous evidence in favour of this Law, and of the bliss and happiness of living and dying under it — and this, testimony of people who were actually living under the Law, not merely theorising upon it, and who experienced it in all its difficulties and inconveniences.[14]

Schechter tries throughout his writings to explain that Jewish law is the fundamental redeeming aspect of classical Judaism, almost parallel to the role of Jesus for Christianity. Observance of the law establishes divine immanence, not distance. Anyone who knows anything about Judaism, argues Schechter, can see that this is true.

2. Biblical Critic and Defender of the Faith

Solomon Schechter was committed to *Wissenschaft*. He did not oppose the methods of higher criticism only its conclusions. This is evident in three of his studies (one a published address from 1899, one an unpublished manuscript in four parts from 1900, and one a published sermon from 1903), which will reveal Schechter's very ambivalent attitude towards biblical criticism. While always supporting scholarly inquiry, Schechter sought to check what he saw as "excesses" in higher criticism.

In "The Study of the Bible," the third essay of the second volume of the *Studies in Judaism*, Schechter articulates his approach towards biblical scholarship better than anywhere else. He delivered the paper as his Inaugural Lecture as Professor of Hebrew at Jews' College of the University of London on January 26, 1899,[15] and delivered a revised version of the same essay before the American Bible Conference on December 7, 1904.[16] In the paper Schechter divides the biblical critics into two schools, an "old school" and a "new school." Both schools are "critical." The "new school" is Wellhausen and his followers who understand the law only as "priestly fetich," while the "old school" more seriously considers the problem of the "compatibility of a real living faith with a hearty devotion to ceremonial law."[17] The "old school" consists of "Ewald, Bleek, Dillman, Strack, Kittel, and many other men of prominence, none of whom could be suspected of being blind followers of tradition. They all accepted the heterogeneous composition of the Pentateuch, and cheerfully took part in the difficult task of its proper analysis."[18] Higher criticism itself was not objectionable. Schechter could respect scholars who treated Judaism with respect, even if they held to the Documenetary Hypothesis. His difficulty was not with higher criticism itself as much as with the conclusions of the members of its "new school." Schechter would not align himself with either school,[19] but by focusing on the academic qualifications of the "old school" he seems to imply that as a professor he will appeal to scholarly research rather than dogmatic faith.

Even if he at times respected it, Schechter refused to teach biblical criticism himself. Announcing that he will focus his lectures on the Hebrew language and the content of the Bible rather than critical theory, Schechter writes:

> I shall be more helpful to the student by lecturing *on* the Bible than by lecturing *about* the Bible. For the great fact remains that the best commentary on the Bible is the Bible itself... I think every student will agree that the best exposition of the "Priestly Code" is to be found in Ezekiel, that the most lucid interpretation of Isaiah is to be sought in certain portions of the Psalms, and that, if we were to look for an illustration of the ideals of the Book of Deuteronomy, we could do no better than study the Books of Chronicles and certain groups of the Psalms. To use a quaint old expression applied to Scripture: "Turn it and turn it over again, for the All is therein," both its criticism and its history. Introductions to the Old Testament, Lives and Times of the various prophets, and histories of the Canon, are excellent things in their own way; but unless we are prepared to exchange the older blind faith for the newer parrot-like repetitions of obscure critical terms, they should not be read, and, indeed, cannot be read with profit, before we hae made ourselves masters of the twenty-four books of the Old Testament in the original.[20]

From Schechter's perspective, the study of biblical criticism should be postponed until one has already mastered the Hebrew Bible, as did Schechter himself.[21] The average student is not qualified to study biblical criticism because he does not know the Bible well enough to judge the criticism. Biblical scholarship is only useful insofar as it explains the text. But Schechter believed that the text was being sidestepped in favor of grandiose theories on the development of Jewish religion. Now Schechter surely knew that Wellhausen knew the Bible in its entirety quite well. His concern, here voiced as the concern of a teacher, was that people were accepting Wellhausen's conclusions without testing them against the Bible itself.

The "new school" of biblical criticism itself championed a methodology which ripped apart the integrity of the text. Schechter, who saw the Bible as a literary whole, was enraged by the critics who, in his mind, sought to reedit the Bible since they could not understand the meaning of the original editors. Schechter wanted his students to let the Bible speak for itself first before they "tore it apart." They should learn Hebrew before they argue with the authors and editors of the Bible. Since Schechter believed that so much of biblical criticism was wrong, to read criticism without a thorough knowledge of the Bible would give one the wrong impression of the Bible.[22] The "older blind faith" is preferable to its newer replacements.

One can understand why Schechter might insist upon a thorough knowledge of the original literature in the original language before criticism is applied. Not only is that a sound educational method, but it describes Schechter's own education. Schechter was born in a small village in Rumania and studied rabbinics in the traditional *yeshiva* (talmudical academy) until his twenty-fourth year, when he moved to Vienna to study at the Bet Midrash of Meir Friedmann, Isaac Hirsch Weiss, and Adolph Jellinek, who trained him in the critical study of rabbinic texts.[23] From Vienna Schechter went to Berlin to study at the *Hochschule für die Wissenschaft des Judentums,* where he continued his training in textual criticism with Israel Lewy. Berlin also offered Schechter the opportunity of studying with Mortiz Steinschneider. Thus, Schechter only immersed himself in *Wissenschaft des Judentums* after years of study of the texts themselves in their traditional settings. For Schechter criticism is valuable only once one understands the subject.

Schechter's reluctance to teach biblical criticism did not mean that he denied all of its tenets (although he certainly denied the Documentary Hypothesis). "That tradition cannot be maintained in all its statements need not be denied," he says. "The Second Isaiah, for instance, is a fact; not less a fact is it that Solomon cannot be held responsible for the skepticism of the Book of Ecclesiastes, nor can David claim authorship of the whole of the Psalms for himself. The question at present, however, is not…whether tradition was not possibly mistaken in this or that respect, but whether it contains elements of truth at all."[24] While the value of the tradition may not have been the question in the minds of Schechter's students in a Bible class, it was the question Schechter wished to address. Schechter was willing to admit that certain traditions of biblical authorship were incorrect. The book of Isaiah is not by one author named Isaiah, Solomon did not write the book of Ecclesiastes, and David did not write all the Psalms. But just because there are some mistakes in tradition does not mean that tradition is useless. Here Schechter's posture of defending rabbinic Judaism becomes, curiously, a priority of biblical study. One notices as well that Schechter's examples of the tradition's errors in biblical authorship are all from the non-Pentateuchal sections of the Bible. He maintains his faith in the unified Mosaic Pentateuch.

"I am in no way opposed to criticism," Schechter emphasizes. "Criticism is nothing more than the expression of conscience on the part of the student, and we can as little dispense with it in literature as with common honesty in our dealings with our fellow-men." Having argued for the importance of studying Hebrew and the Bible, Schechter seems here to be more open to critical inquiry. Is Schechter implying that even a beginning reader of the Bible should not put aside his critical conscience? "Nor, I trust," he continues, "have I ever given way to anybody in my respect for most of the leaders of the various schools of Bible criticism, Lower as well as Higher. The attempt at an analysis of the Bible into its component elements, whether one agrees with its results or assumes a skeptical attitude towards them, is one of the finest intellectual feats of this century."[25] This amazing appreciation of biblical criticism immediately turns sour:

"Though a good deal of brutal vivisection is daily done by restless spirits whose sole ambition is to outdo their masters... [I]f tradition is not infallible, neither are any of its critics."[26] Schechter's point is that while he has nothing against critical thinking, and while he respects the biblical critics, they commit gross errors, and it would be wise for the student to avoid too much of such studies. Indeed, the evidence is sparse and their theories are mostly conjecture.[27]

While Schechter was a traditionalist in opposing the Documentary Hypothesis, an opinion which is somewhat muted in the 1899 paper but very clear in the later two writings, he was no dogmatist. He respected biblical criticism enough to read it seriously. As noted above, he drew a distinction between two schools of biblical criticism. The "new school" consisted of Wellhausen and others whom Schechter barely respected.[28] But there was the "old school" which he did respect, even though it consisted of men who all accepted the heterogeneous composition of the Pentateuch (i.e., the Documentary Hypothesis).[29]

The passage quoted from "The Study of the Bible" and other passages from Schechter's writings show that he had great respect for Kuenen, Dillman, Ewald, and others who were all leading figures in biblical criticism.[30] What he appreciated in such men was their respect for Israelite tradition and their sound philological methods. Schechter himself denied Davidic authorship for all the Psalms and argued along with Heinrich Graetz and other Jewish scholars for the Maccabean authorship of several Psalms, a very late dating. The discovery of the Hebrew Ben Sira text in the Genizah, however, provided evidence that Hebrew verse in the third century B.C.E. was already too evolved from biblical Hebrew to support the hypothesis of Maccabean Psalms, that is, biblical verse from the second century B.C.E. Schechter had to abandon the theory of Maccabean Psalms, "an hypothesis," he writes, "on which I built great hopes. This is a great disappointment to me."[31] He and Graetz had argued for Maccabean Psalms partly because they hoped such a hypothesis would provide evidence for a vibrant Hebrew culture continuing through Hellenistic times.[32]

Schechter accepted the notion that Pentateuchal law underwent extensive development. "The dietary laws," he writes in a different paper, "forming part of the holiness code, and probably kept only by the priests, now [in the time of Ben Sira] helped to hallow every Jewish home which came under the influence of the Synagogue."[33] While not challenging the Mosaic authorship of Leviticus, Schechter proposes that the law code was not followed to its full extent by the people until much later times. The dietary laws might have only been observed by the priests through the entire First Temple period. Only by the time of Ben Sira did the observance of *kashrut* become widespread. As Schechter himself maintained, he was by no means opposed to criticism.

In July of 1900 Schechter wrote four studies attempting to disprove the late dating of Deuteronomy and Leviticus. On July 10 he wrote "On Ruth IV" which deals with the Deuteronomic levirate laws as well as Ruth, and "The Case of the Egyptian who Blasphemed the Name, Leviticus XXIV: 10-23." On July 12 he wrote "The Date of the

Land Laws in Leviticus XXV," and on July 17, "On Deuteronomy XVII: 14-20 (The King)." All four studies were handwritten and apparently never prepared for publication, but preserved in manuscript among Schechter's papers.[34] They provide a rare example of Schechter's own approach to biblical criticism and elaborate views outlined to some extent in "The Study of the Bible."

    1. *"On Ruth IV"* begins with a quotation from S. R. Driver's commentary to Deuteronomy 25:10, where Driver maintains that the marriage of Ruth and Boaz is not a levirate marriage because Boaz is not Ruth's brother-in-law, as Deuteronomy would require.[35] "This passage is a fair representation," Schechter begins, "of the view which would naturally be taken of the chapter in Ruth by a scholar who had no special legal training."[36] But Schechter then goes on to show how obvious it is that Ruth 4 is dealing with a levirate marriage. "If it were true that this was a mere ordinary marriage, how could the name of the dead be raised up [as is made clear by verse 5]!"[37] Thus, in Schechter's acerbic remark against Driver he is saying: (1) only scholars specifically trained in Jewish law should engage in biblical criticism, and (2) even a non-legal scholar should be able to see the obvious, which Driver does not. Driver could not understand the marriage of Ruth and Boaz as a levirate marriage according to the Torah since he believed that Deuteronomy was written later than the Book of Ruth.

    Taking account of the differences between the Deuteronomic law and the narrative in Ruth, Schechter suggests that the account of the marriage of Boaz and Ruth in Ruth 4 represents "an extension of the Deuteronomic law [of levirate marriage]."[38] The differences between Deuteronomy and Ruth are summarized by Schechter:

(1) The Deuteronomic ceremony was full of meaning to those on whom it was enjoined, whereas the actions of Boaz and the next of kin are a mere piece of legal formality necessary to a valid conveyance of the rights but having no contemporary significance.
(2) The spitting – if the silence of the author of Ruth on such a point may trusted – is omitted.
(3) The woman no longer takes a part in the ceremony. Her presence is no longer necessary. He himself takes off his shoe.[39]

Schechter's argument is that by the time of Ruth the law had evolved so that the levir's acquisition of the deceased's wife and property could be performed by any number of next-of-kin, not solely brothers. In addition, the shame associated with the levir's refusal had all but vanished. As Schechter explains: "The spitting was abandoned and the ceremony itself was only retained in a modified form and without any connotation of contempt owning to the extraordinary weight which ancient laws always attach to the performance of the prescribed legal acts long after those acts have ceased to have any meaning."[40]

    At this point Schechter seems extremely liberal in his analysis, acknowledging evolution of law even within the Bible itself. He also is able to refer to statutes of the

Torah as "ancient laws," thus placing them in the context of general legal-historical studies. They are "ancient laws," not "laws commanded to Moses on Sinai."

"But one point [i]s to be noticed," Schechter continues, "if, even in the days of Ruth the ceremony had ceased to mean anything to the people, *a fortiori* it must have been unintelligible at the date to which the higher critics assign Deuteronomy."[41] The narrative in Ruth describes the remnant of an ancient law which is preserved in its earlier fuller form in Deuteronomy. Deuteronomy must be the original law, Schechter argues, since there the ceremony seems to have real meaning whereas in Ruth it is mere formality. Ruth represents the later development of this particular Deuteronomic legislation. How then can Deuteronomy be dated so far after Ruth? Rather, Deuteronomy must date from the ancient period of the inception of Israelite law, i.e., from the period of Moses.

As for the date of Ruth, Schechter suggests that "the book was written before the recovery of Deuteronomy in the reign of Josiah."[42] Besides the evolution of the legal ceremony to mere formality discussed above, the author of Ruth would not have known of the Deuteronomic passage itself at all since the Book of Deuteronomy had before King Josiah, been lost. The claim made by many scholars that the discovery of Josiah might have represented the composition of part of Deuteronomy rather than its mere recovery is not even discussed here by Schechter since he had already, at least in his mind, proved the Mosaic date for Deuteronomy by the analysis of legal evolution. Deuteronomy had to be written far earlier than Ruth since the legal ceremony needed time to develop. But Schechter admits that his proposal for the date of Ruth as before Josiah is "a slight presumption – I do not think it can be put higher that that."[43] The point he cared about was the early dating of Deuteronomy.

2. In *"The Case of the Egyptian who Blasphemed the Name," Leviticus XXIV: 10-23,* an Egyptian who blasphemes the name of God is sentenced to death. This passage is placed in Leviticus amidst a series of laws against murder and assault, including the famous *lex talionis*. Schechter quotes from *The Hexeteuch,* a commentary edited by J. Estlin Carpenter and G. Hartford-Battersby in the same year as Schechter's manuscript, 1900, which attributes the passage to the various different strands of P later to be edited into the final P source of the Pentateuch. The theory of different original authors, argue the higher critics, explains why the story of the blaspheming Egyptian should appear with other laws of no connection. The text we have is a composite. The story of the blaspheming Egyptian is from a different source than the assault laws, only later to be edited together.[44] After criticizing this argument, Schechter remarks that it is "a lamentable example of the hopeless incompetence of the critics and their methods to deal with the task they have been so ill advised as to undertake."[45]

Schechter's critique of the higher critics on this passage is that if the passage is incomprehensible, to argue that it is a composite does not solve the problem. If the text were a composite, then it should be easier to understand, given the many layers of editing the text must have passed through. "If the Tora[h] itself does not date from the time of Moses," Schechter argues, "how came anybody to insert this passage, and that at this place?...And it must be remembered that the critics allege that this part of the Tora[h] had been edited many times before reaching its final form –each time by men who never scrupled to add, excise or alter. How comes it then that such an obsolete and incomprehensible piece of antiquarian law was left in its place?"[46] The purpose of a commentary is to explain the text. If critical studies of philology and legal evolution help with that purpose, as Schechter did employ them, then that is acceptable. But if criticism only serves to make the text more incomprehensible, then it is useless.

If Schechter's biblical studies have any significance besides their illumination of Schechter's thinking, they can be seen as an early forerunner of contemporary biblical scholarship's critique of nineteenth-century scholarship. "The first several waves of modern biblical criticism," writes Robert Alter, "beginning in the nineteenth century, were from one point of view a sustained assault on the supposedly unitary character of the Bible, an attempt to break it up into as many pieces as possible, then to link those pieces to their original life contexts."[47] Schechter argued, along with contemporary biblical critics (or redaction critics as they are sometimes called), that the text has its own context. Whether or not the text originated as a unified document or several documents, it was edited into a final document which has logic and order. Difficulties in the text cannot be explained away as simply due to compositeness.

"That I am not overstating the matter," Schechter adds in his study of Leviticus 24:10-23, "is proved by the fact that the old Jewish commentators who had a practical knowledge of the Hebrew law make head or tail of the passage – to say nothing of the critics, than whom nobody could be more incompetent to deal with matters legal."[48] Even the traditional Jewish commentators, whose explicative ability Schechter respected far more than the higher critics', could not explain the context of this passage.

Schechter proceeds to solve the problem himself. The passage in Leviticus refers to a case which would have happened at the very beginning of Israelite occupation of the land, that is, at the time of the Conquest. Since there were many non-Israelites in the land, the question naturally arose as to whether they would be judged by Israelite law or not. When William the Conqueror invaded England, Schechter recounts, there was one law for the Normans and one for the Saxons. Not so with Israel, where all were judged by the same law, Israelite and non-Israelite. The Egyptian who blasphemed God was treated as if he were an Israelite blaspheming God. The issue at stake was not only God's honor, but the effectiveness of the legal code. The laws of murder and assault are included in this same section since they would also apply during the period of the Conquest when the land was not yet pacified. The context of the passage is the establishment of the legal system at the beginning of Israelite power. The passage must then date from the time of Moses and Joshua, not a later time as the higher critics suggest. The higher critics could not see this since they were committed to the late authorship of Leviticus. The Jewish commentators could not see the context either since they did not analyze the Bible according to the principles of legal-historical evolution. Only Schechter, who respected the unity of the text and was able to apply to it legal and historical analysis, could see that the case of the blaspheming Egyptian and the murder and assault laws would all belong to a very early stage of Israelite legal development. Again, Schechter has used legal-historical analysis against the higher critics.

3. In *"The Date of the Land Laws in Leviticus XXV,"* Schechter argues against the view of the higher critics[49] that the sabbatical and jubilee year legislation must be of very late dating, and of a utopian character. Schechter's basic argument is that the legislation only makes sense if it dates from the time of Moses. Any later hopes to institute such laws would have been ridiculous. Only at the beginning of Israel's legal development could such legislation be sensibly introduced. As Schechter writes: "No mere author of politics and religious codes such as the higher critics presumably picture[d]... could have had the fanatical hopes of bringing about such a revolutionary scheme."[50] Schechter's arguments in this paper seem less compelling than the previous two. He does not adequately address the idea of "utopian" legislation (the program of Leviticus need not have ever been intended as a real political option) or, for example, the possibility of substantial economic reform in the time of Nehemiah. But he uses the same basic mode of argumentation as before: the use of legal-historical analysis to find a plausible historical context. There is, of course, a specific historical context he desires here: a Mosaic dating for Leviticus.

In the course of the Land Laws paper, Schechter does say something very revealing: "We must therefore conclude that in form as in matter we are dealing with the work of Moses. Of course, this is said without prejudice to the discussion of what exactly may be the correct readings in any of these passages under consideration."[51]

Perhaps Schechter is only saying that there are different ways of interpreting the laws here. More likely, he is implying that while the higher critical studies of this passage which attempt to give it a late dating are misguided and incorrect, the lower critical studies which attempt to establish its authentic wording are still worthy endeavors. Just as Schechter accepted the fact of legal evolution in the Ruth paper, so here he accepts the possibility of textual corruption.

4. *"On Deuteronomy XVII: 14-20 (The King),"* the final Bible study of the four manuscripts, is in many respects the most interesting. Schechter begins by quoting Driver's commentary, which argues that the Deuteronomic provisions are to ensure that the monarchy be bound to ethical and theocratic principles.[52] Driver also articulates the theory, which Schechter does not quote directly, that the Deuteronomic laws were composed after the reign of David and of Solomon since many of the Deuteronomic prohibitions were violated during their rule, and 1 and 2 Samuel seem unaware of these regulations.[53] Schechter criticizes Driver's inability to explain Deuteronomy 17:15, which insists that the Israelite king not be foreigner. After accepting four conclusions from Driver, Schechter proceeds to offer his own original interpretation. He first summarizes Driver's conclusions on 17:15:

(1) That the prohibition is remarkable.

(2) That it won't suit the known facts of history of either kingdom [i.e., Judah or Israel].

(3) That it may have been due to some incident in the history of a neighboring country.

(4) That the motive of the provision is probably religious.[54]

Given these points Schechter goes on to suggest (remarkably) that the prohibitions in Deuteronomy 17 are in response, not to David and Solomon as the higher critics propose, but to the Pharaoh Horenheb. Providing us with a brief account of the reign of Akhnaton and that pharaoh's monotheistic religion of Atonism, the worship of the sun, Schechter suggests "how Moses must have sympathized with such a religion when contrasting it with the others he knew."[55] Moses must have then detested Horenheb, the conquering pharaoh who banished Atonism from Egypt and restored the old polytheistic cult.[56] Having suggested this, Schechter goes on to show how almost all the prohibitions against the monarchy in Deuteronomy 17 refer to aspects of Horenheb's reign. He was a foreigner, a general, married for political gain, and was not succeeded by children (the Deuteronomic punishment for the king who does not obey its prohibitions). Moses must have known Horenheb since the Exodus is dated less than a lifetime after his reign. "The facts appear to me to speak for themselves," Schechter concludes his paper. "It is to be noted that they furnish at least as convincing an argument for the date of Deuteronomy as are many that favor with the critics."[57]

In July of 1900 Schechter set out to disprove the higher critics and argue on the basis of critical historical investigation that the Pentateuch dates from the time of Moses. He wanted to prove "the genuineness of the book,"[58] that is, its historical authenticity. He was willing to accept legal development and historical influences on Moses' composition, but not that Moses did not compose the law himself. Schechter's strong commitment to Mosaic authorship was not only due to his piety, but to his desire to defend traditional Judaism against the implicit attack of Wellhausen's theory. While the early J and E sources provided the world with its loftiest ideals, argued the Wellhausen theory, the late D source and even later P source imposed an oppressive cultic legalism upon the Pentateuch and the religion of Israel. But for Schechter, traditional Judaism did not need Jesus, nor Reform "ethical monotheism," for its salvation. For Schechter, the Law itself was the source of salvation. P and D were God's gift of love.[59] Schechter wanted to prove that the P and D material were of Mosaic authorship because that material was the bedrock of rabbinic Judaism. That is why two of the studies argue for Mosaic authorship of Leviticus, the other two of Deuteronomy.

Schechter wrote these four studies in a single week, probably as a reaction to his reading *The Hexeteuch*, also published in 1900. That two-volume study was prepared by a committee of Oxford scholars including Claude G. Montefiore,[60] who had been Schechter's pupil in rabbinics. The publication of the volume, which summarized most of the higher critical theories, and Montefiore's involvement in the project, must have angered Schechter who surely felt the need for a proper Jewish and scholarly response. These four essays could be the germ of that unfulfilled project. Or they might be merely Schechter's personal glosses. He never published them, but he did keep them with his papers. Perhaps he hoped to return to them one day and complete his work. Or perhaps he recognized that it was ill-advised to use the methods of biblical criticism to fight its widely held conclusions. Perhaps it was safer to avoid biblical criticism altogether, which he did accomplish in the curriculum of the Jewish Theological Seminary, refusing to hire a professor who would teach the higher criticism of the Bible.[61]

Another reason Schechter never published his Bible studies must have been his unease with their approach. In these studies, Schechter contextualizes biblical laws into the history of the development of Israelite law without any reference to the divine. This perspective of Pentateuchal legislation is radically different form the traditional view of the Torah as the revelation of God's will at Mount Sinai. Schechter's method was very different from that of Joseph H. Hertz. Although Harvey Meirovich finds a strong influence of Schechter on Hertz and his commentary,[62] their approaches were different. Nowhere in the four studies discussed above does Schechter mention God or any type of divine hand in the composition of the Bible. On the contrary, he argues for historical and legal evolution and claims that historical influences determine the composition of biblical texts. Hertz will, when no other explanation remains, rely on "the Providential view of human history."[63] Schechter discounts the traditional Jewish commentators just as he discounts the higher critics,[64] while Hertz seeks to present the medieval Jewish commentators as eternally relevant. While Hertz sought to use scholarly argumentation, especially archeological evidence, to dispute the Documentary hypothesis, he was ultimately not as committed to critical investigation as was Schechter. Schechter did not merely use critical methods, he was a critic himself. While he denied the validity of the Documentary hypothesis, he still approached the problem as a scholar, and could only argue against the critics in their own language, the language of historical criticism. Perhaps that is why he never proceeded with his project to write a commentary, leaving it to others like Hertz.

Schechter's most famous argument against higher criticism is an address delivered on March 26, 1903, entitled "Higher Criticism–Higher Anti-Semitism."[65] Its fame derives solely from its title, as there are many other places where Schechter's critique of higher criticism and Protestant scholarship in general is more fierce.[66] But in that address he shares a very personal observation: "I remember when I used to come home from the *Cheder,* bleeding and crying from the wounds inflicted upon me by the Christian boys... the pain was only physical, but my real suffering began later in life, when I emigrated from Roumania to the so-called civilized countries and found there what I might call the Higher anti-Semitism, which burns the soul though it leaves the body unhurt."[67]

Schechter's immigration to Central Europe exposed him to two phenomena which determined the course of his life: (1) *Wissenchaft des Judentums,* and (2) anti-Jewish bias in scholarship. The two were of course connected. The academic approach to Jewish literature was adapted by Jews partly in order to dispel misinterpretations of Judaism among the educated. Schechter became a part of that world. He sought to fight higher anti-Semitism with higher scholarship, challenging the academic community to accept his readings of the Bible and rabbinic sources, readings which were, of course, more favorable to Judaism. If his scholarship was polemical, so be it, Protestant scholarship was polemical as well.

This defensive posture of Schechter's studies is reflected in an essay originally published in the *Westminster Review* in 1885, which Schechter wrote on rabbinic research: "But be our opinions of the Rabbis what they may, we may fairly claim, in the name of scientific justice, as well as that of Christian charity, that he who proposes to pass judgment upon them shall first hear their case, and understand it; in other words, that he shall read the Talmud, and critically examine it, before he begins to write about it and expound it."[68] Schechter held this maxim for biblical studies as well. One must understand the Bible in its own context before discussing who wrote it and when. Schechter believed that such responsible scholarship would help dispel the anti-Jewish prejudices of Protestant intellectuals.[69]

3. The Shadow of Zunz and the "Old Adam"

Gerson D. Cohen claimed that "the man of the nineteenth century whom Schechter knew least but venerated most was Leopold Zunz."[70] Zunz was Schechter's hero. He was completely absorbed into German culture, produced monumental works in Jewish scholarship, and opposed Reform within the Jewish community. Among various other references in his writings,[71] Zunz is given a central place in Schechter's introduction to the first volume of the *Studies in Judaism,* which is one of the few places where Schechter attempts to articulate his own theology.[72] In fact, Schechter wrote a lengthy study of Zunz in 1889, which won first prize in an essay contest of the Jewish Ministers Association of America, but he never published it. The editors of the third volume of the *Studies in Judaism* published it posthumously. One page is missing in the manuscript,[73] and apparently contains the conclusion of a discussion on Zunz's theology and how it was meaningful to Schechter. But there is enough in the surrounding pages to inform us of Schechter's meaning. One passage from the paper will summarize its main theme. After noting that in Zunz's time "the Talmud and the Midrashim were considered as a perversion of the Pentateuch and the books of the Prophets, and the Jewish liturgy a bad paraphrase of the Psalms," Schechter writes:

To destroy these notions, to bridge over this seemingly wide and deep gap, to restore the missing links between the Bible and tradition, to prove the continuity and development of Jewish thought through history, to show their religious depth and their moral and ennobling influence, to teach us how our own age with all its altered notions might nevertheless be a stage in the continuous development of Jewish ideals and might make these older thoughts a part of its own progress–this was the great task to which Zunz devoted his life.[74]

Gerson Cohen, in his lecture on Schechter, suggested one emendation: in the last phrase, substitute "Schechter" for "Zunz." Zunz was Schechter's model of the modern Jewish scholar.[75]

What Schechter understood as Zunz's theology, as deduced from his scholarship, became his own theology as developed in the introduction to the *Studies in Judaism*. In that essay Schechter articulates the theology of the "Historical School" by noting that "the center of authority is actually removed from the Bible and placed in some *living body*"...the "collective conscience of Catholic Israel as embodied in the Universal Synagogue."[76] This language was first used by Schechter in his analysis of Zunz in 1889, where he speaks of "the synagogue as a living body."[77] He learned from Zunz that Judaism was a tradition which develops through time. Authority for Jewish tradition lies not in its origins of revelation but in the people's acceptance of the traditions through history. Schechter was not completely comfortable with this position. At times, he confesses, "the old Adam still asserts itself in me, and in unguarded moments makes me rebel against this new rival of revelation in the shape of history."[78] But since that is the "old" Adam in "unguarded" moments, we know that Schechter remained committed to the historical perspective.

The primacy of tradition and the national consciousness of the Jewish people which Schechter learned form Zunz are made manifest in Schechter's Zionism. When he declared himself a Zionist in 1906,[79] he aligned himself with the cultural Zionism of Ahad HaAm.[80] For both, Zionism was a force against anti-Semitism and directed towards the "awakening of the national Jewish consciousness."[81] The national Jewish consciousness was what he and Zunz had been searching for in their researches of the literature of "the Synagogue" or "Catholic Israel," which was the "universal consciousness" of the nation. Schechter's Judaism was a national culture, not a faith alone.

There are two unpublished writings where Schechter makes his appreciation of Zunz clear. One, "Abraham Geiger," was published posthumously in the third volume of the *Studies in Judaism*.[82] (This was never published by Schechter during his lifetime, probably because of its fierce anti-Reform polemic.)[83] In the essay he compares Geiger to Zunz, who "never apologized for the existence of Israel,"[84] but supported Israel's separateness, opposing Geiger in the abolition of circumcision.[85] "That history means remembrance," wrote Schechter, "and that remembrance results in hope, which is the very reverse of absorption, was not foreseen by the few historians the Reform Movement gave us. This could only have been divined by men like Krochmal and Zunz, who were ahead of their time; whilst Geiger was strictly a product of his time."[86] The other unpublished essay which is even fiercer in its anti-Reform polemic and extant only in manuscript is a review of David Philipson's *The Reform Movement in Judaism*. In that essay Zunz again serves as the exemplar of tradition and scholarship in the battle against Reform.[87]

One might ask why, if Zunz was so important to Schechter, he never published his 1889 essay on Zunz's work and thought. The logical place for it to have been published would have been the first volume of the *Studies in Judaism*, which was a collection of Schechter's best essays through 1896. One possible explanation is that while the Reformers believed the two movements in Judaism in the nineteenth century to be Reform and Rabbinism, Schechter saw three, which he defines in his unpublished review of Philipson:

> (1) The Mystical movement, which appealed to the emotions, and was inaugurated by R. Israel Baal Shem and continued by the leaders of the Chassidim.
>
> (2) The "Wissenschaft" movement, which appealed to the philological and historical conscience of men, begun by the Gaon of Wilna and developed by Krochmal, Rappaport, Zunz, and their successors.
>
> (3) The Rationalist movement, which appealed to the instincts of imitation and assimilation initiated at least by Herz Homberg and Peter Beer, continued under Israel Jacobson, David Friedlaender, and their successors.[88]

Schechter included Reform under "Rationalistic" and sees it as opposed to *Wissenschaft*, which is not concerned with assimilation but with Jewish national culture.[89] Although this scheme is quoted here from a late writing in Schechter's life, it seems to have been in his mind in 1896 when he put together the first volume of the *Studies in Judaism*. The first three essays treat the Hasidim, Krochmal, and the Vilna Gaon, respectively. The Vilna Gaon represents the eighteenth-century predecessor of the *Wissenschaft* movement since he approached rabbinic texts with a critical eye. Krochmal represents its development in the nineteenth century. The "Rationalistic" movement is omitted. The representations of the other two are all from eastern Europe, as was Schechter himself. As a student in Germany, Schechter surely felt the antipathy towards eastern European Jewry. Thus in the face of those attitudes of German Jewry, he presented the *Wissencahft* movement as well as the Hasidic movement as hailing from eastern Europe. Only rationalism and Reform came from the West.

There is another aspect as well. Schechter could not bring his study to publication, since he recognized the paradox inherent in his feelings. After all, how could he love Zunz, when Zunz himself was a higher critic of the Bible? Certainly Schechter was aware that Zunz published an article in the *Zeitschrift der deutschen morgenländischen Gesellschaft* in 1873, and then published an expanded form in his *Gesammelte Schriften,* entitled "Bibelkritisches."[90] In that study Zunz concluded that Leviticus was written one thousand years after Moses, and that clear evidence for the existence of the Pentateuch begins no earlier than three hundred years after King Josiah.[91] Schechter was never able to accept higher criticism as a legitimate Jewish pursuit.

Zunz concluded his study with two fascinating sentences: "Rosh HaShanah, Yom Kippur and Purim, unknown to more ancient Judaism, owe their existence to foreign influences and a later era. Meanwhile, history and the development of the human spirit have given them a significance beyond their source. So long as poets and priests [i.e., the biblical authors] continue to exert influence, historians and philosophers must not tire of researching the origins."[92]

For Zunz, the authority of Jewish traditions does not derive from a Mosaic Torah but from the acceptance of the traditions by the Jews through history. While Schechter agreed with this pure *wissenschaftliche* approach in principle, he only articulates it once in his 1896 introduction to the *Studies in Judaism*. The academician and the old Adam struggled within him. It was probably because he could never decide whether there should be limits to *Wissenschaft* that Schechter never published the biblical studies of 1900 nor the Zunz essay of 1889.

The ambivalence which Schechter felt towards the Historical School which he expressed in the 1896 introduction to the *Studies in Judaism* was determinative. While he was committed to research and agreed in principle with all the methods of critical scholarship, he could not publicly endorse biblical criticism, and, therefore, was unable to prepare his Zunz essay for publication. He had to oppose higher criticism since it was riddled with anti-Jewish bias. Far more than Zunz, Schechter was intimately connected with the Jewish world of his time.[93] Zunz abhorred what he called the *Glaubenswissenschaft* (dogmatic history) of the Jewish Theological Seminary in Beslau.[94] He came to hate the use of scholarship as a religious polemic. While Zunz rejected a call to become a rabbi in New York because he feared his scholarship would suffer,[95] Schechter left his professorship at Cambridge University to become President of New York's Jewish Theological Seminary of America. And for Schechter, to doubt the Mosaic authenticity of the Torah went beyond the pale of responsible and traditional rabbinic scholarship.

NOTES

1. For laudatory letters from Weiss, Freidmann and Adolph Jellinek, see *Jewish Theological Seminary of American Students' Annual,* Schechter Memeroral (1916), pp. 13-16. Steinschneider's letter of reference is included in *Application and Testimonials for the Post of Reader in Talmud in the University of Cambridge by* Solomon Schechter (1890), located in the Schechter Collection, Special Collections in the Rare Book Room, Jewish Theological Seminary of America Library (henceforth "Schechter Archives"), 101:13. This paper owes its existence to the encouragement and instruction of my teacher, Professor Ismar Schorsch. I have also benefited from conversations with Professors Edward L. Greenstein, Jeffrey Gurock, Jack Wertheimer, Neil Gillman, Tikva Frymer-Kensky, and my father, Rabbi Robert E. Fine. I am grateful to the staff of the Library of the Jewish Theological Seminary of America, especially of its Rare Book Room, for its help.

2. There is no critical biography of Schechter which seeks to understand him in the context of his times. The full-length biography by Norman Bentwich, *Solomon Schechter: A Biography* (Philadelphia: Jewish Publication Society, 1940), is useful but too laudatory to fulfill this lacuna. The short book by Azriel Eizenberg, *Fill a Blank Page: A Biography of Solomon Schechter* (New York: United Synagogue,1965), is intended for young people, but it is a well-researched anthology of wonderful anecdotes. The documentation of his research has been deposited in the Schechter Archives, 101:14. The only serious treatment I have found on Schechter and his context is a videotaped lecture by Gerson D. Cohen at the Jewish Theological Seminary of America entitled "Solomon Schechter: Transmitter of Rabbinic Tradition," delivered 2 November 1986. The videotape is cataloged in the Jewish Theological Seminary Library.

3. Solomon Schechter, *Studies in Judaism*, First Series (Philadelphia: Jewish Publication Society, 1896), p. xx.

4. The first series of the *JQR* was the English publication used for learned Jewish apologetics as well as scholarly research.

5. Mordecai Kaplan complained in 1934 that "although most of the modern Jewish scholars tacitly assume that [modern scientific] attitude toward the Bible, not one of them has made any attempt to face the issue squarely." From Mordecai M. Kaplan, *Judaism as a Civilization: Toward a Reconstruction of American-Jewish Life* (1934; reprint, Philadelphia: Jewish Publication Society, 1981), p. 549, n. 6.

6. Julius Wellhausen, *Prolegomena to the History of Ancient Israel* (New York: Meridian Books, 1957), p. 509. On Wellhausen and Judaism, see Jon D. Levinson, *The Hebrew Bible, the Old Testament, and Historical Criticism* (Louisville, Kentucky: Westminster/John Knox, 1993), pp. 10-15; S. David Sperling, ed., *Students of the Covenant: A History of Jewish Biblical Scholarship in North America* (Atlanta: Scholars Press, 1992), p. 38 (from ch. 2 contributed by Baruch A. Levine); Lou H. Silberman, "Wellhausen and Judaism," *Semeia* 25 (1982): 75-82.

7. Peter Pulzer, *The Rise of Political Anti-Semitism in Germany and Austria,* rev. ed (London: Peter Halban, 1988), p. 48. On Marr see Paul Mendes-Flohr and Jehuda Reinharz, eds., *The Jew in the Modern World: A Documentary History*, 2d ed. (New York: Oxford University Press, 1995), pp. 331-333.

8. See Mendes-Flohr and Reinharz, *Jew in the Modern World*, pp. 343-346, 356-359.

9. Ismar Schorsch, *Jewish Reactions to German Anti-Semitism, 1870-1914* (New York: Columbia University Press, 1972), p. 170. See the treatment on pp.169 ff., which places Schechter into this context (p. 171).

10. Rudolf Otto's *Idea of the Holy*, first published in Germany in 1917, went against the grain in stressing (or reaffirming) the transcendent element in Christian religiosity.

11. Emil G. Hirsch, "Reform Judaism from the Point of View of the Reform Jew," *The Jewish Encyclopedia*, Vol. 10 (New York: Funk and Wagnalls, 1905), p. 350. See also Michael A. Meyer, *Response to Modernity: A History of the Reform Movement in Judaism* (New York: Oxford University Press, 1988), pp. 202-203.

12. Solomon Schechter, *Some Aspects of Rabbinic Theology,* (1909; reprint, New York:

Schocken Books, 1961), p. 169.

13. Schechter, *Some Aspects of Rabbinic Theology*, pp. 146-147.

14. Solomon Schechter, "The Law and Recent Criticism," in *Studies in Judaism*, First Series, pp. 243-244.

15. Solomon Schechter, "The Study of the Bible" in *Studies in Judaism*, Second Series (Philadelphia: Jewish Publication Society, 1908), p. 309. The essay appears on pp. 31-54.

16. Schechter Archives, 101: 8.

17. *Studies in Judaism*, Second Series, pp. 32-34. "Fetich" was English spelling.

18. *Studies in Judaism*, Second Series, p. 33.

19. *Studies in Judaism*, Second Series, p. 34.

20. *Studies in Judaism*, Second Series, pp. 36-37. For a parallel passage, see *Seminary Addresses and Other Papers* (1915; reprint, New York: Burning Bush Press, 1959), p. 56.

21. "It is said that when he [Schechter] was only 5, when a visitor came to the house, he would throw himself face downwards on the couch and recite the entire portion of the week" (three or four biblical chapters). From Charlotte Schechter, "Solomon Schechter: Rumanian Notes," an unpublished manuscript dated 9 July 1935. Schechter Archives, 101: 13.

22. See *Studies in Judaism*, Second Series, p. 38.

23. See the account in Bentwich, *Solomon Schechter*, pp. 35 ff. Schechter received his rabbinic ordination from Isaac Hirsch Weiss and Meir Friedmann in 1879. I find it telling that, although Schechter was for years an outstanding student in the Rumanian yeshivot, he was ordained by critical rabbinic scholars.

24. *Studies in Judaism*, Second Series, p. 39.

25. *Studies in Judaism*, Second Series, p. 40.

26. *Studies in Judaism*, Second Series, pp. 40-41.

27. *Studies in Judaism*, Second Series, pp. 41-42.

28. For anti-Wellhausen remarks in Schechter's writings, see *Studies in Judaism*, Second Series, pp. 42, 106; *Seminary Addresses*, pp. 4, 5, 38, 70, 173.

29. See *Studies in Judaism*, Second Series, p. 33.

30. See *Studies in Judaism*, First Series, p. 240; *Studies in Judaism*, Second Series, pp. 33, 40, 42, 106, 200; *Seminary Addresses*, pp. 4, 5, 36. I have found one anti-Kuenen remark (*Seminary Addresses*, p. 70), but that is contrasted with at least seven positive remarks.

31. *Studies in Judaism*, Second Series, p. 46.

32. This insight was explained to me by Ismar Schorsch. This is misunderstood by Baila Round Shargel in her *Practical Dreamer: Israel Friedlaender and the Shaping of American Judaism* (New York: Jewish Theological Seminary of America, 1985), pp. 199-200, who assumes that Schechter wanted to disprove the late dating of the Psalms in his Ben Sira studies to oppose an element of the Wellhausen hypothesis. But Schechter wanted the Psalms to be late, contra tradition!

33. *Studies in Judaism*, Second Series, p. 70.

34. They are located in the Schechter Archives, 10: 7.

35. S. R. Driver, *Deuteronomy: A Critical and Exegetical Commentary*, International Critical Commentary (Edinburgh: T. & T. Clark, 1895), p. 285. Deuteronomy 25:5-10 is the source of the laws of levirate marriage where if a man dies childless his wife must be wed to his brother. The first child born of that union is to be raised by the brother as the child of the deceased. However, if the brother does not want to marry the widow then he must appear before the elders of the town where the widow pulls the sandal off his foot, spits in his face and makes a declaration denouncing him, but also, in effect, releasing him from his duty to marry her. This is known as the ceremony of *halitzah*.

36. Schechter, "On Ruth IV," p. 2. Page numbers for the four Bible studies from Schechter Archives 101: 7 all refer to manuscript pages.

37. Schechter, "On Ruth IV," p. 3.

38. Schechter, "On Ruth IV," p. 8.

39. Schechter, "On Ruth IV," pp. 8-9.

40. Schechter, "On Ruth IV," pp. 9-10.

41. Schechter, "On Ruth IV," p. 10.

42. Schechter, "On Ruth IV," pp. 15-16. The Bible recounts (2 Kings 22) that a forgotten "scroll of the Teaching of the Lord" was discovered in the Temple in the reign of King Josiah. Since the subsequent religious reforms of Josiah reflect the Book of Deuteronomy, many scholars believe that scroll to be Deuteronomy, or at least a significant portion of it.

43. Schechter, "On Ruth IV," p. 15.

44. J. Estlin Carpenter and G. Harford-Battersby, *The Hexeteuch,* vol. 2 (London: Longmans, Green and Co., 1900), p. 176.

45. Schechter, "The Case of the Egyptian who Blasphemed the Name, Leviticus XXIV: 10-23," p. 8.

46. Schechter, "The Case of the Egyptian," pp. 13-14, 15.

47. Robert Alter, *The Art of Biblical Narrative* (New York: Basic Books, 1981), p. 16.

48. Schechter, "The Case of the Egyptian," p. 14.

49. He refers specifically to the commentary in *The Hexeteuch,* op. cit.

50. Schechter, "The Date of the Land Laws in Leviticus XXV," pp. 3-4.

51. Schechter, "The Date of the Land Laws," p. 9.

52. Driver, *Deuteronomy,* p. 210.

53. Driver, *Deuteronomy,* pp. 212-213.

54. Schechter, "On Deuteronomy XVII: 14- 20 (The King)," pp. 3-4.

55. Schechter, "On Deuteronomy XVII: 14-20," pp. 10-11.

56. This study of Schechter was written 37 years before Freud's theories in *Moses and Monotheism* were first published. In that book Freud sees Moses as an Egyptian who sought to establish among the Israelites the monotheism of Akhnaton which had been suppressed in Egypt by the "new pharaoh."

57. Schechter, "On Deuteronomy XVII: 14-20," p. 16.
58. Schechter, "The Case of the Egyptian," p. 16.
59. The second benediction before the reading of the *Sh'ma* in the daily Jewish liturgy praises God's love for Israel in granting the statutes and laws. The majority of Pentateuchal legal material is found in the P and D sections.
60. See *The Hexeteuch,* vol. 1, p. v.
61. Israel Friedlaender, whom Schechter appointed as the Seminary's biblicist, was a medievalist with little expertise in biblical criticism (see Shargel, *Practical Dreamer,* esp. ch. 3). Although Louis Ginzberg did accept the Documentary Hypothesis (see his article, "The Codification of Jewish Law," in the *Jewish Encyclopedia,* reprinted in Louis Ginzberg, *On Jewish Law and Lore* [Philadelphia: Jewish Publication Society, 1955], pp. 153-158), he was not appointed to teach Bible.
62. See Harvey Meirovich, "Reclaiming Chief Rabbi Hertz as a Conservative Jew," *Conservative Judaism 46* (Summer 1994), esp. pp. 4-5; Harvey Meirovich, *Judaism on Trial: An Analysis of the Hertz Pentateuch* (Ann Arbor: University Microfilms, 1986), pp. 1-3, 86 ff., and elsewhere.
63. J. H. Hertz, *The Pentateuch and Haftorahs,* 2d ed. (London: Soncino, 1972), p. 555.
64. Schechter knew how to be critical of the Rabbis. He wrote in the *Aspects of Rabbinic Theology:* "The fact is that the Rabbis were a simple, naive people, filled with a childlike scriptural faith, neither wanting nor bearing much analysis and interpretation" (p. 42).
65. *Seminary Addresses,* pp. 35-39.
66. For anti-higher criticism remarks, see *Studies in Judaism,* First Series, p. 154; *Seminary Addresses,* pp. 16, 56-57, 69-70, 124, 131. For anti-Protestant scholarship see, for example, *Seminary Addresses,* pp. 173-174.
67. *Seminary Addresses,* p. 36. The *cheder* is the traditional Jewish primary school.
68. Reprinted in Schechter, *Studies in Judaism,* Third Series (Philadelphia: Jewish Publication Society, 1924), p. 193. For a much harsher statement of the same idea, see p. 4 of an unpublished, untitled, undated manuscript by Schechter on the higher criticism of the Talmud, in Schechter Archives, 101: 9.
69. See *Seminary Addresses,* p. 232.
70. Gerson D. Cohen, "Solomon Schechter," videotaped lecture at the Jewish Theological Seminary, 2 November 1986.
71. See, for example, *Seminary Addresses,* pp. 52, 74, 121, 173-193; *Studies in Judaism,* Third Series, p.4·.
72. *Studies in Judaism,* First Series, pp. xvi-xvii.
73. *Studies in Judaism,* Third Series, pp. 84-142. See p. vi. On this essay, see the *Jewish Chronicle,* January 3, 1890, p. 6; and Siegmund Maybaum, "Aus dem Leben von Leopold Zunz," *Zwölfter Bericht über die Lehrenstalt für die Wissenschaft des Judentums in Berlin* (1893), p. 2, n. 2, who mentions Schechter's intention to publish the essay soon. I have searched for the missing page in the Schechter Archives, and have made inquiries to the New York Board of Rabbis (which was, I believe, the "Jewish

Ministers Association" although that is unclear) and to the archives of the Hebrew Union College and the American Jewish Historical Society, but all to no avail. Jeffrey Gurock of Yeshiva University, who is an authority on American Jewish history at the turn of the century, has advised me that any document from the New York Board of Rabbis from those years will prove impossible to find.

74. *Studies in Judaism,* Third Series, p. 98.

75. See above, n. 70.

76. *Studies in Judaism,* First Series, p. xviii. See my forthcoming article, "The Meaning of Catholic

Israel," and my brief comments on the subject in *Conservative Judaism* 47 (Spring 1995): 76-79.

77. *Studies in Judaism,* Third Series, p. 115. See also pp. 111, 114, for parallels with the passage from

1896 just cited.

78. *Studies in Judaism,* Third Series, pp. xx- xxi.

79. See "Zionism: A Statement," in *Seminary Addresses,* pp. 91-104. On Schechter's Zionism, see Robert E. Fierstien, "Solomon Schechter and the Zionist Movement," *Conservative Judaism* 29 (Spring 1975): 3- 13; David Benjamin Starr, "We Cannot Escape History: Solomon Schechter and Zionism," *Proceedings of the Rabbinical Assembly* 55 (1993): 65- 82.

80. See *Seminary Addresses,* pp. 97, 101.

81. *Seminary Addresses,* pp. 99-100.

82. *Studies in Judaism,* Third Series, pp. 47-83.

83. See Felix Perles, review of *Studies in Judaism,* Third Series, by Solomon Schechter, *Revue des Etudes Juives* 80 (1925): 107, who criticizes the essay on this point.

84. *Studies in Judaism,* Third Series, p. 69.

85. See Leopold Zunz, "Gutachten über die Beschneidung," in *Gesammelte Schriften,* vol. 2 (Berlin,

1876), pp. 191-203.

86. *Studies in Judaism,* Third Series, pp. 71-72.

87. Schechter Archives, 101: 9. See pp. 12-14 of the manuscript. Briefly summarized in Bentwich, *Solomon Schechter,* pp. 304-305.

88. P. 4 of the manuscript.

89. See *Seminary Addresses,* p. 175, where Schechter distinguishes between Jewish *Wissenschaft* and the "Reform or Rationalistic movement."

90. Leopold Zunz, *Gesammelte Schriften,* vol. 1 (Berlin: L. Gerschel, 1875), pp. 217-270.

91. Zunz, *Gesammelte Schriften,* vol. 1, p. 242. See Meirovich, *Judaism on Trial,* p. 113, who points out this conclusion of Zunz contra Schechter and Hertz. But Baruch A. Levine, in Sperling, *Students of the Covenant,* criticizes Zunz for not accepting higher criticism! (p. 23)

92. Zunz, *Gesammelte Schriften,* vol. 1, p. 242. My translation.

93. Schechter seems inspired by what he identifies as "Zunz's motto": "Echte Wissenschaft ist thatenerzeugend" (real scholarship creates action). See *Studies in Judaism,* Third Series, p. 117, and *Seminary Addresses,* pp. 20-21. He does not offer any citation from Zunz for the phrase.

94. Zunz to Gerson Wolf, 16 October 1854, in *Leopold Zunz: Jude-Deutscher-Europäer,* edited by Nahum N. Glatzer (Tübingen: J. C. B. Mohr, 1964), p. 364. See Ismar Schorsch, *From Text to Context: The Turn to History in Modern Judaism* (Hanover, NH: Brandeis University Press, 1994), p. 195.

95. Zunz to S. M. Ehrenberg, 11 December 1834, in Glatzer, *Leopold Zunz,* p. 175.

APPENDIX 4
The Meaning of Catholic Israel

Just over a century ago Solomon Schechter coined the phrase "Catholic Israel."[1] In attempting to describe the theology of the "historical school," Schechter wrote:

> It is not the mere revealed Bible that is of first importance to the Jew, but the Bible as it repeats itself in history, in other words, as it is interpreted by Tradition…. Since then the interpretation of Scripture or the Secondary Meaning is mainly a product of changing historical influences, it follows that the centre of authority is actually removed from the Bible and placed in some *living body*…the collective consciousness of Catholic Israel as embodied in the Universal Synagogue.[2]

While Catholic Israel has, for one hundred years, served as an ideological signpost in the discourse of Conservative Judaism, there has never been a clear consensus on what Schechter meant. Many argue that Schechter referred to the entire body of the people Israel and of their importance in the determination of Jewish law. They say that Catholic Israel is a translation of the Hebrew term כלל ישראל. Others insist that Schechter was only referring to the core group of committed observant Jews who have a stake in halakhah and halakhic change. Still others understand Schechter to have been referring to the collective consciousness of the Jewish people throughout history. Catholic Israel, they explain, refers back to history and makes the claim of tradition for the present age. This paper will argue for this last position. While Catholic Israel may have come to mean other things in the intellectual history of Conservative Judaism, Schechter's meaning must be that tradition, which is formed by the Jewish people through history, is the authority for the Judaism of the Historical School (and Conservative Judaism).

I

Before discussing Catholic Israel as the collective Jewish consciousness through history, it is worthwhile to consider how Catholic Israel has been understood by others. Solomon Solis-Cohen, a founding supporter of the Jewish Theological Seminary, was one of the earliest writers to understand Catholic Israel as referring to the present body of the Jewish people. Defending the legitimacy of Sephardic rites, Solis-Cohen asked, " From the larger view of catholic Israel, is it desirable that such distinctions be maintained? In

---

[1] See Solomon Schechter, *Studies in Judaism* [First Series] (Philadelphia: Jewish Publication Society, 1986), p. xviii. This important introduction to the first volume of Schechter's *Studies* has been reprinted (in part) in Mordecai Waxman, ed., *Tradition and Change: The Development of Conservative Judaism* (New York: The Rabbinical Assembly and the United Synagogue of Conservative Judaism, 1958), pp. 89-97, where it is entitled, "Historical Judaism." An excerpt is also printed in Paul Mendes-Flohr and Jehuda Reinharz, eds., *The Jew in the Modern World: A Documentary History,* 2d ed. (New York: Oxford University Press, 1995), pp. 497-498, where it is entitled, "Catholic Israel."

[2] Schechter, *Studies in Judaism*, First Series, pp. xvii-xviii.

his recent masterful inaugural address the scholar who gave us the term 'Catholic Israel' spoke with special reference to Jewish life in America of the value of diversity of form amid unity of purpose."[3] The scholar to whom Solis-Cohen refers is Solomon Schechter. In his inaugural address as President of the Seminary, Schechter had stressed the Seminary's role as "a theological centre which should be all things to all men, reconciling all parties and appealing to all sections of the community."[4] While Catholic Israel implies a one universal Israel, Solis-Cohen reads Schechter as understanding that diversities are included in and contribute to the universal whole. In a different address Solis-Cohen argued that "America has been a meeting place for Jews representative of all the countries and customs of the dispersion....and from the mingling of various elements will emerge a type better than anyone of its components."[5] Rather than a single type of Judaism, Catholic Israel referred to the complete all-inclusive Judaism. This is a very early example of the כלל ישראל model of Catholic Israel, an embracing of the unity of contemporary Israel.

Moshe Davis agrees with Solomon Solis-Cohen that Catholic Israel refers to the unity of the present body of Israel. In *Yahadut Amerika Be-Hitpathutah*, in citing the above passage from Solomon Solis-Cohen, Davis translates Catholic Israel as ישראל כלל.[6] Davis understands *k'lal Yisrael* to be a central ideological and programmatic concept of the Historical School. He traces the concept of Catholic Israel back to Isaac Leeser and proposes that it was only later developed by Solomon Schechter.[7] In *The Emergence of Conservative Judaism*, a revision of the previous work, Davis notes that when Isaac Leeser spoke of *k'lal Yisrael* he used the term כנסת ישראל, which Davis again translates as the Catholic Israel of Schechter's writings.[8] Leeser wrote in 1884:

What is it that all desire? Is it not the welfare of the faithful, the ישראל כנסת ...For shame men of Israel! Your faith demands your united support; no one can be spared the ranks of the labourers; all are needed.[9]

Leeser is arguing for a unity of action. His *kenesset Yisrael* consists of the body of American Jewry. Moshe Davis explains Leeser's phrase *kenesset Yisrael* to mean "the community of Israel, or 'catholic Israel.'"[10]

---

[3] Solomon Solis-Cohen, "The Sephardic Jews of America,"(1902) in Solomon Solis-Cohen, *Judaism and Science* (Philadelphia: Jewish Publication Society, 1940), p. 69.
[4] Solomon Schechter, "The Charter of the Seminary," in Solomon Schechter, *Seminary Addresses and Other Papers* (1915; reprint, New York: Burning Bush Press, 1959), p. 11.
[5] Solis-Cohen, *Judaism and Science*, pp.121-122.
[6] Moshe Davis, *Yahadut Amerika Be-Hitpathutah* (New York: The Jewish Theological Seminary, 1951), p. 93
[7] Ibid., p. xxi
[8] Moshe Davis, *The Emergence of Conservative Judaism: The Historical School in 19th Century America* (Philadelphia: The Jewish Publication Society, 1963), p. 16.
[9] Isaac Leeser, "The Demands of the Times," *The Occident* 1 (February 1844), p. 521.
[10] Davis, *Emergence of Conservative Judaism*, p. 118. See also p. 419, n. 8.

Davis connects Leeser and Schechter to Alexander Kohut, who argued that the Seminary be named the Jewish Theological Seminary of America to symbolize that it belongs to all of American Jewry and not to any particular party. However, Kohut did not speak of כלל ישראל nor כנסת ישראל, but of universal Judaism and the Judaism of history:

> Judaism is a consistent whole. The Mosaic, prophetic, talmudic-rabbinic Judaism is an organic totality. Nobody has the right to call out, like the false mother in the bible: Divide the living product of faith and of historical development. Nobody has the right to teach, in the name of universal Judaism: I will not give thee the child, and thou wilt not give it to me, let us, therefore, divide it! No, the Judaism of history is a unity, an organic development. May Moses be its head, the prophets its heart, the Rabbis its limbs, one without the other is a halfness, a wanton mutilation, which must in time revenge itself.[11]

While Kohut is not referring here to "Catholic Israel" since this passage predates Schechter's term by ten years, his concept of universal Judaism fits in with the more historical understanding of Catholic Israel. Kohut's terms "universal" and "totality" are synonymous with Schechter's term "catholic." Kohut does not refer to the universality of the present body of Jews, but to a universal form of Judaism attested to by history.[12] The nature of Judaism and the Jews should be defined through history rather than through the sentiments of Jews in any particular time, particularly in a reformist time. "[It is] a good suggestion of Dr. Kohut's," wrote Solomon Solis-Cohen in response to Kohut's article, "that the proposed seminary be called simply a Jewish seminary. For either Judaism is Conservative or it is nothing."[13] Whereas Reform Judaism represented the sentiments of the Jews in a particular time, Conservative Judaism was the Judaism of history.

The passage by Kohut and the reading of Schechter which he anticipates leads Davis to write: "The Historical School in its interpretation of *Klal Yisrael* identified itself with the total experience and commitment of the Jewish people throughout the ages."[14] However, Davis also understands Leeser's כנסת ישראל as Catholic Israel, by which Leeser meant the contemporary body of Israel. Davis, therefore, sees two aspects in the term Catholic Israel. Catholic Israel refers to both the present body of Jewry and the historical experience of the Jewish people. These represent two of the three readings

---

[11] Alexander Kohut, " The Jewish Seminary," *American Hebrew* 25 (February 5, 1886), p. 195. See Davis, *Emergence of Conservative Judaism*, p. 235, but Davis reads; "the Rabbis its links." Limbs is the correct reading from the *American Hebrew*, and fits much better with the organic metaphor.

[12] But Richard Lawrence Libowitz maintains that the purpose of Kohut's suggestion regarding the name of the Seminary was to "symbolize its *k'lal Yisrael* intent, that it was not destined to serve a single sect." Richard Lawrence Libowitz, *Mordecai Kaplan as Redactor: The Development of Reconstructionism* (Ann Arbor, MI: University Microfilms, 1978), p. 22.

[13] Solomon Solis-Cohen, "A Stride Forward," *American Hebrew* 26 (February 12,1886), p. 4.

[14] Davis, *Emergence of Conservative Judaism*, p. 17.

of Schechter's term.

Davis was not the only one to accept these two readings of Catholic Israel. Simon Greenberg, another major figure in the Conservative Judaism of the latter half of the twentieth century, understood Schechter in a similar way. In a 1955 statement on the Conservative movement, Greenberg identifies "the rabbinic concept of *K'lal Yisrael*" as a central concept of Conservative Judaism. Greenberg translates *k'lal Yisrael* as "the Brotherhood of Israel," saying that this follows from Schechter's translation of the same term as Catholic Israel. While admitting that "there have been varying interpretations" given to these terms, Greenberg emphasizes that "those who created those concepts sought to express thereby their inner desire to be identified not with any one sect or party in Israel, but with the whole of the Jewish people."[15] Here, Greenberg seems to favor the view that Catholic Israel refers to the contemporary body of Israel. In 1962 Greenberg wrote a study of the term *k'lal Yisrael* where he again mentions the centrality of the concept for Conservative Judaism. But referring to Schechter's term, Catholic Israel, Greenberg writes: "[Schechter] hoped thereby to indicate that Israel cannot be identified with any one era in the history of Judaism, nor with any one historic community, or ideology or theology."[16] Greenberg argues in his article that *k'lal Yisrael* should not only refer to the contemporary body of Jews but should retain certain aspects of Jewish heritage and tradition. Here, then, Greenberg seems to support the more historical understanding of Catholic Israel.

While Davis and Greenberg seemed to have accepted both the contemporary and historical interpretations of Catholic Israel, most writers have chosen one of the three basic definitions: the present body of Israel, the historical experience of Israel, or a select group within Israel. The rabbis and scholars who understand Catholic Israel as referring to the contemporary כלל ישראל belong, with one or two exceptions, to the generations which did not know Schechter the man.[17] Marshall Sklare, in his summary of Conservative Judaism's ideology, writes that the concept of Catholic Israel means

---

[15] Simon Greenberg, *The Conservative Movement in Judaism: An Introduction* (New York: United Synagogue, 1955), p. 22.

[16] Simon Greenberg, "The Concept of K'lal Yisrael" in Simon Greenberg, *Foundations of Faith* (New York: Burning Bush Press, 1967), p. 231.

[17] Solomon Solis-Cohen, discussed above, seems to be one exception. The only other significant exception which I have been able to find is Norman Bentwich, but his opinion can only be implied by the following statement: "While Schechter taught the authority of Catholic Israel and the progressiveness of the tradition from age to age, he consistently opposed the proposal to establish in America – or elsewhere – anything in the nature of a law-making synod." Schechter opposed the efforts of the Jews in his particular time to organize themselves and actively determine the nature of Jewish law. Bentwich seems to say that since Schechter taught the authority of Catholic Israel, he should have supported the synod. Therefore, Bentwich must understand Catholic Israel as the authority of the Jewish people in a particular time. See Norman Bentwich, *Solomon Schechter: A Biography* (Philadelphia: Jewish Publication Society, 1940), p. 297. Below I will argue that Schechter's opposition to the synods was completely consistent, perhaps even determined by, his idea of Catholic Israel if Catholic Israel is understood as the historical experience of the Jewish people.

that "neither reason nor revelation is the basis for observance, but rather 'the conscience of Catholic Israel' – i.e., the religious practice currently in vogue. Since the majority of the Jewish group, or Catholic Israel, observed *mitzvoth* at the time when Schechter and others elaborated this idea, following group patterns meant conforming to tradition."[18] Clearly, Sklare limits the meaning of Catholic Israel to "the Jewish group at the time." Max Arzt agrees, but expresses it more positively when he understands Catholic Israel as "the unity of Israel the world over."[19] "The world over" refers to the present world, not the historical world.

Mordecai Waxman understands Catholic Israel as the "national sentiment" of the Jewish people.[20] That he understood the national sentiment to be only contemporary is made clear by the first statement of his section on Positive-Historical Judaism: "The natural complement to concern with Catholic Israel is attention to the historical past of Israel."[21] Catholic Israel is not to be found in the experience of the past but in the Israel of the present. The Positive-Historical Judaism of Frankel is concerned with the past, where Schechter's Catholic Israel is concerned with the present. This model, it must be noted, is not supported by the evidence. The context of Schechter's introduction of the term Catholic Israel is an attempt to articulate the "theological position" of the Historical School.[22] Schechter is trying to explain Frankel's position, not complement it.

Herbert Parzen also understands Catholic Israel as referring to the present body of Israel and a translation of *k'lal Yisrael*. He explains the conservative context of Catholic Israel as polemic against Reform. Arguing against Reform leadership, Catholic Israel meant that only the "disembodied Universal Synagogue" had authority to change law. That disembodied totality of the people could not be represented or legislated for by any group. Parzen sees this as an intentional paradox, that only Catholic Israel can legislate, but no one can represent Catholic Israel.[23] Thus, Parzen sees Catholic Israel as referring to a present (though disembodied) Israel rather than a historical Israel.

While Parzen understands Catholic Israel to be a conservative concept, Sidney H. Schwarz and Theodore Weinberger have both recently argued that the correct meaning of Catholic Israel is the Jewish community, which, they say, should be more involved in the process of halakhic decision-making. They see Catholic Israel as a potentially liberating concept and accuse the Conservative rabbinate of not fully realizing this idea

---

[18] Marshall Sklare, *Conservative Judaism: An American Religious Movement* (Glencoe, IL: Free Press, 1955), p. 231.

[19] Max Arzt, "The Legacy of Solomon Schechter," *Conservative Judaism* 11 (Winter 1957), pp. 9-10.

[20] Mordecai Waxman, "Conservative Judaism - A Survey," in Waxman, ed., *Tradition and Change,* p. 15. Gilbert Rosenthal understands Catholic Israel as a "spiritual nationalism." See Gilbert S. Rosenthal, *Contemporary Judaism: Patterns of Survival,* 2d ed. (New York: Human Sciences Press, 1986), pp. 184, 192-193.

[21] Waxman, *Tradition and Change,* p. 16.

[22] See Schechter, *Studies in Judaism,* First Series, p. xvii.

[23] Herbert Parzen, *Architects of Conservative Judaism* (New York: Jonathan David, 1964), pp. 76-77.

and keeping halakhic decision-making for themselves.[24] But the rabbinical establishment, as will be discussed below, has also been behaving according to an interpretation of Catholic Israel. They accept the third definition of Catholic Israel not as the community at large but as the committed core, which in the Conservative Movement is primarily the rabbinate.

II

In order to discuss the committed core theory of Catholic Israel it is first necessary to discuss the historical understanding. This definition claims that Catholic Israel refers to the historical experience of the Jewish people. Just as the Catholic Church refers to the one true universal church, so Catholic Israel refers to the one true universal Israel. According to the Historical School, that one true Israel could only be discerned through the study of history. When Schechter says that the authority of Jewish law is in the hands of Catholic Israel, he means that the collective conscience of the Jewish people through history will decide what is to be sanctified and what is to be forgotten. This is a conservative concept, since it argues that the will of Israel is the will of a two-thousand-year experience rather than a particular synod or community that exists in any particular time. Catholicity is a trans-temporal concept, establishing what is constant from one time to another.

The earliest articulation of Schechter's views can be found in a lengthy and impassioned speech by Henrietta Szold to the New York Council of Jewish Women in 1899.[25] The speech was given as an argument against the synod, which was being proposed for American Jewry by the Reform leaders. Szold expressed the concern that the synod might only come to legitimate the Reform platform. Schechter himself had written a brief and quite terse reply against the synod,[26] and a longer reply six years later.[27] The longer reply, which will be discussed below, was not yet written when Szold delivered her address in 1899. With only Schechter's terse statement, and before he had come to America to head the Seminary, Szold explained the implications of the concept of Catholic Israel:

---

[24] See Sidney H. Schwartz, "Catholic Israel and Halakhic Change," In Ronald A. Brauner, ed., *Jewish Civilization: Essays and Studies,* Vol. 2, *Jewish Law* (Philadelphia: Reconstructionist Rabbinical College, 1981), pp. 171-181; Theodore Weinberger, "Solomon Schechter's (Post-modern) Conservative Jewish Theology," *Conservative Judaism* 46 (Summer 1994), pp. 24-36. See also *Encyclopaedia Judaica,* Vol. 10 (Jerusalem: Keter Publishing House, 1972), p. 898, s. v. "Kelal Yisrael" where Schechter's concept of Catholic Israel is explained as "an elaboration of the talmudic principle "Go forth and see how the public is accustomed to act."

[25] Henrietta Szold, "Catholic Israel," parts 1 and 2, *American Hebrew* 65 (May 5, 1899), pp. 9-11; (May 12, 1899), pp. 45-49. An abridgement is published in Waxman, ed., *Tradition and Change,* pp. 111-127. For a brief discussion, see Moshe Davis, *Emergence of Conservative Judaism,* pp. 280-282; or Davis, *Yahadut Amerika Be-Hitpathutah,* pp. 274-276.

[26] *American Hebrew* 64 (January 13, 1899), p. 372; quoted in Davis, *Emergence of Conservative Judaism,* p. 279.

[27] See Central Conference of American Rabbis, *Views on the Synod* (Baltimore: Lord Baltimore Press, 1905), pp. 134-141.

> With your permission I speak to you of…this broad, universal, Catholic Israel…Israel past and present…the American Jew may fail to grasp it in its breadth. Consciousness of Catholic Israel hallows the ritual…the Synod…ruinous to the catholicity of Israel…allegiance to Catholic Israel embracing, as it does, not only present day Israel scattered the world over, but Israel of all the ages as well…Catholic Israel repudiates the idea that allegiance to itself requires obedience to every utterance in any age or country.[28]

Catholic Israel extends through history. Catholic Israel stands for the weight of tradition. Not synonymous with the present community, Szold notes that the present community may even differ with Catholic Israel. Such was the danger of the synods, which Szold argued against.

Joseph H. Hertz seems to have understood Catholic Israel in the historical sense in the following passage from his Memorial Address for Schechter. Speaking of Schechter's symbol of the burning bush, Hertz continued:

> The voice of God spoke to us from that thorn-bush, a continuous revelation of the Divine with a message for every generation. The Synagogue, Schechter proclaimed, was the collective conscience of Universal Israel, and our sole true guide for the present and the future.[29]

While not explicit, one can infer from Hertz's words that he is speaking of Universal Israel as the continuing identity of the Jewish people through history. Cyrus Adler spoke in a similar manner when he said of Schechter: "He was a great Jew. He rediscovered Catholic Israel and did his most valiant work in endeavoring to eliminate party strife and in creating a universal Judaism."[30] While "universal Judaism" may here refer to a Judaism including all Jews, the Catholic Israel which Schechter "rediscovered" was the common Jewish historical consciousness which would serve to unite Jews in his own day.

One of the earliest academic treatments of Schechter's thought was completed by Myer S. Kripke in 1937. He understood Catholic Israel as "the spirit of the people" and recognized that "a belief or practise or ceremony is Jewish if, and only if, it has become part of the Jewish spirit through continued usage and continued acceptance by the Jewish people through its long history."[31] The authority of Catholic Israel is something which is observed through history. "How we may determine the spirit of the people," Kripke writes of Schechter, "the conscience of Catholic Israel…Schechter insisted could be accomplished in only one way: Study and learning, the cultivation of a science of

---

[28] Szold, "Catholic Israel," op. cit.

[29] J. H. Hertz, "The Chief Rabbi's Schechter Memorial Address," in Jewish Theological Seminary, *Students Annual* (New York: Jewish Theological Seminary, 1916), p. 80.

[30] Cyrus Adler, " A Great and Noble Soul has Passed" in *Students Annual* (1916), p.176.

[31] Myer S. Kripke, "Solomon Schechter's Philosophy of Judaism," *The Reconstructionist* 3 (October 22, 1937), p. 9.

Judaism."[32] The nature of Catholic Israel could be determined not by any sense or vote of the contemporary Jewish community, but by study of the Jewish past. That study will permit "the continuity of Catholic Israel" as David Benjamin Starr phrases it, into the present generation.[33]

The historical understanding of Catholic Israel is represented here by Szold, Hertz, Adler, and as we shall see presently, Mordecai Kaplan, all of whom knew Schechter. Kripke, though too young to have known Schechter, was raised among the generation who did. This is contrasted to those who support the contemporary Israel understanding and the committed core theory, none of whom lived in Schechter's day. What is curious is that so few scholars explain Catholic Israel in this historical mode. The last time this understanding was seriously considered was by Mordecai Kaplan and Robert Gordis, both of whom reject the model as ill-suited for the needs of contemporary Judaism.[34]

Mordecai Kaplan recognized that "the Conservatives have sought to reconstruct the very consciousness of [the] Jewish People."[35] The rediscovery and conservation of Catholic Israel, in the historical sense, is what Kaplan has in mind. In answer to the question, "What is to be gained by reinterpreting the past?" Kaplan answers: "However wrong a tradition may be, from the standpoint of fact, it reveals the collective mind of the people that evolved it. The Jewish tradition, interpreted from an evolutionary and socio-psychological point of view, enables us to recognize and identify the collective Jewish mind."[36] The "collective Jewish mind" is Catholic Israel. Kaplan agreed with Schechter and the Historical School that Jewish studies, *Wissenschaft des Judentums*, had to be pursued in order to discover the nature of Catholic Israel, since that national consciousness was the defining character of Jewish civilization. The idea is articulated by Schechter and the Historical School before him. The purpose of the Historical School, as Kaplan understands, was that the Jew "be made to feel that the People he belonged to had a significant history which reached down to his own day...a living, normal people."[37] The difference between Kaplan and Schechter is that Kaplan did not accept

---

[32] Ibid.

[33] See David Benjamin Starr, "We Cannot Escape History: Solomon Schechter and Zionism" *Proceedings of the Rabbinical Assembly* 55, (1993), p. 68.

[34] Since Kaplan and Gordis, the only writers I have been able to find who interpret Catholic Israel historically are Louis Jacobs and David Rudavsky. Jacobs writes: "Catholic Israel...the source of Jewish authority is not in the Bible but in the historical experience of the people of Israel." Louis Jacobs, *A Jewish Theology* (New York: Behrman House, 1973), p. 222. Rudavsky writes: "Catholic Israel, or the Universal Synagogue, as envisaged by Schechter, transcends both geographical and temporal boundaries. It applies not to a single community, but to all of Israel in time and place." David Rudavsky, *Modern Jewish Religious Movements: A History of Emancipation and Adjustment* (New York: Behrman House, 1967), p. 333. In addition to this paper, I had begun to discuss these ideas in The Open Forum: Positive-Historical Judaism, *Conservative Judaism* 47 (Spring 1995), pp. 76-79.

[35] Mordecai Kaplan, *The Greater Judaism in the Making: A Study of the Modern Evolution of Judaism* (New York: Reconstructionist Press, 1960), p. 358.

[36] Mordecai Kaplan, *The Future of the American Jew* (New York: Macmillan, 1958), p. 379.

[37] Kaplan, *The Greater Judaism in the Making*, p. 357.

the past as necessarily normative for life in the present.

Kaplan explains that a key concept of Jewish law for Conservative Judaism "is the principle of historical continuity, which was expounded under the term positive historical Judaism by Zechariah Frankel…and under the term Catholic Israel, by Solomon Schechter." Here Kaplan clarifies that Catholic Israel is the same concept as Positive-Historicism.[38] Kaplan continues: "That principle was intended to guide us in accepting or rejecting any proposed changes in Jewish law. Changes in law, according to that principle, must not be made arbitrarily, to accommodate a local or temporary situation." This should eliminate all doubt that Kaplan understood Catholic Israel historically. But Kaplan rejects this principle. "The principle as such is unworkable. It merely illustrates the definition of 'Conservative' as one who does not believe in doing something for the first time."[39] Understanding Schechter correctly as referring to the weight of history and tradition, Kaplan rejects the model. He cannot wait for history to move on its own. American Jewry must pursue a Reconstructionist program if it is to survive. Judaism is a civilization and can evolve like all other civilizations. The first responsibility of halakhah must be towards the contemporary body of people rather than the collective consciousness from the past else there will be no forward movement. The great irony here is that while Kaplan rejects Catholic Israel, his alternative is the way Catholic Israel came to be understood by so many in the latter half of the twentieth century, that halakhah will reflect the needs of the people.

Before turning to a discussion of Gordis, it should be noted that Kaplan did not reject Schechter as radically as it may seem at first glance. In answer to the question, "Have we any moral obligation to perpetuate our heritage from the past?" Kaplan answers:

> Judaism has realized that truth [that man is a social animal], and has embodied it in the ideal of the covenant. The first covenant entered into between God and Israel committed not only those who took part in it; it committed also their descendants (Deut. 29:9-14). Loyalty to the covenant is not ancestor worship, for it implies faith in the future no less than loyalty to the past. It is an expression of the sense of the community of *k'lal Yisrael* in time as well as in space. Without accepting our inheritance from our forefathers, we can bequeath no inheritance to our children, and we ourselves are left both without roots and without fruits.[40]

This passage by Kaplan beautifully summarizes Schechter's philosophy. The only major distinction between Kaplan and Schechter is the nature of the inheritance.

---

[38] Cf. discussion of Waxman, above.

[39] Kaplan, *The Future of the American Jew*, pp. 387-388.

[40] Mordecai Kaplan, *Questions Jews Ask: Reconstructionist Answers* (New York: Reconstructionist Press, 1956), p. 24.

III

Robert Gordis agreed with Kaplan that "the outlook of Conservative Judaism may be formulated in one sentence: Judaism is the evolving religious culture and civilization of the Jewish people."[41] He also agreed with Kaplan that Catholic Israel (understood in the historical sense) is "fundamentally a static principle, barring the way to change."[42] Catholic Israel was, in its time, "a historical necessity…when Reform threatened to sweep everything before it." Gordis recognizes, as does Kaplan, that the needs of America are different than those of Europe. But he differs from Kaplan in his program. "Today," he writes "our concern is no longer with preventing extreme innovation but with establishing norms for orderly growth and progress. Yet because of its basic truth, Catholic Israel can prove equally fruitful in our present situation."[43] Rather than sacrifice the halakhic system to contemporary needs, Gordis proposed to activate it for new decisions and legislation which would suit the times. But surely the principle of Catholic Israel would cause some to caution against change. Therefore, Gordis proposed a redefinition Catholic Israel. "Catholic Israel must be conceived differently from hitherto accepted views," he wrote, continuing:

> Catholic Israel is the body of men and women within the Jewish people, who accept the authority of Jewish law and are concerned with Jewish observance as a genuine issue.[44]

Robert Gordis, in 1942, redefines Catholic Israel as referring neither to the entire Jewish historical experience nor the contemporary body of Jews, but only to a core group of committed observant Jews who have a stake in the halakhic process. If Gordis were to have adapted the contemporary Israel definition of Catholic Israel then one might argue that because most Jews do not observe Shabbat, Shabbat no longer needs to be observed. By inventing a third definition Gordis is able to get past the static nature of the historical definition and avoid the anarchic dangers of the *k'lal Yisrael* definition. Gordis clarifies that "Catholic Israel is vertical as well as horizontal, that is to say, it includes generations gone before…their practice cannot permanently bar the way to growth, but it must necessarily exert influence on our decisions regarding changes from accepted tradition."[45] Thus, a core group of committed Jews, informed by the past but given permission to continue to move forward as they did – that is the Catholic Israel that

---

[41] Robert Gordis, *Conservative Judaism: A Modern Approach to Jewish Tradition* (New York: United Synagogue, 1956), pp. 15-16.
[42] Robert Gordis, "Authority in Jewish Law," *Proceedings of the Rabbinical Assembly* 8 (1941-1944), p. 78. This critical address of Robert Gordis to the Rabbinical Assembly in 1942 was reprinted with some minor revisions in *The Reconstructionist* 8 (November 13, 1942), pp. 8-17, and (November 27,1942), pp. 8-14. A version also appears in Robert Gordis, *Judaism for the Modern Age* (New York: Farrar, Straus, and Cudahy, 1955), Ch. 9 and Robert Gordis, *Understanding Conservative Judaism* (New York: The Rabbinical Assembly, 1978), Ch. 7. All citations, however, will be from the original source, the R.A. *Proceedings*
[43] Gordis, "Authority in Jewish Law," p. 78.
[44] Ibid., p.79.
[45] Ibid., p. 80.

Gordis now reads into Schechter.

Gordis's program became the ideology of the Conservative rabbinate. Through the Rabbinical Assembly's Committee on Jewish Law and Standards, the rabbinate set on a course of prolific halakhic decision-making, often at odds with traditional practice, but all framed within the context of the halakhic system. And after all, the rabbinate was the Catholic Israel which Schechter said was more authoritative than revelation.

Kaplan, in a response to Gordis, declared that it was "the heart of arbitrariness for Dr. Gordis to imply that people who validate their departure from traditional norms by legalistic interpretation belong to Catholic Israel, while those who validate their departure by the voluntarist approach to Jewish observance are to be excluded."[46] But this did indeed become an essential difference between Conservative and Reconstructionist Judaism. Where Reconstructionism permits a measure of individual autonomy, Conservative Judaism insists that changes of practice must be legitimated by halakhic reasoning. For Conservatism, that is the link to the past.

An irony of Gordis's position is that while he, like Kaplan, understood Catholic Israel to mean the consciousness of the Jewish people through history, he redefined the phase, changing its meaning from a conservative to liberal concept. While this act of redefinition was noticed by some,[47] it is amazing how often it has not been noticed, while people have come to understand Gordis's self-admitted redefinition as Schechter's original intention.

"Of course," writes Gerson Cohen, "the concept of catholic Israel did not include those who had renounced the obligations and demands of their faith. To be counted in the consensus one had to be knowledgeable in the traditional literature and to have set oneself to live by the results of the exegesis and reasoning that formed the tradition."[48] This reasoning was the invention of Gordis, who argues that while in theory democracy should apply to everyone, it only really applies to those who have a stake in and participate in the system.

"Catholic Israel," writes Neil Gillman, "that consensual 'living body' of caring, learning and committed Jews which, Schechter argued, had always served and would continue to serve as the ultimate authority for determining the shape of Judaism in every generation."[49] Paul Mendes-Flohr and Jehuda Reinharz define Catholic Israel as "the universally accepted sentiments and practices of devoted Jews."[50] There are more

---

[46] Kaplan, "In Reply to Dr. Gordis," *The Reconstructionist* 8 (November 27, 1942), p. 20. Kaplan's reply is reprinted in Kaplan, *Questions Jews Ask*, pp. 263-276.

[47] Kaplan, ibid.; Sklare, *Conservative Judaism*, p. 234; Seymour Siegel, *Conservative Judaism and Jewish Law* (New York: The Rabbinical Assembly, 1977), pp. xviii, 47; Schwarz, "Catholic Israel and Halakhic Change," in *Jewish Civilization,* p. 173; Weinberger, "Solomon Schechter's (Postmodern) Conservative Theology" *Conservative Judaism* 46 (Summer 1994), p. 33.

[48] Gerson D. Cohen, "Conservative Judaism" in Arthur A. Cohen and Paul Mendes-Flohr, eds., *Contemporary Jewish Religious Thought* (New York: Free Press, 1987), p. 95.

[49] Neil Gillman, Introduction to Solomon Schechter, *Aspects of Rabbinic Theology* (Woodstock, VT: Jewish Lights, 1993), pp. iv-v.

[50] Paul Mendes-Flohr and Jehuda Reinharz, *The Jew in the Modern World*, 2d ed., pp. 498-499.

examples of people identifying Gordis's redefinition with Schechter's use of the term. These should suffice.[51]

What became established after 1942 (Gordis's speech) was, as Seymour Siegel writes, that "the idea of Catholic Israel is basic to any understanding of the approach of Conservative Judaism to Jewish law."[52] But in the context of the intellectual history of the Conservative Movement, Catholic Israel is a concept in flux. Everyone uses it for one's own purposes. Those who wish halakhah to better reflect *amkha*, the people, claim that Schechter meant by Catholic Israel that the highest halakhic authority is the Jewish people or community of any one time. Those who wish to stress inter-denominational activities claim that Catholic Israel was Schechter's term for emphasizing the importance of the wholeness and unity of the Jewish people. Those who wish to legitimate the halakhic activity of the rabbinate claim that Schechter meant by Catholic Israel that the committed few are the final authority of halakhah in every age. And finally, those who wish to preserve as much of the tradition as possible claim that by Catholic Israel Schechter meant that the historical experience of the Jewish people through history is the authoritative voice of God's will. The irony is that this last option, which few claim, is, in fact, what Schechter really meant.

IV

That Schechter meant the historical definition of Catholic Israel will become evident from an evaluation of his own writings. The central text is the introduction to the first *Studies in Judaism:*

> The centre of authority is actually removed from the Bible and placed in some *living body*, which by reason of its being in touch with the ideal aspirations and religious needs of the age, is best able to determine the nature of the Secondary Meaning.[53]

This passage is often used by those who argue that Schechter referred to the community of Jews of a particular time, since they understand the needs of their own age. But that reading does not necessarily follow. If the *living body* of Catholic Israel transcends the generations, in each generation it would be in touch with the needs of that age. That is what it means to say that it is "living." This is made clear from what follows:

[51] See also Bernard Mandelbaum, *The Maturing of the Conservative Movement* (New York: Burning Bush Press, 1968), p. 33. See also Daniel H. Gordis, "Positive-Historical Judaism Exhausted: Reflections on a Movement's Future," *Conservative Judaism* 47 (Fall 1994), p. 7, n. 16. In that note, Daniel Gordis first mentions Schechter's conservative intent, raises the issue of halakhic power to the laity (which is a corollary of the contemporary Israel definition), moves on to mention that Schechter only referred to a committed core, then finally mentioning Robert Gordis's attempt to limit the "potential danger" of having too much halakhic power, he then states that the "reconfiguration" didn't work. Of course it did, for Daniel Gordis has already internalized R. Gordis's redefinition and takes that for granted as Schechter's intent.
[52] Seymour Siegel, "The Meaning of Jewish Law in Conservative Judaism: An Overview and Summary," in Seymour Siegel, ed., *Conservative Judaism and Jewish Law*, p. xviii.
[53] Schechter, *Studies in Judaism*, First Series, p. xviii.

This living body, however is not represented by any section of the nation, or any corporate priesthood, or Rabbihood, but by the collective conscience of Catholic Israel as embodied in the Universal Synagogue. The Synagogue 'with its long, continuous cry after God for more than twenty-three centuries,' with its unremittent activity in teaching and developing the word of God, with its uninterrupted succession of prophets, Psalmists, Scribes, Assideans, Rabbis, Patriarchs, Interpreters, Elucidators, Eminences, and Teachers, with its glorious record of Saints, martyrs, sages, philosophers, scholars, and mystics; this Synagogue, the only true witness to the past, and forming in all ages the sublimest expression of Israel's religious life, must also retain its authority as the true guide for the present and future.[54]

The "Synagogue" for Schechter represents the entire history of the Jewish people's expression. By the Synagogue Schechter meant the high culture and literature of the Jews. Leopold Zunz had said in 1818 that the literature of a nation is the gateway to a complete knowledge of its culture through the ages.[55] Schechter uses the term "Synagogue" because Zunz said that after the destruction of the Temple, the Synagogue became the single base for Jewish peoplehood.[56] The introduction to the first *Studies in Judaism* should make clear how much Schechter admired and was influenced by the figure of Zunz.[57] But where Zunz studied the poetry of the synagogue, Schechter studied all aspects of rabbinic culture which he lumped under the rubric "High Synagogue." The list of contributors to the Synagogue spans the ages and should make clear that the "living body" of the Synagogue, that is, Catholic Israel, transcends the generations. One must also note Schechter's aversion to a corporate Priesthood or Rabbihood. That leaves one to wonder what he would have thought of Gordis's Rabbinical Assembly and Law Committee.

The list of contributors to the Synagogue appears two other times in Schechter's writings. In the essay, "The Law and Recent Criticism," Schechter writes:

One the one side, we have the opinions of so many learned professors, proclaiming *ex cathedra*, that the Law was a most terrible burden...On the other side we have the testimony of a literature extending over about twenty-five centuries, and including all sorts and conditions of men, scholars, poets, mystics, lawyers, casuists, schoolmen, tradesmen, workmen, women [*sic*], simpletons, who all from the author of the 119th Psalm to the last pre-Mendelssohnian writer – with a small exception which does not even deserve the name of a vanishing minority – give unanimous evidence

---

[54] Ibid.

[55] Leopold Zunz, *Gesammelte Schriften,* Vol. 1 (Berlin, 1875), p.6.

[56] Leopold Zunz, *Gottesdienstlichen Vorträge* (Frankfurt a.M., 1892), p. 1.

[57] On Zunz's influence on Schechter, see my "Solomon Schechter and the Ambivalence of Jewish Wissenschaft," *Judaism* 46 (Winter 1997), especially pp. 17-24.

in favour of the Law.[58]

What one notices from the list is its attempt at comprehensiveness. It is an all-inclusive universal or catholic Israel. And this Catholic Israel extends from the Bible through to the eighteenth century, the last century not included. It is a catholic collective consciousness of the people through history minus a few "vanishing minorities" which fell short of the universal Judaism. The final appearance of the list is in Schechter's posthumously published essay on Leopold Zunz:

> Zunz wanted that as we read the history of Judaism, we should ourselves become, if not priests and zealots, then at least prophets, Soferim, sages, philosophers, poets, and if it should become necessary, also martyrs for the idea.[59]

When we commune with the literature we become a part Catholic Israel. At once we are prophet, *sofer*, sage, philosopher, ranging the centuries of experience. Priests and zealots are excluded because they did not write and contribute to the Synagogue in the way that the others did. Only experience that is recorded can truly become part of the collective experience of the common consciousness of Catholic Israel.

The phrase Catholic Israel is rare in Schechter's academic writings, although there are various references to the Synagogue.[60] There is one more passage, however, from the Zunz essay, which should be quoted:

> Here you have the Synagogue as a living body with the two great institutions of praying and teaching. The prophets and the Soferim come, and when these disappear they are followed by the sages…What now prevents us from building on this basis and from enlarging this treasure by the best ideas of our time for the benefit of posterity as our ancestors did for us?[61]

What one learns from the history one can infuse into the present and the future. The focus is not so much on resisting the present as it is on preserving the experience of the past. The role of the scholar is to transmit Catholic Israel from the past to the present so it may continue to live.

Most of the references to Catholic Israel are in Schechter's sermons and speeches collected in the volume, *Seminary Addresses and Other Papers*. In his inaugural address as President of the Seminary Schechter said: "There is no other Jewish religion but that taught by the Torah and confirmed by history and tradition, and sunk into the consciousness of Catholic Israel."[62] In "The Seminary as Witness," Schechter says that the Seminary curriculum "should be wide and comprehensive, containing within itself

---

[58] Schechter, *Studies in Judaism*, First Series, pp. 243-244.
[59] Solomon Schechter, *Studies in Judaism*, Third Series (Philadelphia: Jewish Publication Society, 1924), pp. 114-115.
[60] See, for example, Schechter's preface to *Some Aspects of Rabbinic Theology.*
[61] Schechter, *Studies in Judaism*, Third Series, p. 115.
[62] Solomon Schechter, *Seminary Addresses and Other Papers*, p. 23.

elements of eternity and catholicity."[63] That is, the curriculum will cover the complete corpus of the Synagogue, the literature of the Jews. Further in that address, Schechter refers to "the great body of Jewish doctrine and Jewish law taught by Catholic Israel."[64] This seems to prove that Catholic Israel is an historical entity and not the present community of Jews, since "taught by Catholic Israel" means of which Catholic Israel is the source. The precepts, usage and customs of Judaism "are consecrated by the consent of Catholic Israel through thousands of years," [65] Schechter says in "Spiritual Honeymoons." Catholic Israel is the source of tradition, and of its sanctity.

Schechter's appreciation of the cultural Zionism of Ahad Ha-am stems from his interest in "the awakening of the national Jewish consciousness." [66] In a Jewish homeland Catholic Israel, meaning Jewish tradition, might flourish once again. The Jewish national consciousness must be somehow related to the "Jewish historical conscience" [67] which must be related to Catholic Israel, which is translated in an academic essay as "the conscience of Israel."[68] But in the preface to *Some Aspects of Rabbinic Theology,* we have the phrase, "and forming an integral part of the religious consciousness of the bulk of the nation, or 'Catholic Israel.'"[69] The "bulk of the nation" is a troublesome phrase which will appear again below. Perhaps in this case Schechter refers to the historical Israel and contemporary Israel at the same time?

In "The Problem of Religious Education," Schechter speaks of "Keneseth Israel, where the spirit of Catholic Israel dwells." [70] In "His Majesty's Loyal Opposition," Schechter's dedication speech at the Hebrew Union College, he said, "And thus may God's blessing be upon this College, among all other colleges of Catholic Israel, ישראל ככל"[71] Like all of the other citations, these can be understood either according to the historical definition of Catholic Israel, or the contemporary Israel definition. But there is one more source which will argue very strongly for the historical view.

Mention has already been made of the Synod controversy and of Schechter's opposition. In 1905 Schechter wrote his second and more lengthy response where he argues against the synod which would only increase the spread of Reform. "A Synod in which such a [non-traditional] spirit would be prevalent is bound to dissociate us from the large bulk of Israel."[72] Here perhaps bulk means just contemporary Israel other than America, such as Eastern European Jewry. Further in the essay, though, there comes a key sentence:

---

[63] Ibid., p. 44.

[64] Ibid., p. 50.

[65] Ibid., p. 62.

[66] Ibid., p. 100.

[67] Ibid., p. 178.

[68] Solomon Schechter, *Studies in Judaism,* Second Series (Philadelphia: Jewish Publication Society, 1938), p. 116.

[69] Schechter, *Aspects of Rabbinic Theology,* p. xxviii.

[70] Schechter, *Seminary Addresses,* p. 117,

[71] Ibid., p. 244.

[72] CCAR, *Views on the Synod,* p. 139.

Then the schism is sure to come and we shall be cut off from the universal synagogue.[73]

If a Reform program is passed by a democratic synod representing the entire Jewish community, then that contemporary democratic entity will be cut off from the universal synagogue, or Catholic Israel. Hence, Catholic Israel does not refer to the contemporary body of Jews. The only other explanation is that it refers to world Jewry including Eastern European Jewry, from which America would be cut off. This is conceivable since just above we had the reference about the "bulk of Israel" which could have referred to Eastern Europe. But if the above reference refers to Eastern Europe, then the bottom reference would not also refer to Eastern Europe. It should refer to something else, especially since it uses different words. And also, Schechter would not use the term "Synagogue" to refer to the population of Eastern European Jewry.

The key to understanding Schechter is to recognize the roots of the term Catholic Israel. Schechter was never claiming to be original. In the 1896 introduction to *Studies in Judaism* he had only meant to describe the theology of the Historical School. The preceding discussion should have established that Schechter's term does not stem from the כנסת ישראל of Isaac Leeser, as Moshe Davis suggests, because Schechter fought against the synods which were meant to meet Leeser's charge of a union of American Israel. Part of the confusion is the evolution of terms through the past two centuries. Today, *k'lal Yisrael* refers to the unity of contemporary Israel, which was what Leeser meant when he said *Kenesset Yisrael*. A further confusion is that Schechter probably was thinking about כנסת ישראל as it is understood in the rabbinic literature, which is not quite the way Leeser used it.[74] In the Midrash, כנסת ישראל is the voice of Israel when it speaks to God, especially in the midrash for the Song of Songs. The כנסת ישראל speaks to God representing all of Israel, not just one group in one age.

In the Talmud, Sanhedrin 102a we read:

אמר רב חנינא בר פפא כל הנהנה מן העולם הזה בלא ברכה
כאילו גוזל להקב״ה וכנסת ישראל שנאמר גוזל אביו ואמו...
ואין אביו אלא הקב״ה . . . ואין אמו אלא כנסת ישראל
שנאמר שמע בני מוסר אביך ואל תטוש תורת אמך.

Rabbi Haninah the son of Rav Papa said that anyone who enjoys anything without saying a *b'rakhah* it is as if he stole from God and the *Kenesset Yisrael*. For as it says, if one steals from his father and mother...and none is the father except God...and none is the mother except the *kenesset Yisrael* since it says in Proverbs, "Listen my son to the advice of your father and the teaching (Torah) of your mother."

Advice comes from God so Torah must come from *Kenesset Yisrael*. This is but one of many midrashim where Schechter's concept of Catholic Israel is very discernible. It is

---

[73] Ibid.

[74] Schechter connects *Kenesset Yisrael* with Catholic Israel, *Seminary Addresses*, p. 117, cited above.

quite clear here that *Kenesset Yisrael* is not referring to the present body of Israel. Unfortunately, Schechter does not quote any rabbinic passages in connection with Catholic Israel. But since he certainly was learned in rabbinic texts, it is likely that he had in mind passages like the one above.

Norman Bentwich and David Rudavsky both suggest that Schechter derived the concept of Catholic Israel from Adolf Jellinek who taught him the principle of *Kenesset Yisrael*.[75] This is possible since Adolf Jellinek was head of the Bet Midrash in Vienna where Schechter pursued his rabbinical studies and received his ordination. Unfortunately, neither Bentwich nor Rudavsky supply a reference for Jellinek and *Kenesset Yisrael,* and I was unable to find such. However, Jellinek, a master preacher, would always bring rabbinic midrash into his sermons. That distinguished him from many of his more liberal colleagues who would not use rabbinic texts in sermons. Jellinek did and his sermons would cover the whole depth of Jewish history as well. And it has been noted that Jellinek was concerned with "*Stammesbewusstein*" ethnic consciousness.[76] Jellinek was surely an important influence for Schechter.

Of more general influence on Schechter were the ideas of German Romanticism as they made their way into the consciousness of the Historical School of *Jüdische Wissenschaft.* Two very influential figures were Johann Gottfried Herder and Friedrich Karl von Savigny. Herder stressed the individuality of cultures among different peoples, whereas Savigny argued that the law is an expression of a people's consciousness.[77] The Jewish scholars of *Wissenschaft des Judentums* believed that through research they would discover the unique essence of Judaism, the collective consciousness of the people, Catholic Israel. The influence of German Romanticism, which stressed conservatism of custom and law in order to revive old national spirits, should not be underestimated. Hermann Kantorowicz writes concerning the Historical School of Law founded by Savigny, but the same words could be said about the Historical School in Judaism:

> The historical school teaches that the contents of the law are necessarily determined by the whole past of the nation, and therefore cannot be changed arbitrarily. Thus, like the language, manners, and the constitution of a nation, all law is exclusively determined by the nation's peculiar character by what was later called the *Volksgeist.* Like language, manners and constitution, law has no separate existence, but is a simple function or

[75] Bentwich, *Solomon Schechter*, p. 285; Rudavsky, *Modern Jewish Religious Movements*, p. 427, n. 25.
[76] See M. Rosenmann, *Adolf Jellinek: Sein Leben und Schaffen* (Vienna, 1931), p. 195.
[77] See Kaplan, *The Greater Judaism in the Making*, pp. 350-365 on the influence of German Romanticism on the *Jüdische Wissenschaft* and Conservative Judaism. See also Rivka Horovitz, "HaShpa'at HaRomantikah al Hokhmat Yisrael," *Proceedings of the Eighth World Congress of Jewish Studies* (Jerusalem: World Union of Jewish Studies, 1982), Hebrew section, pp. 107-114; and Fritz Bamberger, "Zunz's Conception of History: A Study of the Philosophic Elements in Early Science of Judaism," *Proceedings of the American Academy for Jewish Research* 11 (1941), pp. 1-25.

facet of the whole life of the nation.[78]

Schechter's concept of Catholic Israel can, in part, be identified with the concept of *Volksgeist*, the spirit of the nation. Research aims to understand that *Volksgeist*, which is a facet of "the whole life of the nation" is the nation in its entirety or catholicity. While the historical understanding of Catholic Israel can be identified with *Volksgeist*, its use as a synonym for contemporary Israel or the Gordis redefinition suggested instead the concept of *Zeitgeist*, the spirit of the community at a particular time. It is far more likely that Schechter was concerned with *Volksgeist* than with *Zeitgeist*. Where *Volksgeist* was a Romantic and conservative concept, *Zeitgeist* was more rational and revolutionary. Mordecai Kaplan writes concerning Zechariah Frankel's program: "The spirit of the age should not be relied upon as a guide."[79] The "spirit of the age" is *Zeitgeist*. Rather, one should look to the *Volksgeist*, Catholic Israel.

The final influence on Schechter with regard to Catholic Israel is the work of Leopold Zunz. This has already been discussed above in relation to Zunz's and Schechter's focus on the "Synagogue." But Zunz influenced Schechter with regards to Catholic Israel in a far more direct way, a way which has never been noticed before. In an 1870 essay on the religious poetry of the Jews published in his *Collected Writings*, Zunz speaks of Catholic Israel. His language is German rather than English, but the phrase is "Israel das Allgemeine," of which "Catholic Israel" is a direct translation.[80] The German word "allgemeine" means "universal," of which another word is "catholic." Zunz says that there are three central elements of the development of Judaism over three millennia: 1) *Israel das Allgemeine*, 2) the *gottesdienstliche* nature of Israel, and 3) *Poesie*. Catholic Israel, a religious nature, and poetry were the three defining forces in Jewish development. Catholic Israel established the national over the individual, a historical entity; a religious nature determined the spiritual and lasting tone of the national expression; poetry gave the medium for expression. It is clear in Zunz that *Israel das Allgemeine* is a historical concept, corresponding to the historical understanding of Catholic Israel. And we know for a fact that Schechter read this passage since he quotes from the page in his essay on Zunz.[81] He quotes a different part of the page, but there is no doubt that *Israel das Allgemeine* would not have escaped him. Schechter wrote the Zunz essay seven years before his 1896 introduction to the *Studies in Judaism*. Certainly Schechter developed the idea of Catholic Israel in that introduction, but the actual term is a translation of a phrase from Zunz.

Schechter's Catholic Israel, then, refers to the collective consciousness of the

---

[78] Hermann Kantorowicz, "Savigny and the Historical School of Law," *Law Quarterly Review 53* (1937), p. 332.

[79] Mordecai Kaplan, *Judaism as a Civilization* (Philadelphia: Jewish Publication Society, 1981), p. 160.

[80] Leopold Zunz, "Israel's gottesdienstliche Poesie," in *Gesammelte Schriften*, Vol. 1 (Berlin, 1875), p. 123, and again on p.125.

[81] Schechter, *Studies in Judaism*, Third Series, p. 111.

Jewish people through history. The object of research was, for Schechter, to distill the nature of Catholic Israel so that it, traditional Judaism, could be lived in the present and transmitted to the future. However, Catholic Israel as a term grew and developed with the Conservative Movement in America, eventually becoming an ideological signpost, used variously by competing factions in the debates over Jewish law. The irony is that despite all the debate, Schechter meant something completely different.